Cities without Crisis

Mike Davidow

INTERNATIONAL PUBLISHERS   NEW YORK

Library of Congress Cataloging in Publication Data
Davidow, Mike.
  Cities without crisis.

  1. Cities and towns—Russia. 2. Russia—
Social conditions—1970-   I. Title.
HT145.R9D38   309.1'47'085   76-5415
ISBN 0-7178-0448-8
ISBN 0-7178-0449-6 pbk.

ABOUT THE AUTHOR

Mike Davidow was born in 1913. His father was a photographer and his mother worked in the garment industry. He attended Brooklyn College and took an active part in the turbulent student movement of the 1930s. During the early years of the Great Depression, Davidow was also the New York City organizer of the Unemployed Councils, and then active in the Workers Alliance which succeeded it.

Davidow served with the 165th Infantry of the "Fighting 69th" Division during World War II and participated in the invasion of Okinawa in the Pacific theatre of war. After the war, he worked for a number of newspapers including the *Daily World* (1961-68) and specialized as a writer on urban and political problems. In 1969 he went to Moscow as a correspondent for the *Daily World* and returned to the United States in 1974.

Mike Davidow is also the author of a number of plays. His work *The Long Life*, about garment workers, won first prize in a nation-wide one act play competition in 1964. *The Eagle Doves,* another play, was among the top contenders in the American National Theatre Academy's National contest in 1966. Recently the American Conservatory Theatre gave a dramatic reading of a more recent work, *The Closest Battlefield.* A new book of cultural criticism, *Soviet Theatre: People's Theatre From the Box Office to the Stage,* will be published shortly by Progress Publishers in Moscow.

The author and his wife, Gail, now make their home in San Francisco where he is doing further writing on the Soviet Union.

To Gail, who lived this book with me and made it possible,
To Bobby, who loved the human world of socialism and now rests in it.

Contents

1 / THE MOST HUMAN WORLD

One of the greatest forces shaping the destiny of our planet is the present competition between the two systems—socialism and capitalism. The overwhelming majority of humanity wants this to be a peaceful competition. The people want to know, not who has the biggest bomb, but where is there greater concern for the welfare of people? Where is there a more purposeful life, especially for youth? Where is there a more secure life when crisis and tragedy strike, and for the sick, the handicapped and the aged? Where does life hold forth a brighter future? Where is there truly a more liberating life for women? Where is there a greater fraternity of peoples? Where do working people, the mass of the people, have a greater and more meaningful say in running their country? Where are culture and education made more available to the people? Where are cities in crisis and where are the complex problems of modern urban existence being solved? Where are there cities of fear and cities offering a secure life? In short: where is there a better, a more happy life, not for the privileged few but for the mass of the people?

This book will address itself to such vital questions. Though figures are vital indicators and will be referred to when necessary, this will not be a battle of statistics. My story is a comparative account of what life in the Soviet Union is like as seen through the eyes of an American who lived not only in Moscow but traveled widely through 14 Soviet Republics.

To an American coming from what is often a painfully inhuman way of life, the lectures by our liberals and radicals on the need for "socialism with a human face" sound incredibly ludicrous and arrogant. For what has, above all, impressed me is the often stark contrast in this respect between our two countries, our two societies. However, life in the Soviet Union is no utopia, and I am well aware of, and will deal with, serious problems and shortcomings. But Soviet life is the most human life yet devised by people. Soviet socialist-humanism reveals itself in little as well as big things—and, above all, in its people and their relationship to one another.

For more than 58 years, a people have lived without exploiting each other and without being exploited. They have grown up in a society where a person's worth is measured not by his pocketbook, but by his contributions toward improving the welfare of his fellow man; where mutual concern and cooperation are ways of life; where there is no fear of tomorrow; where the base instincts and predatory habits inherited from the past are not given license in the name of "individual freedom," but are collectively combatted and uprooted. More than half a century of such existence has left its imprint on the Soviet character that is, perhaps, more apparent to us inhabitants of the "free" world, than to Soviet citizens themselves.

In the Soviet Union goodness and kindness are regarded as the normal characteristics of human beings and not as weaknesses to be seized upon by those not burdened with such "frailties." A half-century of life without dog-eat-dog morality, without racism and national discrimination, without corruption and pornographic pollution has erased a considerable amount of centuries-accumulated dirt. Soviet men and women are the most morally clean people we have ever met. Observing the large areas of moral filth and decay in our capitalist society, we could perhaps note this contrast better than most and certainly more clearly than our Soviet friends, who now take their moral qualities for granted. After all, Soviet life is the only life most of them really know. They, in fact, are more critical than we. With their eyes set on the Communist future, they are very much concerned with eliminating the vestiges of filth that still besmirch their way of life.

Here let me comment on a common failing among friends of the Soviet Union who are not too familiar with the daily realities of Soviet life. Many friends of the Soviet Union actually expect to see the ideal Communist man and woman when they visit the USSR. And they swing from unreal elation to unjustified dejection when the "ideal" they themselves imagined does not measure up to the standards they set for the Soviet people (pedestals the Soviet people never requested).

We can understand this because we, too, were possessed with some of these unrealistic conceptions when we first arrived, the natural result of inexperience with socialist life, the lack of understanding of what it takes to achieve one of the new society's most difficult, yet most beautiful goals—the molding of a new man and woman. Shortcomings of some Soviet people came as a shock to us. Like many who struggled all our lives for socialism, we had created the idealized image of a pure human being. It was as unfair to the Soviet people as it was unreal. We had not fully grasped that socialism is a period in which the grime of the past is removed step-by-step. The building of a new society and, above all, the pioneering of a path toward such social reconstruction is an incredibly difficult process, involving costly sacrifices as well as mistakes.

To understand this — to really understand it — is a vital necessity for all who seek an honest picture of Soviet life. That is why anti-Soviet propaganda concentrates on the hangovers of the past, focuses on difficulties, exaggerating and distorting them. That is why it ignores or underplays achievements and maintains a curtain of silence on the most meaningful contrasts between Soviet life and our own.

One of the current myths fashioned by the more sophisticated anti-Soviet propagandists is that of a revolution that has spent itself, of a Soviet Union that is aging and conservative. This myth is peddled primarily among radicalized but politically inexperienced people, many of whom see revolution primarily as a destructive, cleansing force, and confuse its far more complex and significant constructive aspect with conservatism. The October Revolution in the Soviet Union has far from spent itself. On the contrary, it is now in the process of ascending its highest peak—communism.

In no society in history is construction so much a part of a way of life. The crane in the Soviet sky has joined the hammer and sickle as an emblem of socialism. A vast land stretching from the Baltic to the Pacific is the setting for this unprecedented effort. It is as if several new countries and hundreds of new cities are being constructed in one gigantic project. And the process of construction is itself transforming the builders.

In a way my book can be called *The Most Human World* because that best describes the world I've been living in the past five years. I want to stress that it is not a perfect world—it is a human world. It is a restless, demanding world characterized by an incessant struggle to perfect itself and, above all, the people who live in it.

I have found life in the Soviet Union a most exciting adventure. I was seized with the once-in-a-lifetime feeling that all journalists treasure: I found myself impatiently awaiting the next day to see what exciting new features the world I was living in would bring. And I was rarely disappointed. I seek to take the reader with me in reliving some of this adventure.

2 / FIRST IMPRESSIONS

arrived in Moscow on March 5, 1969. I had left the "free world" twice before to visit the "other world"—in 1961 as part of a U.S. delegation, and in 1967, as a special correspondent for the *Daily World* to report on the Fifth Moscow International Film Festival. But there's a world of difference between living in a country and being a guest or a visitor.. The Soviet Union was not now on "its best behavior." It seemed to say: "Here I am in daily, real life, not just as I am on holidays."

It is the little things that first hit home. They are indeed to be treasured. Like the fresh smell of early morning or the last weary but brilliant rays of a sunset, they live with you forever. And I will try to relive with you some of these "little" experiences that first introduced me into the sight, smell and feel of the New World we had entered.

There is no better way to get to know a country and its people than to walk its streets. I was walking along Gorky Street with Alla Borisovna Grechuhina, my interpreter and secretary. Walking with Alla was an experience in itself. An extremely attractive and knowledgeable woman who spoke fluent English with an American accent (most here acquire an Oxford accent), Alla was an indefatigable and enthusiastic guide. She quite understood the significance of these walks for me, and notwithstanding the added work, threw herself into them with relish. Part of the reason was, of course, that she was seeing her Moscow (and her Soviet Union) through the eyes of an excited arrival from the "other world."

11

I stopped suddenly to impress the scene before me into my memory. Fluffy puffs of snow were carpeting Gorky Street and embroidering in white the bearlike fur coats of passersby. Tiny tots wrapped in their long fur coats, peaked hats perched on their heads, looked like oversized bunnies. Technically it was spring in Moscow (spring, we were told, arrives March 1st), but evidently no one had informed Old Man Winter and he was hanging around for a while. From the looks of it, he seemed to be in no hurry. But then I was in no hurry for him to leave. I love winter and for those who love that cold season of whiteness, Moscow and much of the Soviet Union are quite inviting.

Men, bearing bouquets of snow-covered flowers, rushed by me. Spring and snow! Alla explained. March 8th, International Women's Day, a legal holiday celebrated here on a far wider and more meaningful scale than our commercialized Mothers' Day, was approaching.

But it wasn't the flowers that made me stop. All along our walk I had a strange feeling. Somehow it was very different from the walks I had taken only a few days ago in the world I had just left. Then I realized: it wasn't the wintrylike spring, nor mass of walking furs, nor the parade of flowers. People were walking—some hurrying (Muscovites, I later discovered, like people in all big cities, do everything at a faster tempo), but there was no tension.

I had on several occasions observed one man jostle another. I had waited for an angry exchange of words, possibly blows, as is quite common on U.S. streets. The colliding men either excused themselves or just continued on their separate ways. These things were expected in crowds and no one suspected his neighbor of ulterior motives.

A Ride on the Moscow Metro

I had been particularly impressed with this calm when I found myself in a subway crush in Moscow's Metro that could rival our own in New York. *Ploschad Revolutsii* (Revolution Square) is the conjunction (it can also be described as the bottleneck) of three major stations. The other two are Sverdlov Square and Karl Marx Avenue. It is one of the major transportation problems on which Moscow is concentrating. The crowd Alla and I were swept into as we changed trains, could only be compared to the outpouring from a Yankee Stadium World Series game. Muscovites were not only jostling and pushing one another; they were literally breathing down each others' necks—men, women, children of all ages. Yet there are no subway police to keep you in your lane, to prevent dangerous crushes or break up fights (no police patrol Moscow's Metro trains as in New York). I must confess I became tense, uneasy, and eyed my fellow subway "sardines" with some suspicion and even hostility. I was just reacting normally—as a New Yorker. I looked at Alla to see her reactions. She was as patient and as relaxed as other Muscovites. The crowd moved imperceptibly—but it moved. Not an angry word was exchanged. No one was watching to maintain order and no directives were being blared over loudspeakers. People were either moving along, silently lost in their own thoughts or were spending the time in light, lively conversation with their friends or new subway acquaintances.

My thoughts flashed back to a frightening subway experience I had had in New York the summer before I left for my assignment in Moscow. I was coming home from work during the five o'clock crush on a typically humid summer day. I had been propelled into the train by the burly subway guards whose function it was to pack in the "sardines." Angry words as well as threatening elbow digs accompanied our entrance. The first fight—and it was a no-holds-barred struggle—was for seats. They were, of course, occupied by the fastest and the most aggressive, and least of all by those who most needed them—the elderly and tired women long past their prime. Few indeed surrendered the prized seat to these women after such a struggle. Instead, the victors sat stony-faced or hid their faces in their newspapers, while the weaker, older riders clung to each other and the overhanging train straps.

Nowhere is the free enterprise principle of the "survival of the fittest" better revealed than in the daily subway struggle. And the reasons for this inhuman behavior were written on the faces of my fellow New York subway riders. They were the faces of people exhausted by the rat race that begins with awakening—when you gulp down your cup of coffee, and gobble up your toast and rush to catch the train; that rises in intensity with the inhuman speedup that is the foundation of our unparalleled mass production, profits and nervous breakdowns; that is unrelieved by the hurried lunch, coffee and sandwich break, and that meets its most grueling test in the rush-hour ride home. The subway ride home is not just another train ride—it is a trip in an underground that gives one a good conception of what hell must be like. It is the last straw—the running over of the daily cup of bitterness. And for Black and Puerto Rican workers to whose bitter cup is added the daily dash of racist discrimination, who know they are returning to rat-ridden ghetto slums where the battle for survival is far from over at the end of a day's work—the train ride is, indeed, the last straw. These are the invisible but very much present passengers that accompany New York working people on their daily subway rides.

Suddenly the New York subway train came to a dead stop. The electric fans, which had been circulating the humid polluted air, stopped. The lights, too, went out. The sweating, tightly packed passengers gasped for breath and recoiled from each other in fear. Someone shouted angrily at his neighbor. A woman screamed in terror. The fear was made more contagious by the darkness. A few voices began to reflect the rising panic. There were cries for air. Only the fortunate quick restoration of the train's operation prevented what may well have resulted in a terrible panic. This was the event I now recalled as I shuffled along with my fellow Moscow subway riders.

Later on, as I came to know the daily life of the Soviet people better, I understood why in Moscow a subway ride was a pleasant means of transportation, and a crowd was just an unusually large number of people gathered together at the same time and at the same place. But during my first ride, I could already see the reason. It was present in the very subway itself. A most delightful place in Moscow—and in all Soviet cities with metros—is the subway. In another chapter I will describe in detail how they are operated and maintained. If New Yorkers could spend just one week riding to and from work in the Moscow subway, an awful lot of the anti-Soviet, anti-Communist pap they had been fed about the suppression of the individual under communism would evaporate in those subway rides.

My First Trolleybus Ride

My first trolleybus ride provided another "little" insight, this time without Alla. Moscow's huge, box-shaped trolleybuses, run quite frequently in most areas—far more so than our buses. But Muscovites, like New Yorkers, are in a great hurry, even if it's to get nowhere in particular. No one waited for the next trolleybus, which could already be seen approaching. Instead, all piled into the first bus to arrive, which was already almost full. And like a New Yorker, I squeezed in with them.

But the trolleybus did not move. It was stalled. The cables had slipped off the overhead wires which fed it power. In a flash, a slip of a girl nimbly climbed to the roof of the trolleybus and restored the paralyzed vehicle to life. There was a natural assurance and grace in her movements, an undisputed control over this mechanical monster that had been entrusted to her.

I was well aware of the role women play in every phase of life, and I had even observed them working side by side with male co-workers on construction sites. But that was from the outside, as an observer. I was so engrossed in the activity of our attractive driver (who was hardly noticed by the other passengers) I had forgotten to pay my fare. Alla had told me the fare was 4 kopecks on a trolleybus. I searched my pockets but my smallest coin was a 15-kopeck piece. Where could I go for change? I was aware that except on rare occasions there were no conductors on surface lines. Fares are paid on the honor system. You put your fare into a coin box and tear off your paper receipt. Every once in a while there is a spot check. If you can't show a receipt, you pay a rouble fine.

There was no difficulty finding the coin box—it was the center of activity. A schoolboy who was closest to it was acting as the voluntary, unpaid conductor. From all directions hands were raised and coins were passed from hand to hand until they reached the young conductor, who seemed to be enjoying himself immensely. The boy neatly clipped off receipts and they were deposited into the hands of the waiting passengers via this overhead human conveyor belt. But what does one do for change? Puzzled, I decided to make a contribution to Moscow's transportation system, and dropped my 15-kopeck piece into the coin box. I made a mental note to raise this problem with Alla and that was the end of it. But not as far as my fellow passengers were concerned.

Soviet citizens, as I later discovered, are collective busybodies. Just ask someone for directions on a street and you are informed not only by the person to whom you directed your question but by everyone within whispering distance. Very often the result is a lively sidewalk discussion on your destination. I felt a hand on my shoulder and turned my head around. My neighbor, a middle-aged man, smiled and said: "You put in too much, comrade." Then, without another word, he proceeded to organize my refund. The woman before me gave my friend a three-kopeck piece and deposited one kopeck in the box. My friend turned the three-kopeck piece over to me. Then he announced:"The comrade needs eight more kopecks." A young man who had not yet paid his fare cried out:"Here, I have four." By this time I had lost track of the count. But not my fellow passengers. An elderly woman tapped a young girl about to put four kopecks into the box. "We need four kopecks for this comrade," she explained. The girl nodded and handed her coins to the woman, who turned them over to me. As I pocketed the last coin, a warmly clad, ruddy-faced man gently felt my thinly lined New York overcoat. "You are cold, aren't you?" he asked kindly. I nodded agreement. He shook his head worriedly as he got off.

More than five years have passed, and yet as I write I see as vividly as on that day the faces of my fellow passengers on my first trolleybus ride. I have since come to take this daily, simple but ever so revealing demonstration of collectivity for granted. I, too, have since participated in the ticket and coin passing and the organization of refunds on numerous occasions. But I realize that my first trolleybus ride pointed up perhaps the most significant fruit of more than half a century of socialist living—the Soviet citizen's concern for his fellow man, expressed not in hail-fellow-well-met words that are forgotten as soon as they are uttered but in daily acts of cooperation.

I have also witnessed and myself felt many acts of rudeness, indifference and selfishness that unpleasantly reminded me of our own dog-eat-dog competitiveness. They are the bitter remnants of the past which cling tenaciously to people and are the heritage of centuries of habits. Much can be and is being done to eradicate them by the powerful Soviet medium of education and culture. But it is the force of new socialist habits such as I experienced on my first Moscow trolleybus ride that is the decisive factor in molding people, imparting to them new, truly human standards of morality and behavior. I have often thought: Why should such a simple act of neighborly cooperation impress me so? Why should it not be the norm for us, too?

When I first mentioned this incident to my Soviet friends, they were puzzled that I found it so unusual. Now after five years of living in the Soviet Union I can understand their reaction. But when I told it to my American friends, I could detect their skepticism.

One of my readers wrote an irate letter to my newspaper in response to my article describing the trolleybus scene, taking me to task for "idealizing" the Soviet people. She even accused me of belittling our own people because I stated it would be hard to imagine such a scene on U.S. buses. I was quite upset by the letter. Not because it scolded me—I soon got over that—but because it hit home to me the difficult problem I faced: to be believed. It is hard for Americans, even those sympathetic to socialism, to imagine the reality of everyday Soviet life.

No people on earth have been subjected to anti-Sovietism and anticommunism so intensely and so long. It pollutes our lives. But for the poison to seep into our systems, there must be an opening giving it access. And the opening—well understood and utilized by anti-Soviet propagandists—is that ours is an entirely different way of life.

It's not that people in the United States are not as good as their fellow humans in the Soviet Union. The real American tragedy is that a society that breeds a Lieutenant Calley, spends $150 billion to destroy the villages and towns of Indochina while our cities decay, that is symbolized by the Attica massacre and the Watergate scandal, that measures success by dollars and regards those who permit principles to stand in the way of such success as failures or suckers makes it "unprofitable"for people to act with consideration toward each other. Powerful objective forces make the struggle to secure and maintain human decency very difficult indeed. Whereas, in the Soviet Union, life and society combine to bring out the best in people and to eradicate the worst, in our dog-eat-dog society, the contrary is the case. An honor system on our buses wouldn't work because our people know that the buses are not ours and that the entire transportation system abuses rather than serves us.

Thus, American passengers have little incentive to act like Soviet passengers. How can one participate in an honor system with those who have no respect or consideration for you, your welfare, your comfort and safety? How can one think of helping to collect fares and organizing refunds for the transportation owners or public authorities whose only concern is placing on the working people the burden of maintaining an ever more costly, ever deteriorating transportation system?

Of course, there are those in the Soviet Union who violate the honor system and at times avoid paying fares. It is not always the fault of the passenger; the trolley and autobuses are often so packed that it is difficult to get to the coin box. And passing coins up (especially where change is involved) makes it quite a complicated operation. It is all the greater tribute to the inbred sense of public responsibility that there are relatively few "free riders." What happens to those who violate the honor system? I was in Moscow only a week when I found out. A matronly woman tapped me on the shoulder as I sat on the trolley. "Where is your receipt?" she demanded as she flashed her credentials. I must confess I was a little flustered. It was not an easy thing to find the flimsy bit of paper which I had shoved in my pocket containing gloves, notebook and cigarettes.(I have since learned to keep it in an available spot.) The stern look on the inspector's face hardly helped me in making my search. Finally I found it and displayed it proudly. The woman examined it and returned it to me.

The man occupying the seat before me was not so fortunate. A young man, he smiled sweetly and weakly tried to explain that he was just getting ready to pay. But the look on the inspector's face stopped him short. With a shrug of his shoulders, the young man reached in his pocket for the ruble fine. But this hardly satisfied the inspector. *"Molodoi chelovek* (young man)," she began, and the *"molodoi chelovek"* alone made him shrink into his seat. All eyes turned on the *"molodoi chelovek."* Her sharp words, reminding him that he had cheated Soviet society out of much more than four kopecks, were unnecessary. The look on his face made it clear that he was prepared to pay far more than the ruble to forget the entire incident. The most powerful and most effective punitive and educational force in Soviet life is public disapproval and in aspects of social relations, it is increasingly being brought into play.

Subbotnik

I shall never forget my first *"subbotnik.*"* It was a glimpse into the Communist future when all will labor for the common good and work itself will be a labor of love.

Appropriately enough, it was at the Moscow Locomotive Depot (Sortirovichinaya),in those grim days more than fifty years ago, on April12, 1919, that the first *subbotnik* took place. Vladimir Ilyich Lenin, the founder of the world's first socialist state, saw in the voluntary labor of fifteen workers the great beginning, the seeds of the future Communist society.

It was Saturday, a day off for most Soviet workers, but there was rush hour traffic on Moscow's streets, buses and subway.There was a May Day atmosphere— this time, however, the march was not to Red Square but to the factories and farms, and the holiday attire consisted of working clothes. Matronly women, *babushkas*, elderly men, and sturdy young girls and boys, carrying shovels on their shoulders, were walking along Leningradski Prospekt. They were part of the huge army who were giving Moscow its spring cleaning.The elderly folk wielded their

Subbotnik—voluntary unpaid work for the benefit of society in the workers' spare time (Saturday evening, Sunday). The Russian word *subbota* means Saturday.

shovels with gusto, a pink glow on their cheeks and a sparkle in their eyes. The younger set made their work a sport, kidding and vying with one another. Alla and I passed factories dressed for the occasion with crimson banners and flowers. From every factory there came the sound of music.

At the Moscow Railroad Depot, in the yard, bedecked with flowers and emblazoned with red streamers, stood the old locomotive which was repaired and dispatched to the threatening front in 1919. Close by, eyeing it with loving eyes, were the three surviving old Bolsheviks who had made it battle-ready. The old veterans seemed to cast off the years as they basked in the warmth of the spring day. Assembled at this place of honor were 70 old-timers—railroad workers who had retired. They had come to work on their old jobs and had brought their grandchildren with them. Gathered, too, were musicians from the Bolshoi Theater, actors from the Mayakovsky Theater and a colorfully dressed song and dance ensemble.

After a brief ceremony, all went to work. The clang of hammers and wrenches and the whirring sound of drilling machines mingled with the gay Russian folk tunes and old revolutionary songs. Komsomol teams competed with each other as they labored to free the depot of the residue of winter's grime. White-collar workers and Pioneers struggled with shovels beside them. Inside, the old-timers and those who had replaced them—their hands dripping black oil—were working on the underbellies of the huge metal monsters. Pride in their labor was written on the faces of all. And as they worked, artists sketching with charcoal, pen and watercolor sought to catch that look on paper.

I noticed reporters and television cameras assembled around one particular worker. He was Aleksei Lebedev, winner of the coveted Order of Lenin for exemplary work, who was pointed out to me by his fellow workers with the pride bestowed on hometown heroes. The Soviet press accords heroes of labor the kind of respect our monopoly-controlled newspapers reserve for corporation executives.

The lunch break turned out to be a concert and the repair shop was the concert hall. Standing and sitting on the locomotives, machines and window ledges were the "concert goers" in their oil-spotted work clothes. The women had managed to clean the smudges off their faces and to primp up their kerchiefs. The audience leaned confidently from their precarious positions to catch a glimpse of their favorite artists. And in this remarkable setting we listened to the Bolshoi orchestra play excerpts from a Tchaikovsky symphony and watched theatrical performances by Mayakovsky actors. I tried to imagine such a concert in a General Motors or Ford plant!

I noticed a grizzly old veteran, tears of joy streaming down his cheeks. He was Yakov Kondratyev, 80 years old, one of the three survivors of the Great Beginning. Kondratyev had heard Lenin speak to the railroad workers on the significance of their *subbotnik*. Alla introduced us and Kondratyev hugged me. He pointed to the scene about me and exclaimed: "Look how Lenin's words have come true."

Much still has to be done to make Lenin's prediction come fully true—that's what the construction of the material and technical base of communism and the molding of the new Soviet men and women is all about. But Kondratyev's wise old eyes encompassed the vision of more than half a century of socialism. And nowhere do you better see the historic transformation that Soviet life represents than in the Soviet factory, especially in the attitude toward labor. At the Moscow railroad repair shop a young worker asked me to describe my impressions. "It's a joy to be in a land where workers are honored," I told him. A puzzled expression appeared on his face. "But why should that be so unusual? "Isn't that the way it should be?" he asked simply. There you had the two worlds meeting—it is summed up in: "Isn't that the way it should be?"

I'm no engineer or economist. I know a factory as a worker, and I inspected the factories I visited as a tenant does a prospective apartment. The question I asked myself was: How would I like to work in these factories?

I, like most American workers, counted the minutes I spent in my shop. At quitting time, we ran from it as from the plague. In the mornings we returned, sullen and glum, to sweat it out until the hour of liberation struck again. Friday was our day of deliverance. We lived for weekends. Soviet workers, too, count the time on the job and look forward to their weekends. Not all are doing the work they like to do. And work here, as everywhere, demands effort and self-discipline, is physically hard and, at times, dangerous. But what I saw at the Moscow *subbotnik* was a glimpse of the Communist future when all will labor for the common good and work itself will be a genuinely creative process and a source of joy. How that will expand living!

But the Soviet factory (and that goes for all places of labor) today already provides a sort of preview of that future. It is not yet the finished product but it is in the refining process. I saw this preview in countless Soviet plants—everywhere. I saw it in the giant Likhachaev Auto Plant in the flower pots that adorned the automated machines. I saw it in the plant's libraries where workers, leafing pages with grimy fingers, read novels and books on engineering. I saw it in the new comfortable homes built by Leningrad port organization and trade unions for the longshoremen, only a few minutes walking distance from their jobs. I saw it in the Odessa longshoremen's polyclinic located right on the docks. "We need only two minutes to answer an emergency," Dr. Ivan Komaneyetz, the chief physician, told me. There is a medical staff of 105, including 28 doctors whose sole responsibility is to take care of 6,500 port workers.

I saw it in the prophylactic rest stations not far from the factories, which play so vital a role in preventing serious illness. I saw it in the galleries of heroes of labor that adorn the approaches to Soviet factories as well as their corridors. I saw it in the palaces of culture, which are clubs, socal centers, music halls, ballet theaters, all rolled into one. Everywhere the factory is not only the center of construction but of culture. Everywhere it is a place to live in as well as work. I grasped for the first time, words I was quite familiar with: workers' power. Now I realized I was living in a country that was the embodiment of the power of the working class.

I read with amusement the Olympian pronouncements of the "one world" and "convergence" theorists, who see the scientific-technological revolution as the great leveler, erasing differences between all modern industrial countries, regardless of social system. What world do they live in? Surely not the one I have inhabited most of my life. The very opposite is true, as anyone who spends some time in the Soviet Union and other socialist countries will soon realize. Never have the two worlds been in such stark contrast as now.

3 / SOVIET SHOPPING

Soviet shopping is quite an experience and an eye-opener. The store is an excellent barometer of a country's economic health. Soviet shopping extends literally from the store to the street. People shop hectically all day and into the night, everywhere: on the street, in the numerous underpasses; in GUM department store (the Macy's of Moscow); in the *Universalny Magazines* (on the style of department stores); in an ever increasing number of well-stocked supermarkets; at street stalls and kiosks. Moscow seemed to be on a continuous buying spree—no one appeared to be concerned about saving up for that "rainy day."

My first sight of groups of Muscovites gathered around someone or something—and they were everywhere—prompted an automatic reaction. I grabbed astonished Alla by the hand and ran to see what was up. But it was just a street scene I have since become accustomed to— Muscovites of all ages gathered around an itinerant bookseller who was displaying his wares on a makeshift shelf. They were buying books as we buy hot dogs or hamburgers and most books did not cost as much. Many paperbacks were selling for 30 to 40 kopecks and quite a few for less. I picked up an up-to-date hardcover, 250 page textbook on radio mechanics. It was priced at one ruble and eight kopecks.

What I was observing were some living statistics the world is familiar with: the USSR may have had a shortage of quality toilet paper (the supply has since considerably increased) but one quarter of all the books published annually in the world are published in the Soviet Union. I mention books as part of my description of Soviet shopping because they are considered as much a necessity as bread.

Moscow not only does much of its shopping outdoors, it nibbles and munches in the street on hot meat, cabbage, rice or jam pies *(pirozhki),* and gobbles up unbelievable amounts of the best ice cream I have ever tasted. At first, I found the sight of Muscovites biting into the cream cones enveloped by their steaming breath incredible. But I learned to eat this frozen delicacy in every season, including bitter wintry days.

You can eat a meal on the streets for about 50 kopecks. The pie costs 5 kopecks (meat pies, 10 kopecks) and the ice cream from 10 to 20 kopecks. The ingredients are tasty and unadulterated. For weeks I lunched in the streets.

It was as much to catch the hum of this dynamic, exciting city as to bite into the goodies. I watched and listened and compared. I first compared what I saw to the Moscow I visited in 1961. The stores were stacked with far more commodities and Muscovites were far better dressed. In fact, it became increasingly difficult to distinguish Muscovites from New Yorkers by their dress. The fruits of the 8th and 9th Five Year Plans are easily seen in the more plentiful supply of most consumer goods, in the steady improvement of services, and in the better dress of Muscovites in the street.

When we first came to the Soviet Union I found prices of many food items and consumer products high in comparison with ours. But five years of inflationary prices back home (rising 5-6 percent annually and in 1974 over 10 percent) have considerably narrowed the gap on many basic commodities, especially foods, and on a number of products even boosted prices higher than in the Soviet Union. Thus, the *International Herald Tribune,* on February 16, 1974, noted: "It cost $150.40 last month to buy at wholesale, goods that cost only $100 in 1967." During that same period, prices in the Soviet Union have remained stable and even declined. According to the UN's International Labor Organization, consumer prices in the USSR dropped 7.8 percent during 1963-71. (There was a steep increase in the price of vodka and cognac and a decrease in the cost of haberdashery and televisions and radios. Synthetics were considerably reduced.)

We found many food items cheaper or about the same price as ours. Fish is far more plentiful and far lower-priced. We had been buying excellent halibut filets (called *paltus,* in the Soviet Union) these four years at 1 ruble 40 kopecks a kilogram (a kilogram is 2lbs. 2oz.) By comparison, the price of halibut in the USA is two or three times higher. Cod fillet is about 32 cents a pound—far cheaper than in the USA. Unlike in our country, fish in the Soviet Union is far cheaper than meat. Per capita consumption of fish in the Soviet Union in 1971 was 15.4 kg. as compared to 6 kg. in the USA.

Meat, I believe, is now on the whole cheaper than in the USA though the choice of cuts is a good deal less. Beef for soup or pot roast costs from 1 ruble 65 kopecks to 2 rubles a kilogram (from 80 cents to $1 a pound). Pork is the same price. Lamb, including chops and leg of lamb, is a little cheaper, about 90 cents a pound.

Compare this to these meat prices (per pound) in the USA *(International Herald Tribune,* March 29, 1974): round steak $1.65 to $1.72; lamb chops $1.91 to $2.13; leg of lamb $1.37 to $1.51; rib roast $1.44 to $1.63; pork chops $1.54. On the other hand, chicken is far more expensive than ours, it sells for 2 rubles 65 kopecks a kilogram. At the rate prices are rising, however, this will not hold for much longer. It is true we found the chicken we ate in the Soviet Union of far better quality than the average we bought in our supermarkets.

One of the things we discovered in our Soviet shopping is that the wide gaps in quality our shoppers are familiar with, do not exist here. The food products are largely of one quality—the best. But fine quality or not, we were puzzled by the high prices of chicken. The most logical explanation for this we received much later during our visit to Bulgaria, from a large-scale producer and exporter of chicken. The higher cost, we were told, is the result of the higher cost of feed and less mechanization. From what I have seen, however, of the new huge poultry and meat factory complexes being constructed all over the Soviet Union, close to large cities, chicken and meat should be far more plentiful and lower-priced in the near future. One thing is clear: with no monopoly meat packers to manipulate the prices, the lower costs of production will benefit Soviet consumers.

As one familiar with the highly inflated cost of medicines and drugs in the United States, I found the price of drugs in the Soviet Union unbelievably low. I was introduced to this startling contrast in a rather humorous way. Our family was struck by the grippe (flu) soon after our arrival in the Soviet Union. Our doctor had prescribed an equivalent of terramycin drugs, which we knew from our experience were quite expensive (about 50 to 60 cents a tablet in the United States five years ago). I handed the cashier a ten-ruble note. You pay her before the purchase and receive a tab which you then hand over to the saleslady, a time-consuming operation they are moving to eliminate. The prescription was for ten tablets. The cashier gave me the tab and 9 rubles and 10 kopecks in change. I was sure she had shortchanged herself. I waited, certain that she would readily recognize her error. But the young lady eyed me belligerently. "What are you waiting for, *grazhdanin* (citizen)?" she asked in a rather irritated tone. She was backed up by audible protests from the long line of customers. "You made a mistake," I informed her in my halting Russian. But this only made her angrier. She picked up the receipt and, addressing herself to the customers (who by this time had gathered around her to see if she were truly taking advantage of the foreigner), she read out the prescription emphasizing that it called for *ten* tablets, and triumphantly displayed the 90 kopeck tab to her fellow Muscovites. By this time one or two attempted to explain to me that I was not being overcharged! I could not help bursting out into laughter, much to the bewilderment of my fellow customers. I have since grown accustomed to picking up drug tabs for 5 and 10 kopecks without batting an eyelash. There are medicines that are imported which are more expensive and are more difficult to get. And there are drugs which are in short supply. This can be a problem.

But perhaps the greatest relief to a former New York shopper was the realization that no one was out to do me in. From force of habit, I entered each store warily, on guard. Shopping in our country is run on the Roman adage:"Let the buyer beware!" Gradually it hit me that no one was out to overcharge me, give me short weight, stale or damaged merchandise (there's a scale in clear view for customers to check their purchases, and it is used). I came to the comforting realization that there were no giant food monopolies like A&P or Safeway to fleece me from counter to cash register. Shopping in the Soviet Union is a normal, natural exchange, if a hectic one, not our ceaseless battle against exploitation that starts at the point of production and continues with every purchase. Any given commodity is the same price everywhere, with the exception of fruits and vegetables, which are cheaper in some warmer areas. The same goes for quality. There are times when some food prices fluctuate, particularly those of fruits and vegetables during the winter. Many vegetables are now lower-priced than ours. Potatoes cost less than 5 cents a pound, carrots the same, cabbage 3 cents a pound in season, and beets, the same. Fruits, especially citrus, are a good deal more expensive since they are largely imported from Arabic countries.

But there are no monopolies to maintain artificially high prices in times of abundance. This, after all is said and done, is the fundamental lasting difference between shopping in Moscow and in New York.

There is another very important medium of Soviet shopping, one that plays an enormous role in saving time and household chores, the *culinaria*. Nothing comparable exists in the United States. The *culinaria* is a store which supplies Soviet citizens with freshly prepared cooked foods (meats, fowl, fish, salads, sour cream, cookies, cakes, as well as ready-to-cook foods), all at prices that hardly make it economical to cook at home. Any similar outlet in our country at that profit level would either have to skimp on weight or quality, or both, or go bankrupt. And there's a *culinaria* within walking distance in every neighborhood. Most large plants or enterprises have one or more on their own premises to service their workers. The present 9th Five Year Plan calls for a vast increase in their number. The *culinaria* in our area did a rush business every day, and particularly as suppertime approached and workers stopped off on their way home to pick up their evening meal. There are also places where you can order a fully cooked meal in the morning and pick it up at suppertime.

Supper, incidentally, is not the main meal there as it is in our country. In fact, an amusing folk saying I've heard sums up the disparaging attitude toward this evening meal: "Breakfast for yourself, lunch (or dinner) for your friends and supper for your enemies." Lunch, the most solid meal, is usually eaten at the plant or enterprise *stolovia* (dining room). I've eaten at many of them in factories and enterprises all over the country. Nothing fancy—but good, wholesome food. The quality of the cooking varies, and in some places leaves much to be desired. But, on the whole, I've found it tasty if not sumptuous. And the price is ridiculously low. I've eaten a full-course meal, including meat, potatoes, cabbage or beet salad, soup, tea and cookies for less than a ruble. Most *stolovias* are partly subsidized by the enterprise.

With the main meal eaten out, shopping is that much easier. But in spite of all this, shopping still constitutes one of the Soviet citizen's main bottlenecks and time consumers. The amount of time one spends on the omnipresent *ochered* (line) cuts considerably into the Soviet citizen's free time, especially that of the Soviet woman. Notwithstanding the fact that nowhere else in the world have women achieved so high a level of equality in all spheres of life, the main burden of the shopping is still borne by women. Here the *babushka* (grandmother) is a godsend and highly treasured. The *babushka* is a great help to the family.

Another problem that complicates shopping is the shortage of workers. The Soviet Union is a fully employed society. Any debate there on whether 4 percent unemployment is tolerable (even 9 percent does not seem to occasion alarm in our "free-enterprise" society) would itself be regarded as intolerable. With the well-nigh unlimited opportunities for training and advancement in all skills, and the attractiveness of industrial, scientific, and technical fields, the service trades have difficulty competing for and holding workers. The 24th Congress of the Komsomols, at which I was present, took note of this problem and there is a special stress on the importance of the service trades as well as special efforts to make them more attractive. The main emphasis is on modernization of services. At a Sokolniki park exhibition I saw many of the new modern facilities now under production that will considerably facilitate servicing. The struggle (and it is an all-out one) is to get these models more quickly into mass production. The emphasis is now being placed on supermarkets, which are beginning to spring up in many areas. But the modernization of Soviet retail stores constitutes one of the main problems and tasks. The main guarantee that there will soon be considerable improvement is the direction charted by the 24th Congress of the CPSU with its stress on making drastic improvements in living conditions and in the quantity and quality of services and goods.

Very little is syphoned off from Soviet pay envelopes. Alexander Birman, Soviet economist, estimates that "after payment of income tax, rent, trade-union dues and insurance, a Soviet family has at its disposal no less than 80 percent of its cash income." By contrast, rent and taxes alone slice off close to 60 percent of the average U.S. family income. The famous American high wage shrinks beyond recognition before it ever gets to the supermarket. About one-third is chewed off in federal, state and city taxes, not to mention a host of sales and invisible taxes. A congressional survey found "higher tax payments outstripped all other price increases in the 1974 consumer budget and that this rise had a greater impact on low income and middle income tax payers than on wealthy." *(N.Y. Times* 2/10/75) The Soviet citizen, by comparison, hardly knows the meaning of taxes. The only tax deductions are nominal for many Soviet citizens, reaching a top of 13 percent.

I discovered that my Moscow friends pay an average of 10 to 15 rubles a month for rent, about what they pay for 5 to 7 kilograms of beef. They pay nothing for the most complete medical care, and nothing for their children's education. Cultural events are minimally priced. (Theater seats are from 40 kopecks to 2 rubles.) Unions pick up 70 percent of the bill for 24-day vacations at palatial sanitoriums and rest homes. Transportation, as I already indicated, is almost what we would call free. A telephone call costs 2 kopecks and a home phone bill is a ruble and 50 kopecks for unlimited local calls. Stack this up against our bill for these everyday living needs: $10 to $15 or more for a visit to the doctor's office; more than $100 a day for a hospital room; $3,000 to $4,000 and up, a year for a college education; movies $3.50 and up; theater tickets, $5 to $15; a week in a hotel resort, from $125 per person and up; telephone, $20 a month and up; and close to $30 a month for gas and electric. There is no one over there to skim off the cream in gigantic profits. There are no General Motors, Ford or Rockefeller Standard Oil to vote themselves huge annual dividends. There are no loan sharks to prey on working people hard up for cash.

There is an income differential in the Soviet Union—socialist society is based on the principle "from each according to his ability and to each according to his work." By our standards, the "gap" between high and low incomes in the USSR is hardly noticeable—though for Soviet citizens, who do not measure with our yardstick, it is a source of concern. It is a gap they, their government, and their Communist Party accept as only temporary and are working to eliminate. That's what the construction of Communist society—based on the principle "from each according to his ability and to each according to his needs" is all about.

The result of all this is a *truly mass purchasing power* that is in the hands of the *entire population*. The main problem faced by Soviet society and its rapidly expanding, modernized industrial and agricultural machine is to *keep up* with this mass purchasing power. Unlike the situation in our country, there are no bulging warehouses with goods people sorely need but can't afford to buy. At times commodities lie on the shelf. When they do, it is not because they are priced out of the reach of the average consumer but because of poor quality. The process is almost a direct one from the factory and farm to the consumer via the store or the street. Salespeople rarely have to wait for customers and almost an entire day's supply is bought up daily. Food products rarely lie on the counter long enough to lose their freshness.

Yet, for all its basic considerable advantages and recent improvements, Soviet shopping reveals that essentially neither production nor distribution has yet caught up with demand and the purchasing power in the hands of the mass of the Soviet people. Correspondents of the big-business press concentrate on this aspect of the subject to contrast our society's supposed affluence with the scarcities under socialism. Americans are not told of the ridiculously low price of drugs and books; the stable, even declining, prices and low rents; but they do hear about those commodities which are higher priced than ours and those in short supply. And they are certainly told of the long shopping lines.

The shortages in the Soviet Union are not *man made*. Anyone who would dump milk on the ground, slaughter pigs, plough under cotton, burn grain and corn to keep prices from falling, as has happened in our country during the Great Depression of the 1930s or hold back and reduce the supply of meat, sugar, gasoline and oil to boost prices artificially, as the food and oil monopolies are now doing, would be taken to the nearest insane asylum or prison. Soviet shortages are the product of a history of ordeals no other country in the world can match—the price it had to pay to pull itself up, by its own bootstraps from a backward past.

It is worth recalling the price paid by the Soviet people to save their country and the world from fascism. These figures never really deeply penetrated into the minds of our people, who themselves have not suffered the ravages of a war on their soil for more than a century. Perhaps one should remember when mentioning that meat is still not so plentiful in the Soviet Union as it is in the United States, (though high prices keep it off many U.S. tables), that the Nazis seized and took to Germany more than 60 million head of cattle, in addition to demolishing thousands of collective and state farms.

If the 24th Congress of the CPSU sounded one clear and determined message, it was that the sinews of the entire powerful Soviet industrial, scientific, and agricultural machinery are being mobilized to increasingly satisfy consumer demand. Something had entirely escaped me previously, even though I was theoretically familiar with the operation of Soviet socialist society. Now I really understood the meaning of the words: the main law of socialist economy is the continuous and increasing satisfaction of the material and cultural needs of the people. Our own society is motivated by only one "law"—the drive for maximum profits.

Everything that Soviet society produced was thought of in terms of the entire population, not just the more affluent sections of society. In our country, the 25 million Americans officially listed as living below the poverty level are hardly regarded as serious consumers. For them shortages are permanent. Very little of our unparalleled industrial machine and our bountiful agricultural resources are geared for this market. But in the Soviet Union there are no such categories in its population. The market toward which the Soviet economy is directed is far greater than the one any capitalist country sets itself.

By comparison with the past, Soviet people are beginning to experience abundance and their appetite is growing with the eating. The gripes I heard, as I waited on a line in stores, were the complaints of a people who know they are moving onto the long-awaited, hard-earned highway of plenty and who are impatient with inefficiencies which can no longer be justified. This goes for poor quality of goods, inadequate services, and rude salespeople. Leonid Brezhnev at the 24th Congress gave clear expression to this impatience with such weaknesses and sounded the call to battle to eliminate them.

Soviet shopping reflects both the advances and the problems still to be solved. But there is no question that, given peace, the USSR is now well on the road to becoming a mass affluent society in the best meaning of that much-abused concept. This is so because the entire Soviet society, from the Soviet Council of Ministers and Central Committee of the CPSU to the factory and farm, is striving to accomplish this goal. Soviet newspapers, radio and television keep a daily scorecard on how each unit of society is contributing toward reaching it. The heroes and heroines who grace the front pages of *Pravda, Isvestia,* and are the stars of television, are the best workers and farmers. For the first time in history, the welfare of an entire people, above all, its economic, cultural, and social well-being, is the prime business of a government.

4 / CAN MODERN CITIES BE "LIVABLE"?

When I left New York, Mayor John Lindsay was getting a bit tired, walking the streets of Black and Puerto Rican ghettos in a well-publicized effort to convince the slum dwellers, who were desperately fighting rats, roaches and racism, that City Hall cared. Lindsay's handsome profile was a poor substitute for the homes, schools, and hospitals that were never built; the jobs that never materialized; the garbage that festered in Harlem, Bedford-Stuyvesant, and Brownsville streets; the dope pushers who destroyed the kids; and the brutal racist cops who shot them.

In my more than five years in Moscow, I never once saw Mayor Promyslov take a similar walk to soothe Muscovites. Promyslov didn't have to. Muscovites have more substantial proof that their city and their government, on every level, care. The difference between the mayors of these great cities is far more than a matter of style.

The *New York Times* of June 5, 1969, noted that Lindsay, as a candidate for mayor in 1965, promised to build 160,000 low- and middle-income apartments in four years. Considering New York City's housing needs, this was hardly an extravagant pledge. The *Times,* however, pointed out that Lindsay fell far short of his commitment. It noted that in the subsequent three and one half years "the city started only 34,167 apartments and just 8,920 of these were for low-income families." Moscow's plan, on the other hand, called for 120,000 apartments a year and 120,000 were constructed. The difference goes to the root of the contrasting social systems.

One of the most important stories the Soviet Union has to tell is why its great cities are cities without crises—why they are flourishing. The Soviet Union is not only pointing the way to bridging the age-old gap between town and country; it is showing the world how to resolve the complex problems of modern cities; how to make them livable. Nothing has so jolted the 70 percent of our own population who live in cities, as the realization which hit home with particular force in the 1960s, that our great cities are rapidly becoming unlivable. This realization exploded into a revolt, involving increasingly greater sections of our urban population, especially in the Black, Puerto Rican and Chicano ghettos. It was (and is) a rebellion against crisis living, against indifference and inhumanity on every governmental level, from the White House to City Hall.

As a reporter on New York affairs for the *Worker,* I already noted, in May, 1964, that the cities in our country were facing many-sided, increasingly severe crises. This background induced me to make a study of city life and problems in Soviet society. Living in Moscow for more than five years, as well as visiting many cities in the fourteen republics, gave me a pretty good idea of the differences between life in the Soviet cities and those in the United States.

Is it safe to walk Moscow's streets at night? Is it safe to breathe its air? How do Soviet schools teach their children—*all* their children? Americans, familiar with the situation in so-called difficult schools in Black, Puerto Rican and Chicano ghettos and barrios and in poor working-class areas will understand the stress on *all.* How do Muscovites and Soviet people generally get to work? How are they cared for when they are ill? How are the most afflicted, the physically and mentally handicapped, provided for? How are Soviet cities kept clean? What is their cultural and recreational life like? What do Soviet urban dwellers pay in taxes? Do Soviet cities face annual budget crises? How are they financed? Do Soviet cities have slums, ghettos and neighborhoods such as divide our cities? Are Soviet cities tinderboxes of tension, as are ours? And, last but not least: What is the relationship between Soviet citizens and their police—militia, as they call them?

Modern urban life poses a major challenge to the two social systems existing in the world today. And, above all, the world will want to know: How are the major representatives of these two world systems meeting this challenge? To put it bluntly: Where are cities more livable?

Soviet cities are not only incomparably more livable than our own,

but they are cities with bright futures. If U.S. big city dv
spend some months walking Soviet city streets at all hour:
contact with its militia, going to its schools, riding its subways,
its parks, theaters and concert halls, and being cared for by its docto₁.,
polyclinics and hospitals, they would come back with many questions
(and many answers) for the big-bank dominated government officials
who answer our cities' crises by heaping more lay-offs, tax and price
increases, and less and poorer services onto the backs of the working
people.

Not that they would find a utopia in the Soviet Union. There is still
plenty to complain about in Soviet cities and Soviet citizens are not
restrained in their complaints.

Many of the problems have their source in historic factors: in the
remnants of the czarist past; in physical surroundings, practices and
habits that still cling tenaciously to people; in the lingering effects of the
massive destruction and the cataclysmic social uprooting of World War
II. Only by living here can one truly realize how much further Soviet
life would now be advanced toward the construction of communism had
it not been set back by the incalculable physical and human losses in the
war against fascism.

But there are also problems that stem from inefficiency, poor organization, and petty bureaucracy. They are, indeed, irritating problems
which one meets in all phases of Soviet life. Bourgeois correspondents
delight in reporting and distorting them for good measure. Such problems do exist—expecially in services which, as a result of understandable past preoccupation with laying the industrial foundation of the
Soviet Union, are in a relatively early stage of development here. There
are also urban problems which the Soviet Union faces, in common with
all highly industrialized countries: pollution, transportation, and the
relationship between community life and industry; the stresses of big
city life (not the tensions produced by the class, racial and national
conflicts and antagonisms of "free-enterprise" society); noise, and the
control of that mechanical "monster"—the automobile.

Soviet cities face *problems;* ours face *crises.* That is the great divide
between the cities of our two great countries. Problems can and will be
solved with time, experience, and effort. But what can be said about the
crisis of our cities? In the past decade, it has been the subject of
countless studies and reports. In that decade, according to official calculations, $150 billion was spent to destroy cities and villages of Vietnam

and to create countless My Lais. According to a *New York Times* study, June 5, 1969, the New York City Planning Commission estimated that "to make a visible dent in the city's housing problem, $580 million a year must be allocated for ten years at least." Yet the same article notes that Washington allocated only "about $100 million to New York for all its housing program in 1968." The same abysmal gap between word and deed, the same monstrous sense of values, characterizes the abuse to which our capitalist society and the successive administrations representing it have subjected the bountiful resources of our beautiful country and the talents of our industrious working people.

Our crisis-ridden great cities, from which increasing numbers are fleeing in terror, stand as the most powerful indictments of the inhumanism as well as obstructionism of our social system. Where are they to run, the *New York Times* asks, in its study. And it correctly notes that the flight to the suburbs, which only the more affluent can afford, is no escape because the social ills will only catch up with them in time. This is so because, as many Americans are beginning to learn, it is a diseased social system and not geography that is at the bottom of the urban crisis.

The essence of Soviet living is that there is no unbridgeable gap between work and deed. Deeds do fall short of plans at times. The failures are the result of human weaknesses and errors, either in planning or execution. Planning in the Soviet Union is a law of life in every phase of living and cities are no exception. A plan (once adopted) is not a pledge; it is a commitment, a law. Failure to fulfill a plan is the subject of sharp public discussion and accounting that usually result in overcoming the obstacles hindering its fulfillment.

I met with city officials of Moscow, Kiev, Lvov, Kishinev, Riga, Leningrad, and with many members of local Soviets in town and village. All lived by Master Plans that extended from ten to twenty-five years, as well as by yearly plans. The plans are based on scientific estimates of the needs of the cities as well as the resources required to realize them. Both are only possible in a socialist society that has eliminated anarchy of production and the leeches of capitalism.

For example: Soviet cities can construct homes on a scale unprecedented in history because, among other things, they do not have to pay real-estate hogs for the right to build on the land (a price that in New York and other major U.S. cities often is as great or greater than the cost of construction itself). The land is the property of the state and belongs to all the Soviet people.

For the same reason, Soviet cities can be planned. Moscow is planned by a centralized body of 1,500 highly trained architects. The mustering of such a force would be beyond the means of any U.S. city. Moreover, the architects would fight a losing battle with the powerful real estate and banking interests for every inch of park space and every landmark they sought to preserve. One has but to recall how these interests ran roughshod over the protests of New Yorkers to tear down one of our most beautiful structures, the Pennsylvania Railroad station, in order to make room for the more profitable new Madison Square Garden. Such a situation is unimaginable in the USSR. Moscow annually spends huge sums to preserve and restore more than 1,000 historic buildings, monuments and homes. A walk through Moscow streets is like a stroll through its ancient and revolutionary history. I found this to be the case in every Soviet city I visited. Houses where great writers, actors, artists, scientists and revolutionaries lived are noted by plaques. For example, Nezhdanova Street in Moscow is a stroll into Russian and Soviet theatrical history. This not only pays tribute to those who left their mark in history, but preserves, perpetuates and enhances the character of a city. This is one of the most delightful characteristics of Soviet cities.

What particularly impressed me is that I found nowhere that sense of futility and blind groping that characterizes discussions on the problems of cities in our country. In fact, living there, it is difficult to think in such terms as a crisis of cities. You think of problems—big problems—but never are they viewed as beyond Soviet society's means of solution. And the basic reason for this lies in Soviet urban reality. Soviet cities are not decaying—they are flourishing. They are becoming increasingly livable. Soviet cities are living proof that it is not population size (though Moscow's plan limits the city's size to 7.5 to 8 million), nor the complex problems of modern urban life that determines whether cities are in crisis or flourishing, manageable or unmanageable, livable or unlivable. It is the *social system*.

While the crisis of our cities can be to some extent lessened, the vast and complex problems of urban existence cannot be solved under capitalism. Big cities, like big industry or large-scale agriculture, can no longer function in the interests of the mass of the people in an outmoded social system based on private gain and profit rather than on common welfare. The scientific-technological revolution has everywhere tremendously sharpened and laid bare the contradictions of capitalism and nowhere is this more oppressively reflected than in the crisis of our cities—for cities are the concentrated centers of capitalist contradictions. What the crisis of our cities demonstrates, above all, is that the capitalist system is no more able to grapple with the complex problems of urban life than it can resolve problems arising from the anarchy of production. Socialist cities, on the other hand, can resolve and are resolving such problems for the same reasons that they have overcome the problems of unemployment, poverty, racism and national divisions. As in all aspects of modern social existence, the more than half-century of Soviet socialist examples point up the lessons which show the way out of our urban crisis.

5 / LIFE WITHOUT LANDLORDS

We had not lived in the Soviet Union very long when it occurred to us we had completely forgotten about a very important person in our lives—our landlord. The first of the month held no terror for us here. At home our landlord was our first concern. You gave him his cut—from 25 percent to 30 percent or more of your monthly income—and then you turned to your other worries— the utility monopolies which sliced off $20 or more for gas and electricity, and another $25 on the average for telephone. Then there were doctor bills, insurance payments, and college tuition for the children.

One of the greatest pleasures in our living in the Soviet Union came from our acceptance of the first of the month as just another day. One of the chief factors contributing toward making Soviet cities tension-free is that the inhabitants are free of landlord worries.

Those who make it their business to protest the alleged denial of individual rights of Soviet citizens can put this "abrogated right" on the top of their list: *Soviet citizens are denied the right to worry about landlords.* Moreover, these "defenders" can add to their list still another curtailment in Soviet socialist life: the denial of the right of existence to landlords.

What is it, after all, that makes a city tense? Basically it can be traced to the individual citizen's worries. Americans who walk our cities' streets are bundles of worries. They worry about their landlords. They worry about getting or keeping a job. They worry about the calamity that would strike them should they get sick; and when serious illness does strike, they worry about paying the doctor and the hospital, and about losing their jobs. They worry about walking the streets at night. They worry about their youth getting sucked into the expanding whirlpool of drug addiction. And if they are Black, Puerto Rican, Chicano, a Native American Indian, or an Asian-American, then not only are all these worries considerably magnified, but to them is added the daily humiliation of the economic and social barriers of racism.

Soviet people, city dwellers included, have their worries—but these are not among them. Socialism, though it has freed people from most of the deadly social and economic worries that beset citizens of our "free" world, has far from eliminated personal unhappiness and tragedies. Personal worries resulting from problems of love, marriage, sickness, etc., have not been eliminated. They just exist in a society that does not aggravate and complicate them and does its best to minimize and overcome them.

Communism will, of course, greatly extend man's capacity for happiness. But those who look to a social system, even the most advanced and most human in history, to do away with all personal unhappiness are seeking a utopia. This has never been claimed for socialism and communism by either the founders of scientific socialism or the leaders of the Soviet Union. The social worries facing the Soviet people arise largely from unresolved problems that still exist in Soviet society in the period of socialism and are complicated by the effects of World War II. Among them is the serious housing shortage. But the Soviet people know that these are temporary worries. This knowledge is based not on blind faith or self-delusion, but on solid reality.

This is hardly the outlook our urban dwellers have. Let me just illustrate it with this one fact. The *New York Times* (June 5, 1969) notes that at the rate of public-housing construction of homes people with low incomes could afford in the United States, such families "could expect to move into a project in 51 years." It points out: "To solve this problem, New York City needs right now 780,000 new subsidized apartments but the federal housing program, in its *34-year history, has produced only 800,000 units across the entire country.*" [My emphasis, M.D.] By contrast, the Soviet Union constructed 11,350,000 new or improved apartments in the five-year period 1966-70, about 2.3 million a year, and another 12 million during the 9th Five Year Plan (1971-75).

These homes will be constructed for those who need them and not for those who can afford to pay most for them. Homes are built *for people – not for profit*. There is large-scale housing construction in the United States. The entire world recognizes the tremendous productive capacity of our extremely skilled construction workers. In the 1960-1970 period, the yearly rate of apartment building in the United States was 1.4 million units a year (as against 2.3 million in the Soviet Union). The current crisis has resulted in a 50 percent reduction in construction in the United States.

What makes the contrast between Soviet and U.S. apartment building more meaningful is the answer to the question: For whom are apartments being built? Take New York as an example. Here is how the *New York Times*, in its article titled "The Changing City: Housing Paralysis" (June 5, 1969) described the situation: "The state of housing in New York seems as hopeless as an abandoned tenement whose broken windows stare blankly out on a slum." For whom are homes being built? "Private industry is building apartments for only the wealthiest 7 percent of the population, except in cases where it receives government subsidies." The *New York Times* points out: "Private industry has built and owns 92 percent of the city's 2.8 million residential units without government subsidies." And the *Times* adds: "But privately financed apartment houses are now going up only in the most prestigious neighborhoods, such as Manhattan's East Side, and monthly rents are in the range of $100 to $130 a room." This rental rate has since risen.

The building of homes is regarded as one of the main duties of socialist society. To place such a vital social task in the hands of those who would use it to extract profits from high rents, and who would use that inhuman yardstick to pass on who gets an apartment and who doesn't would be regarded as the height of irrationality by any Soviet citizen. The construction of housing in the Soviet Union is one of the chief functions of Soviet government on every level. I will describe later how this is organized and give some of the background of its historical development.

Soviet citizens have no rent worries. This is not only because they have no landlords but because they hardly pay rent: 4 percent or less of one's income. U.S. rent payers would "laugh" at Soviet rents. Take our family. When we left the States we were paying $150 a month rent—not too high by U.S. standards. But when my wife Gail visited our apartment in the Bronx in May, 1972, the rent had gone up to $235 a month. By contrast, our rent in Moscow remained static for five years, at 18 rubles 30 kopecks a month! (About $20 at the official exchange rate.) We had three large rooms (they don't count the kitchen as a room there) with all modern conveniences. I have before me our rent book. Here is how it breaks down: 12 rubles, 32 kopecks for the apartment itself; 4 rubles, 19 kopecks for heat (all apartments are centrally heated); one ruble, 20 kopecks for water and sewage; 50 kopecks for radio; 15 kopecks for the TV antenna. And in comparison with our friends, ours was a higher than average rent. As for our utilities: for gas, the average monthly charge was 22 kopecks per person. (It was recently reduced from 32 kopecks—can Americans remember their last utility reduction?) Electricity was a little higher, about 4 or 5 rubles a month in winter and about 5 rubles in summer. We paid 2 rubles, 50 kopecks a month for telephone for unlimited local calls.

The amount of the rent does not determine who gets a decent apartment. Who can't afford to pay these rents? It should be noted that because of the serious housing shortage that still exists, the method of distributing apartments is clearly delineated and strictly enforced in public view. Only in cooperative housing (about 6 to 7 percent of housing construction in Moscow) is income an important factor and even here it is negligible compared to U.S. standards. The cardinal criterion determining the distribution of Soviet housing is *need* not *income*.

Here is how it works. Persons with the greatest need get preference in the distribution of housing. Those with less than five square meters per person in housing space (it was three meters before 1969), the minimum prescribed by law, are given first priority. Special consideration is given to war invalids, sick people, disabled workers, large families and Heroes of Labor. Families living in very old substandard houses are also given preference. Exemplary workers are accorded preferential treatment by their unions in the distribution of new apartments built with the plants' funds.

State-owned apartments are allocated by special housing committees set up in each of Moscow's 30 local Soviets. These committees openly consider housing requests and complaints. Allocations are discussed publicly at meetings of the executive committee of the local Soviet. The names of all those receiving new apartments are placed on public wall bulletins. At the beginning of each year, the names of those waiting for apartments are listed on these bulletins in order of priority.

Vast construction programs, particularly during the last twelve years, have considerably reduced the waiting rolls and shortened the waiting period. From 1965 to 1973, 840,000 Moscow families (more than every second family) received new or improved apartments (more than the total constructed in the U.S. federal housing program during its 34-year history).

Moscow and Soviet cities generally still have serious housing problems, a sizable number of Soviet citizens still share apartments, and there is a considerable waiting list for new apartments. This particularly affects small families and single persons. The State first concentrated on meeting the most pressing demand for large flats for families. It is also more expensive to build small apartments. But as the volume of housing construction mounts, attention is increasingly being paid to the singles' problems. More small apartments are being built.

The Soviet Union is well on the road to becoming the *first country* in history to solve the housing problem for its people. No social system besides socialism ever set itself such a goal, let alone demonstrated that it can be done. What this means in respect to resolving the problems of modern cities can hardly be overestimated—for the problem of urban living is first of all—homes. I often thought: what would be the effect on the lives of the mass of U.S. urban dwellers, especially in the Black ghettos, Puerto Rican and Chicano barrios, if they were truly guaranteed the "security of their homes," if they lived with the realization that they were assured "the comforts of home" as their normal right? And what effect would all this have on reducing the tensions which are ripping our cities apart?

The Soviet Union is one vast construction site—especially in the cities. And first priority is being given to building adequate housing for the people. This is so apparent even to visitors that A. Allen Bates, director of the Office of Standards Policy of the U.S. Department of Commerce, told a congressional hearing: "The Soviet Union is the first, and thus far the only, nation which has solved the problem of providing acceptable low-cost housing for the mass of its citizens. . . . In the USSR, all housing built in the last twenty years has been deliberately designed as low-cost housing. In the United States, no housing built during that period, or now designed for future construction, can be characterized as low-cost housing." And Bates added: "Slums are not profitable under the Russian form of economy." And one may well ask: Why should they be profitable in our country?

In 1971-75 twelve million apartments were built, more than the total housing space the Soviet Union had in 1950. More than 60 million people (in addition to the 55 million in the 1965-70 period) have *improved* their housing. More than 73 billion rubles was spent from 1971-75, 22 percent greater than the previous five years.

I asked Nikolai Ullas, deputy head of the capital's Architectural and Planning Department, this question: When do you think Moscow's housing problem will be largely solved? Ullas gave the question a serious, thoughtful answer. Solving Moscow's housing problem means: the 30 percent who still share apartments (mostly members of the same family) will move into their own; the still sizable waiting list for new apartments will be largely accommodated and the waiting period reduced to what may be expected of a metropolitan city. It also means the elimination of 9 million square meters of old housing (the equivalent of 300,000 apartments). The latter constitute Moscow's major residue of the substandard housing inherited from czarist days—largely wooden single-family homes.

Ullas divided his answer into two parts. In respect to the first two problems, he declared that they will be solved largely by 1980 (the end of the 10th Five Year Plan). As regards the last point, the most difficult since it involved dealing with private homes, Ullas stated it would take another five to ten years.

Thus, the outlook is by 1985-90 Moscow will be a city *completely without substandard housing.* No major city in the capitalist world can look forward to such a future. I don't know what the prospect is for the Soviet Union as a whole. Certainly, special attention is given to Moscow which, the 24th Congress of the Communist Party of the Soviet Union decreed, must become the model Communist city. But I would hazard the guess that the Soviet Union (given peace) will enter the twenty-first century with the housing problem largely solved.

The Soviet Union has the right to boast of its socialist "miracles"— in this case the housing "miracle" is all the greater when we consider the situation in the country fifty-eight years ago when the young socialist republic started. More than 60 percent of the urban housing was made up of one- and two-story wooden dwellings; less than 10 percent of the homes in the central parts of big cities had running water; less than 3 percent had sewage and only 5 percent had electricity. Moscow, the capital of the czars (notwithstanding its palatial homes for the nobility, rich merchants and capitalists), was a city of incredible slums. More than 325,000 (out of a total Moscow population in 1917 of 1,850,000) lived, fifteen persons to a room, in slums of wooden barracks. And for this kind of housing, rents took 15 to 22 percent of a working family's income. The conditions among the peasant poor in the villages was even worse.

The humanism of the new social system is best revealed in the Soviet Union's housing story. This is truly "socialism with a human face." One of the first acts of the government following the October Revolution was the expropriation of the homes of the rich and their conversion into apartments for the working people. This was done under the decree issued November 8 (one day after the Revolution), "On Requisitioning Flats of the Rich to Relieve the Plight of the Poor."

Even though each exploiter had several apartments and estates, the redistribution hardly made a dent in the abysmal housing situation the new socialist state inherited. The Soviet Union faced an unprecedented *concentration* of housing problems. It had to build new housing almost from the ground up (and underground, since sewage, water, and a gas supply were nearly nonexistent). It had to construct not only for those who lived in the cities at the time of the Revolution but for the millions who were streaming into the cities from the countryside under the impact of the socialist industrialization program. This program transformed the Soviet Union in record time from a backward agricultural country into an advanced industrial country.

In terms of urban problems this meant that between 1926 and 1971 the population of the cities increased by more than 110 million (it is now more than 140 million out of 250 million). In 1940, after substantial progress had been made in urban housing construction, the Soviet Union was struck by the Nazi holocaust. No country in history ever suffered such destruction of life and property as did the Soviet Union in the four war years: 1,710 towns and urban settlements, 70,000 villages, 32,000 industrial enterprises, thousands of medical, educational and cultural establishments were destroyed. Great cities like Kiev, Stalingrad, Minsk, Sevastopol, Odessa, Novgorod, Pskov, and Orel were turned into ruins. Heroic Leningrad lost one-third of its population (900,000) and much of the city was severely damaged. Not only were there 20 million war dead but 25 million people were homeless. This was the housing problem the Soviet Union confronted: *The inheritance from a backward past, the demands arising from unprecedented industrialization and the destruction wrought by the most barbaric war machine in history. Never before did a country face such a combination of problems all packed within the space of half a century.*

One does not have to speculate on what would happen if our "free-enterprise system" faced comparable problems. A look at what happened to rents in the United States in a tight housing situation, and particularly in New York City, where 70 percent of the population are tenants, can give one a good idea. Even New York's rent control law, the last to hold out against unrelenting landlord assaults, offers little protection.

The big landlords and big real estate interests conduct guerrilla warfare against tenants in rent-controlled buildings in a campaign to undermine and destroy the rent control law. Wielding their power, they punish tenants by refusing to make necessary repairs, curtailing the supply of heat in winter, allowing rats and roaches to invade apartments. They organize "tax strikes" to bring pressure on City Hall. Noting that an estimated two to three thousand buildings are abandoned by landlords every year, the *New York Times* said:"As a result, more and more vacant structures are left standing, with a depressing and demoralizing impact on surrounding property and residents. Their infection spreads quickly through whole blocks, until some sections of the city now *resemble bombed-out areas of wartime Europe."* And the *Times* points out, "abandonment is a national problem, even in major cities without rent control."

Abandoned apartment buildings in the Soviet Union? Landlords who discard old buildings like worn-out socks? This is like conjuring up the Middle Ages, like applying the standards of an insane, inhuman world to a sane and human society.

I spoke to Soviet people who told me of the days they lived in abandoned buildings. But that was during or shortly after the war. Inhabitants of demolished Minsk told me they were compelled to live for some years in caves and underground shelters. No Soviet citizen has ever been denied decent shelter by the whim of someone who could no longer make a suitable profit out of it.

The Soviet Union, as I already indicated, had to confront a far more critical housing situation than we ever did. It still does in some areas, particularly in rural regions. It certainly does not compare with the United States with respect to luxury housing or middle-class private homes. It has to catch up with U.S. know-how, particularly in plumbing and the finishing touches of apartment construction. But in the critical matter of providing decent homes for the mass of working people at rents that they can afford, there is no comparison.

The Soviet housing success story is summed up in this: like the hammer and sickle, the building crane in the sky has become the symbol of Soviet power.When I visited Moscow's Central Construction organization, Abram Isaacovitch Birger, dynamic chief engineer of the designing bureau, told me: "In our gigantic construction everything depends on the crane." It really does. Cranes with 8-ton capacity lift huge iron-reinforced concrete slabs, making up a wall of a good-sized room, as if they were toys in a child's erector set. It's a common sight to see "a slip of a girl" manipulate these monsters with dexterity and ease. The crane is a key to Soviet housing construction because buildings are largely prefabricated.

Most construction is done indoors. This not only makes for assembly-line production methods but is extremely important in a country where winters are long and severe. Not that building is restrained by winter. Construction is not seasonal— it is a year-round affair. Work in Siberia and the Far North, for example, is halted only when the temperature hits 45 degrees below zero (centigrade). Success in housing was made possible because the Soviet Union did for housing construction what industrial production in the auto industry did for the United States. It put home building on the assembly line; it *prefabricated construction.*

Whereas, in our "free-enterprise society" workers are compelled to resist such progress because it spells death to their jobs, this advanced prefabrication process was welcomed by the building workers in the Soviet Union who, like all other workers there, have no need to fear unemployment.

Whereas in the 1930s, 10,000 to 15,000 apartments a year were built by the traditional methods, beginning with 1966-67 it rose to 120,000 annually. Of these, 80 to 85 percent are prefabricated. Once the apartments have been "manufactured," it's largely a matter of assembling them. It takes 28 days to assemble a 9-story building containing 144 apartments. Another 12 to 14 days are required for finishing work. A building of that size would take six months to construct under traditional construction methods. The prefabricated method requires 4 to 4.5 times less labor and saves considerably on the use of raw material.

I visited two factories (in Moscow and Leningrad) where prefabricated units are manufactured on the assembly line. There were two conveyors in the plant, one for production of inside walls and the other for outside walls. A huge concrete mixer poured its mixture into metal frames already containing all the necessary wiring units and pipes for central heating. Thus, most of the electrical and plumbing work was already done. The heating pipes are encased in the walls. This not only saves time and labor but keeps the walls warm. Vibration along the conveyor settles and hardens the mixture and the walled surfaces are polished. The walls are then heated in an ovenlike process. The entire operation takes from two to eight hours. Light-weight sand is used. The aim is to find the lightest materials with the strongest and most lasting qualities, able to withstand Russian winters as well as intense heat.

Housing construction and all building in the Soviet Union are organized and conducted by huge *combinats*, which combine manufacture and assembly. There are three such *combinats* in Moscow. The work of laying the foundation is done by specialized organizations whose work is also coordinated by the *combinat*. The advantages of this unified industrialized method of construction have proven themselves. The Soviet Union's unmatched, unceasing construction would be unthinkable without it. Although in the United States the cost of construction has skyrocketed to such a point (in 1969 it was 118 percent above the 1949 level and is much higher today) that it has priced housing beyond the reach of many Americans, housing costs in the Soviet Union are being steadily reduced. And this is not at the expense of the workers or through speedup resulting in increased accidents,as is often the case in our construction industry. In construction, as everywhere in the Soviet Union, the word of the union and the job safety committee is law and no work is done without its O.K.

According to Dr. John R. Gates, chief of building and housing of the U.S. Department of Commerce, profits, financing, and land costs account for 44.7 percent of the cost of constructing a house in the United States: land, 19 percent; contractor, 12.3 percent; financing, 6.7 percent; and real-estate fees, 6.4 percent. These are all expenses that are alien to Soviet housing construction. Incidentally, labor costs for housing construction are only 26 percent in the United States—far below the "expenses" listed by Gates. A 1969 report on Soviet housing by an eight-man delegation headed by Dr. James R. Wright, Chief of the Building Research Division, National Bureau of Standards, Department of Commerce, noted that many of the basic advantages enjoyed by Soviet housing construction cannot be applied to construction in the United States, where interest, land, operating expenses, and taxes are more important in the price of housing than labor and materials (*Daily World*, May 19, 1973).

An additional charge paid by home owners and tenants in the United States is unknown in the Soviet Union—graft. This, as Americans know, is viewed as an indispensable element in construction in our society. The *New York Times*, June 29, 1972, after a six-week investigation, reported that the New York City construction industry pays "at least $25 million a year in bribes to city building inspectors, highway officials, policemen, state safety inspectors, agents of the Federal Housing Administration, clerks in various agencies, union representatives and certain powerful blue-collar workers."

Notwithstanding all its basic advantages, there are serious problems in Soviet construction. These are the subject of sharp discussion in the Soviet press. In the report of the Central Committee at the 24th Congress of the Communist Party of the Soviet Union, Leonid Brezhnev, General Secretary of the party, noted the major shortcomings in construction:"Plan and financial discipline are sometimes violated. Insufficient use is made of new effective materials and building elements. The quality of construction remains poor." It is on the last point that a particularly sharp struggle is being waged, resulting in improvements in the quality of new housing.

Soviet architects will admit that the problem of combining mass production with utility and beauty is a complex one. Because of the critical housing shortage, the overriding need was speed—speed and more speed in construction. Some of the results of this can be seen in the early prefabricated apartment buildings. They were pointed out to me in Vilnius by my genial host and colleague, Domas Snuikas of *Tiesa,* Soviet Lithuania's *Pravda.* "Our first pancakes in the batch," Snuikas called them. And "first pancakes" is what they look like in Vilnius and wherever else they are found. Boxlike, poorly finished and montonous in uniformity, they hardly graced Old Vilnius. The "second batch" was a vast improvement. (Vilnuis received a Soviet award for its "second batch".) The finishing was smoother, the designs more attractive, and the beginnings of variety in form were discernible.

The "third" and latest batch is now appearing in increasing numbers in all Soviet cities, the culmination of years of effort and experience in the struggle to combine beauty and utility. There is still far to go in this respect, but the progress is unmistakable. Monotonous uniformity is beginning to give ground to variety. The basis for this, explained to me by Birger, head of Moscow's experimental designing bureau, is the panel system, which allows for flexibility in construction. Panel units, like blocks in a child's set, can be positioned in an unlimited number of ways. Rooms are now more attractive and comfortable, with all modern conveniences. The progress that has been made is attested to by the praise of U S. architects. Scott Ferebee, the president of the American Institute of Architects, who visited the Soviet Union in December, 1972, said that he was impressed by the major qualitative changes in Soviet town building in recent years.

More stress is also being placed on taller buildings (nine to twelve stories and lately twenty-five stories) in Moscow. Larger units are more economical and use land more rationally. Spread-out cities like Moscow, tax transportation. There is lots of room—a little too much to make it easy to get around. And it's quite a job for the Metro and buses to keep pace with the construction of what amounts to little cities within the big city. The aim is to reduce the time required for workers to get to and from work to no more than a 30-minute ride each way.

Contrary to the false picture of a propertyless population under socialism, Soviet citizens can and do own their own homes. Under Soviet law, however, they can't use their property to exploit tenants. Soviet citizens are permitted to build one- or two-story private homes, generally with not more than five rooms. They are allotted plots of land by the state *free of charge*. Such individual private homes are quite widespread in rural areas and small towns, and they constitute one-third of the total housing. These homes, which compare favorably with our own workers' and farmers' homes, are usually built by collective or state farm construction organizations with state assistance. Loans are provided at about 2 percent interest. Incidentally, summer homes are quite numerous. Those who want to build *dachas* are given land free.

Contrast this with the situation noted by *U.S. News and World Report,* March 17, 1969: "If a house costs $20,000 and you get a $19,000 mortgage at an 8 percent rate [much higher now—M.D.] for 30 years, you will end up paying $31,206 *for interest alone* by the time you get the loan paid off."

In the Soviet Union considerable assistance is provided for those who desire and can afford to buy cooperative apartments. Cooperative apartment buildings are organized by enterprises, institutions, and executive committees of the Soviets in cities and rural areas. Here is how it works. A cooperator makes an advance payment of 40 percent of the cost of his apartment. One half of one percent is paid in interest on the state loan. The apartment is paid for in equal installments over a 10 to 15 year period. Local authorities allocate the ground space to the cooperative. When the full payment for the apartment is made (the period depends on the tenant), the member pays only the maintenance cost, which is about 15 rubles a month for a three-room apartment (the kitchen is not counted). Until then the member pays about 35 to 40 rubles a month rent. Unlike our cooperatives, there are no rent or maintenance increases. Cooperative housing has helped cut down the waiting period for new housing.

To sum up, Soviet construction is well on the road to solving the housing problem for the entire population—something never before even attempted by any society or country. It is becoming increasingly able to solve the problem faced by all mass-production industries—that of combining beauty and utility. Moreover, no country in the world can compare with the Soviet Union in the painstaking care and expenditure of effort and money to preserve the architectural heritage of the past. For the multinational USSR this means literally preserving the national flavor of over 100 peoples. All this makes for cities of both comfort and charm. These are the physical attributes of cities without crises.

Soviet housing is much more than bricks and concrete. It is trees and greenery. I'm not speaking now of parks which occupy so much of their cities' areas. Moscow, for example has 20 square meters of greenery per person; its surrounding environs bring the numbers up to 30. I'm referring to the little parks that make up the "back yards," courtyards. Every cluster of houses has one. It consists of a wooded area with park benches where one can rest and relax and children can play. One of the duties of the maintenance workers is to keep this area in good condition. Just the sight of the trees provides Soviet urban dwellers with relief from the oppressiveness of brick and concrete.

Trees can form a natural part of the Soviet housing scene because they constitute a natural element in the planning of housing construction.

Soviet housing grows with the city. It is part of a carefully thought-out plan whose aim is convenience, comfort and culture brought to where people live. When a new area goes up, nurseries, schools, polyclinics, cinemas, sport fields, stores—all go with them. The name given to these "little cities within a city" is "micro-area."

What about maintenance and repair of buildings and apartments? In our landlord-owned buildings, especially in ghetto slum areas, a guerrilla war between landlord and tenant is fought over every housing improvement. Abandoned buildings stand as damning evidence of the social destructiveness of the struggle.

Rats and roaches are not major problems in Moscow as they are in New York. As for the shrieking sounds of fire engines so familiar in New York, I have only on rare occasions heard them in Moscow.

Neither is the fight against winter a bitter tug-of-war between tenant and landlord. It is a common battle against cold led by the city Soviets and an elaborate housing organization. The severe Russian winters are made comfortable indoors by the vast city central heating system that warms every home. As for repairs, buildings are not permitted to deteriorate into slums. The idea that buildings are private property which can be neglected when they are no longer profitable is completely alien to the Soviet people. They have been brought up to regard and respect their buildings and their apartments as socialist property—belonging to the entire people. Thus, the responsibility for maintenance and repair is generally regarded by the Soviet tenant and the vast organization servicing him as a mutual one. This is not always the case but it is the law of the land and the spirit in which Soviet citizens are brought up and live.

I am familiar with this not only through study at all levels of the Moscow housing organization but as a tenant in an apartment building in which we were the only foreign family. The size and scope of Moscow's housing setup denotes in itself the care and consideration to tenants' needs that would be unthinkable in our country. Moscow's government-owned buildings are maintained and serviced by an army of 100,000 workers: mechanics, electricians, carpenters, painters, plumbers, roofers, etc. This does not include those who service the cooperative buildings.

Here is how the setup functions: Each of Moscow's 30 districts has its own maintenance department, commonly referred to by its initials, ZHEKH. I spent a day with ZHEKH in the Kalinin district. I would strongly urge that U.S. tenants' organizations visit the Soviet Union and arrange tenants tours of ZHEKH. It would bring home to them how pleasant life without landlords can be. Just consider this fact: Kalinin's 4,000 tenants living in 1,433 apartments are serviced by a staff of 167 full-time workers. For purposes of efficiency and closer contact with residents, each ZHEKH is subdivided into six branch offices, each headed by a *tekhnik-smotretel* (supervisor). Each branch office services nine to ten apartment buildings or four to five buildings in more densely populated areas.

The Soviet Union lives by *plan*. And ZHEKH is no exception. Kalinin's ZHEKH has its One Year and Five Year Plans. It has its seasonal as well as long-range objectives. The yearly plan is worked out during October to November on the basis of apartment visits and close consultation with house committees made up of tenants to determine specific needs. Winter plans begin every September 1. Russian winter is no joke and demands early and thorough preparation. Every household seals its windows with paper strips well ahead of the expected wintry blasts. But winterizing is the responsibility of ZHEKH and its subdivisions. It must see to it that the heating system is in good order; windows properly sealed; and floors and roofs in good condition. There are also many tasks in preparation for spring and summer. The ravages of winter place demands on maintenance and repair that are far greater than those in temperate climates.

Climate, I have come to appreciate, plays a considerable role in every aspect of social life. With most of its vast territory affected to varying degrees by severe winters, the Soviet Union in its industrial, agricultural, and transportation plans, as well as in respect to housing and maintenance, faces considerably more difficult problems than we do. Spring in Moscow and most Soviet cities means much more than a cleaning. It means repairing—particularly the outside walls of buildings. That's why it is common to see workers, many of them sturdy women, on scaffolds filling in cracks with cement. One also sees workers perched on roofs and balconies, clearing away the ice that could be dangerous to passersby.

Repairs are part of the *preventive* approach that guides every aspect of Soviet social living. You *prevent* sickness and you forestall or delay decay. The regulations are all written into law. We, too, have laws. But there's no one there in the USSR to bribe inspectors to look the other way. And most important, there's no one there to skimp on repairs. Problems arise and these pertain largely to minor household repairs caused by the neglect of individual maintenance workers.

Fire hazards have been reduced to a minimum, among other reasons, because electric wiring, a major cause of fires in big cities in the United States, is regularly checked and repaired (all new buildings, of course, are fireproof). Another important contributing factor: heating is piped from a central source instead of being produced in thousands of hazardous furnaces. This also does away with explosions, and considerably reduces pollution. More then 800 Soviet cities and towns are fully served by central heating systems, The Soviet Union is self-sufficient in oil, gas, and coal and is hardly menaced by an "energy crisis." But it seeks to avoid waste of fuel. Central heating is a great conserver of fuel.

Just as Soviet factories are much more than places to work, Soviet homes are more than places to live. They are centers of educational, cultural, sports activities—all supervised by ZHEKH. Each local area has its Red Corner for the children where they are taught to dance, sing and are also organized into amateur groups. Each ZHEKH has its people's court, composed of the tenants themselves, which settles local grievances arising among the tenants. It can impose fines.

In all Soviet cities housing must undergo capital repairs at least once every three years. These include plumbing, central heating, floors, etc. These are in addition to routine repairs occasionally necessary. Buildings must be completely restored, from the inside out, every 30 years.

Moscow has an elaborate setup for emergency repairs. There are 30 stations—one for each district. I visited the one in the October district and saw: huge cranes, mobile repair stations, 30 trucks, fire-fighting equipment and bulldozers. The station is fully equipped to handle any emergency around the clock—for this purpose it has 66 workers. In addition, the October station has a staff of 230 workers to handle all kinds of major repairs. But the work of this emergency setup is made considerably easier by the excellent system of regular inspection.

Our first week in our Moscow apartment we were introduced to this feature of tenant life which, as recent arrivals, we were hardly used to. A matronly woman rang our bell. She was a member of the tenants' house committee. "Do mice disturb you?" she asked. I could hardly suppress a smile. She didn't know quite what to make of this, so I told her, "No, they don't disturb us." From then on our doorbell was rung regularly for one or another checkup: every three months for general and fire inspection and every month for gas checkup. Incidentally, checkup is carried out not only by regular official inspection but by tenant house committees. These committees play an important and necessary role—not only in inspection, but in keeping maintenance workers on their toes. They listen to complaints and act on them. The maintenance worker at fault is deprived of a bonus, while good work is rewarded by higher bonuses.

However, maintenance is not considered solely the responsibility of the maintenance workers. Tenants, in the main, have a collective, socialist attitude toward buildings which, after all, belong to them as well as to Soviet society. They are held responsible for leaving their apartments in good condition when they move and for cleanliness and care of buildings. In the U.S. ghetto slums, property is not even treated with respect by its landlord owners. Service workers have no landlord in the USSR to tell them to skimp on heat or stall on repairs. Nor are they, as in the United States, underpaid and overworked. And they do not, as in our country, have to also bear the brunt of the frustration of abused tenants.

Unlike our maintenance workers, who are largely unorganized, Soviet maintenance workers are 100 percent unionized and enjoy the rights and benefits of all Soviet workers: free medical care, 24-day vacations (of which the union pays 70 percent of the cost), full sick benefits, retirement pensions for men at 60 and for women at 55. Like our *tekhnik-smotretel* Alla, they can go to special technical schools to increase their skills (two days a week with full pay). Maintenance technical schools and institutes are training a sizable corps of workers and technicians to make homes the comfortable pleasant place they are meant to be.

No setup, even one that is so oriented towards providing tenants with the utmost in services, is self-regulating. I came across neglect and delay in the handling of repairs and in responding to complaints, notwithstanding the vast army of workers charged with the responsibility of servicing Moscow's apartments. It is as irritating there as it is anywhere; it calls forth the justifiable wrath of Soviet tenants. But there is a vast difference between fighting your landlord and combating the inefficiency and indifference of some maintenance workers. The landlord's neglect is activated by his economic interests, which are in conflict with those of his tenants. Fewer services mean more profits. The neglect and delay in handling complaints we met in the Soviet Union stem from human deficiencies, lack of a conscientious attitude toward their jobs on the part of some maintenance workers, and poor organization and poor direction by individual housing units and ZHEKH. It was also often due to an insufficient supply of parts.

The Soviet tenant does not come up against the stonewall resistance of the landlord, backed by the entire legal and social structure of a society that places profits above people. The tenant faces no City Hall bureaucracy, and no landlord-biased courts to smother complaints and frustrate corrections.

The struggle against inefficiency and an indifferent attitude to one's work is waged by the entire Soviet society, all levels of government, the Communist Party, the press, radio and television. It is a vital element in the fight for a Communist attitude toward work. But Soviet tenants also have effective instruments at hand which they are not at all hesitant in using. First of all, there are the housing committees which meet regularly and check on the work of the maintenance organization. Then there are the people's control units, largely made up of the more civic-conscious retired workers who exercise a check on the maintenance organization itself.

In the more then five years I walked the streets of Moscow and numerous cities in 14 Republics, I never came across any racial or national ghettos. I never came upon slums or "poor neighborhoods." I saw old run-down houses but no areas where the underprivileged live. No district in Moscow or in any Soviet city can be identified by race or nationality. This is true even in cities in the non-Russian republics where, of course, citizens of that particular nation or nationality predominate. In Alma Ata (Kazakhstan) for example, Russians, Ukrainians and other national groups live side by side with Kazakhs and Uigars. In Moscow, Leningrad, Kiev, Odessa, Kishinev, Riga, Vilnius, and Minsk, there are large numbers of Jews but I never once came across a "Jewish neighborhood."

There are no "poor" neighborhoods because there are no poor, no underprivileged. Though under socialism there are those of higher income, you can never tell by the neighborhoods they live in. There are no slums because there are no slumlords. Thus, the buildings as well as those living in them are respected and cared for. There are no ghettos because racism and national discrimination which create and profit from ghettos have long been eliminated. Nothing more distinguishes Soviet cities from our own than the absence of these social sores that have made our urban centers cities of crisis. No Soviet citizens return from a day's work to depressing areas defined by their class position or the color of their skins. This is the meaning of life without landlords. *Where* one lives in our society determines *how* one lives. All this is wrapped up in the class character of our housing. This is the essence of ghetto slum living.

In 1872, Friedrich Engels noted that under capitalism the brutal exploitation of workers at the point of production is "not abolished" after working hours; it is "merely shifted elsewhere." The "elsewhere," as workers know, is "home," from the boss to the landlord or, as Engels put it, "the same economic necessity" which produced the miserable conditions at work "produced them in the next place also." And Engels concluded: "As long as the capitalist mode of production continues to exist, it is folly to hope for an isolated settlement of the housing question or any other social question affecting the lot of the workers. The solution lies in the abolition of the capitalist mode of production and the appropriation of all the means of subsistence and instruments of labor by the working class itself." (*The Housing Question,* Progress Publishers, Moscow, 1970, p. 71.) Nothing demonstrates more forcefully Engels' century-old truth than contrasting the housing stories of the United States and the USSR.

6 / SCHOOLS WITHOUT CRISIS

One of my first acts upon arrival in the Soviet Union was to "go to school." I spent three weeks in Moscow classrooms of all levels and I watched the children and youth with pleasure and pain. Pleasure, because nothing is more beautiful than the sight of happy children in the process of discovering a new world. Pain, because only a few weeks before, I had witnessed quite different scenes in our New York schools. I had come from schools that were battlegrounds, not places of learning. I recall how from February 3 to March 16, 1964, a period of little over a month, 728,616 children, led by their parents, boycotted New York schools. I had seen ugly scenes where reactionary-led mobs shouted racist epithets at children as they entered integrated schools, scenes now being repeated in Boston, Louisville, and elsewhere in our country. I had seen teachers, most of whom once regarded walking a picket line as beneath their "professional dignity," taking to the New York streets in militant strikes, because they were fed up with conditions which made it impossible for them to teach and denied them an adequate living standard. Teachers' strikes today, like parents' boycotts, are part of the U.S. school scene. They reflect two sides of our deepening school crisis.

As I entered Moscow schools, I reveled in their calm, in the natural harmonious relationship among children and youth of many races and nationalities in the normal atmosphere of learning that surrounded them. I mentioned this to my teacher-guide, who seemed puzzled by what appeared to her as an odd observation. She, like most Soviet citizens, found it hard to grasp the decay in our free enterprise society. Why shouldn't schools be able to teach? And why shouldn't there be the pleasant, calm atmosphere that makes it possible for teachers to teach and children to learn?

As I went from class to class in the Moscow schools, I thought to myself: suppose the situation were reversed, suppose Moscow parents, their children and teachers visited our New York schools, especially those euphemistically designated as "difficult schools" in Black and Puerto Rican ghettos or areas bordering them? They would see schools that relied on police patrols and corporal punishment to maintain classroom discipline. They would meet U.S. parents who send their children off to junior high and high schools with the dread fear that they can be induced to drug addiction by preying drug pushers.

U.S. News and World Report, May 25, 1970, noted that of the 900 who died from overuse of drugs in 1969 in New York City alone, 224 were teenagers and 24 were *under* 15 years of age. It stated, "in virtually every *major* metropolitan area of the country, drug use and abuse has increased by leaps and bounds and is now getting into the junior high schools."

As in housing, one can only fully appreciate the advances in Soviet education by looking back at its beginning. Czarist Russia was a land of illiteracy; three-quarters of its population could not read or write. Not only was illiteracy almost complete in the national provinces, but 40 of the 100 nationalities had no alphabet. This was the czarist heritage the new Soviet Republic had to build on. Alexander Arsenyev, member of the USSR Academy of Pedagogical Sciences, noted, "by the most 'optimistic' forecasts of czarist officials, the introduction of general primary education in the country, would take at least two centuries." The more than half-century of Soviet existence is the story of a cultural revolution that is unprecedented in mankind's history.

The milestones along this path denote the giant strides. In the first ten months of its existence, the young socialist Republic abolished all restrictions on education based on religion, race, nationality, and sex. A mass campaign wiped out illiteracy and in a single decade cultural backwardness was overcome. Though it had to spend huge sums and devote its energy to rebuild on the ruins of World War I, the Civil War and intervention, the young socialist Republic allotted huge sums to education. Never, even in its most bitter days, did it skimp on educating its children.

In the late 1930s, a general 7-year schooling was put into operation. In 1939, the USSR was on the verge of going over to a general secondary education in urban areas and compulsory 7-year schooling in rural areas and in the national republics. But the savage Nazi invasion interrupted and postponed this step.

To Bring Up Good Human Beings

The Soviet people's goal is the construction of Communist society that will eliminate the inequalities still existing under socialism, bring abundance to all, and make possible the fullest creative development of the people. Therefore, the schools and Soviet society concentrate on the molding of the new man and woman. The Soviet Union trains more than 285,000 engineers annually, as compared to about 60,000 in the United States. In 1972, the USSR had 2,600,000 engineers; the United States had 945,000. But though no one recognizes more fully the importance of training scientists and technicians in this age of the scientific-technical revolution (and there is recognition that Soviet schools have much to do to catch up with the needs of the time in this respect), the prime aim of Soviet schools is to help bring up genuinely humane human beings. This goal was put to me with poetic beauty by an outstanding Soviet mathematician, Aleksei Markushevitch, who is also vice president of the Soviet Academy of Pedagogical Sciences. The goal of Soviet education, he told me, is to harmonize the individual and collective development of Soviet children. "We want to imbue them with the realization that without association with other people, without the spirit of comradeship, without the ability to restrain and suppress one's egoistic inclinations and emotions, *one cannot merit the proud title of human being.*" This is the philosophy not only of Soviet schools but also of Soviet society. Thus, the Soviet child, unlike his U.S. counterpart, is not shaken by the awesome and disillusioning gap between what he is taught in school and what he meets in life. The Soviet child's world is in full harmony with the world he meets outside as a student and the world he joins as a producer.

The Soviet child does come across people who are far from being builders of the Communist society. The Soviet child does meet self-seeking careerists and petty bureaucrats. He does come across situations in real life that are at odds with the principles of socialism. And, in some, these experiences do produce cynicism. But they stand out because they are in sharp conflict with the mainstream of Soviet life.

These blots are just that, blots of dirt inherited from the past that time and a good social scrubbing are diminishing. The Soviet child sees all Soviet society, including his school, participating in that scrubbing. Markushevitch's words are not just those pious platitudes with which we in the United States are all too familiar. They are the guidelines of Soviet schools and Soviet society.

The major problem Soviet schools face is that of catching up with the demands of a dynamic society moving toward the construction of a Communist society and, above all, with the demands of the scientific and technological revolution. I found that the Soviet press discussed these problems even before the 24th Congress of the CPSU. A probing statement by the Central Committee of the CPSU and the Council of Ministers of the USSR, published in 1969, noted that "the level of training of skilled workers in vocational and technological educational establishments lags behind the growing requirements of socialist production." It pointed to "substantial shortcomings also in the ideological education of the students engaged in vocational training." These problems, linked with demands of dynamic development, are the problems Soviet schools face and grapple with.

But what is the major problem confronting our city schools? Here is how school expert, Fred M. Hechinger puts it in the *New York Times Encyclopedic Almanac,* 1970: "The major issue confronting public education is the crisis of the urban centers, with their concentration of disadvantaged Black, Puerto Rican and/or Mexican-American children." And who are those disadvantaged children? The majority of children in many, if not most U.S. city schools. Hechinger points out "in many urban centers, the minorities had, in fact, become majorities, in terms of school enrollment. For example, in New York City, the Negro and Puerto Rican enrollment now stands at 54 percent and is rising 2 percent annually." [It is now 64.4 percent, M.D.] Hechinger cautiously notes that a "gap" exists between these children and their "predominantly white teachers because most of these youngsters come from seriously deprived environments." In plainer English than Hechinger evidently wants to employ, this means most come from ghetto slums, from homes hit twice as hard by unemployment and disease, from areas rife with crime, dope pushers and corrupt, brutalized police. It means that these "deprived" children are deprived of nurseries, and roam dangerous streets after school while their parents are at work.

Soviet children do not have to use streets for playgrounds. They have

3,865 Pioneer Palaces and 36,000 Pioneer Camps that have everything in them that children can dream of. They have more than 100 theaters, 33 railroads (fully run by children), their own newspapers (e.g. *Pionerskaya Pravada,* 10 million circulation). Dope pushers? These fears are alien to Soviet parents. Who is to profit from dope in a society that has long eliminated profiteers? Unemployed parents? There has been no unemployment in the Soviet Union since 1930.

There are problems related to broken homes and drunken parents— usually the father. Schools, teachers, young Communists, Pioneers, militia—all collectively work to help children in such situations. The child is, above all protected, even if this means taking him or her out of a bad home environment. Gap between Soviet child and teacher? In the economic and social sense that Hechinger alludes to, it's unthinkable in Soviet society because, though there is a difference in income under socialism, it is almost meaningless in terms that Americans are familiar with. Nowhere in the world (as some U.S. educators themselves have noted) is there a closer or more affectionate relationship between teacher and pupil than in the Soviet Union. True, there are, at times, gaps in understanding between teacher and child. There are teachers who lack understanding of their pupils. This was the subject of the popular Soviet film, "Let's Live Till Monday." But the entire atmosphere breathes the kind of spirit of teacher-pupil relationship that our teachers and children truly long for. The discriminatory racial and national gap Hechinger refers to has long been eliminated in the Soviet Union.

Soviet children are taught the equality of peoples in practice because many of their principals, teachers and later professors come from peoples who only half a century ago did not have alphabets. During the 1960s, Black students, all over the United States, rose up in militant mass demonstrations, demanding that their history, long ignored, be taught in schools. In contrast, the history of more than 100 peoples making up the Soviet family of nations is not only taught to all Soviet children, but lessons are conducted in 51 of the languages of peoples inhabiting the Soviet Union. Each year the Soviet Union publishes 300 million copies of textbooks in 47 languages. They are prepared by the Soviet Union's outstanding scholars in every field.

Soviet children start school later than ours—at 7 years of age. Mothers can enter their children into crèches when they are about 6 months old. Preschool training is not regarded here as a privilege spooned out to a handful of "disadvantaged" children, as in our "Headstart" program, only to be snatched away by the economy knife. It is the normal right of the mass of Soviet children. Crèches and nursery schools are attended by 13 million children—more than half of all children of preschool age. Of these, 9.5 million attend nursery schools. And room is being made for an additional 2 million.

Harmony Between Soviet Schools and Soviet Life

Moscow has more than 300,000 children, ages three to seven, in 2,200 nurseries. The fee ranges from three rubles 50 kopecks to 12 rubles 50 kopecks a month, depending on the family income. The Moscow Soviet pays the additional cost, which averages 45 to 50 rubles a month. You have to visit these nurseries to appreciate the combination of affectionate care with skillful training and inculcation of the spirit of collectivity and discipline Soviet children receive.

Take the nursery No. 342 in the Krasnaya Presnaya district of Moscow. The 145 children are taught music, dance, art and foreign languages by 12 highly trained teachers. Besides the 12 teachers, there is a staff of doctors, nurses and a dietician, cooks, and household workers—with a ratio of one staff member to two children. Each group has its own dormitory, playrooms and toys. The nursery also has its own puppet theater and sports ground.

What impressed me in my visits to classrooms was not only the serious atmosphere of study I found but that the children seemed to be enjoying their work. I saw this in a third year class of eight and nine year olds studying English in Moscow's special secondary school, No. 31. It is one of 50 where English is taught starting with the second year and some subjects are taught in English, beginning with the fifth year. The children seemed to enjoy the discovery of each new word. In the sixth year geography class, geography and grammar were skillfully combined. Alexander Markov, the teacher, barely paused to correct a verb tense here, a geographical location there. The boys and girls— aged 13 to 14—not only answered questions but debated the sources of the Nile in commendably fluent English. I participated in a 10th year class (17 to 18 year olds) where Socrates and the participles were discussed in quite literate English. Irene Ureena, the teacher, was equally demanding in both grammatical and philosophical precision. I was happy she didn't call on me, especially to answer her probing questions on participles.

What gives Moscow's classrooms the atmosphere of serious study that would delight the hearts of frustrated U.S. mothers, is that at no time is learning looked upon as pointless, as it is by so many of our schoolchildren, especially the "disadvantaged," who, at an early age are familiar with the economic, social, and racial "facts of life." What makes the classroom seem pointless to Black youth is not only that they are economically handicapped by the second-class schooling they get, which Hechinger characterizes as "the system's inability to educate the poor and culturally deprived," but that racial barriers doom them to the most menial jobs, despite their education, and to joblessness "in congested areas."

Soviet youth know that the classroom leads to waiting jobs for all: in schools to teach others, in laboratories, in factories, on collective farms, or on the stage or concert platform. It is the link with this Soviet reality which gives purposefulness to the Soviet classroom. Soviet youth speak of their ambitions with a confidence born of a knowledge that their vast, dynamic country needs them, their skills and their boundless energy. This every school child knows and takes for granted.

This is not to say that all find the place in life they seek or fulfill their ambitions. Abilities are not equal nor do all apply themselves equally to their studies. I met Soviet youth who were far from satisfied with the position they achieved.

But even in such cases it was rare indeed that I came across someone who felt he was cheated by Soviet society or his schools. They know that the doors of learning are still open to them in evening courses and correspondence courses that can lead to as many entrance exams to higher educational establishments, institutes and colleges as they wish to take. In 1971-72, 647,000 took evening courses and 1,643,000 studied by correspondence. This is in addition to 603,000 who studied evenings and 1,178,000 by correspondence in specialized secondary schools. Going to school or studying at home continues in the Soviet Union at any age. Almost 80 million Soviet citizens—about one out of three—study. About 4 million workers go to school evenings in 11,000 schools, or learn by correspondence. They receive from their enterprises all the aid they need to continue their studies. Those who study and work at the same time get time off to prepare for exams, are exempted from night work and the more arduous types of labor, get additional paid holidays that could extend from 20 to 40 days (in some instances as much as four months), and are provided with a 50 percent discount on travel fares to and from places of study.

With this living link between Soviet society and the school, it is understandable why the connection between theory and practice is a natural one and present in all studies. Soviet schools take seriously their job of equipping young men and women to play their role in advancing their country toward communism. This calls for people who have absorbed the best contributions of past societies, who are in step with the swift pace of the scientific-technological revolution. It means much more than that: it means bringing up not only proficient engineers and technicians, but human beings who have absorbed the finest cultural contributions of mankind.

L. Timofeyev, corresponding member of the USSR Academy of Sciences, aptly summed up the Soviet approach to specialization and the humanities in these words: "Literature, history and the arts are the spiritual antidotes which prevent people from turning into mere producers and consumers of material influence."

Mikhail Prokofiev, Minister of Education, publicly stated that in the new school curricula introduced September 1, 1972: "Art subjects account for 40 percent of the hours, considerably more than before, and in non-Russian schools where pupils study their own language and literature in addition to Russian and other subjects, for 47 percent."

Soviet schools are not divided into elementary, junior high and high school. The general secondary school roughly embraces the three, though, as the curricula will show, it is on a considerably higher level. Secondary education continues in vocational schools, which train skilled workers, and in specialized schools, which produce intermediate-grade technological personnel for various branches of the economy as well as intermediate specialists for public schools, health, and cultural establishments. All classes are on a six-day week, six-hour day.

In 1969, preparations were under way for the introduction of the new curricula Prokofiev referred to. Soviet educators were not satisfied that the schools were adequately tapping the full potentials of Soviet children and youth while keeping pace with scientific progress, or adequately educating them in the spirit of Communist upbringing. When I discussed this question with Markushevitch, vice-president of the Academy of Pedagogical Science, who was heading a commission that was revising textbooks and curricula, he told me that it was the opinion of Soviet educators that the learning capacities of children, especially as regards mathematics and scientific subjects, still have unexplored potentialities. Markushevitch emphasized the creative character of childhood "when everything appears new and significant, when inquisitiveness is inexhaustible, and when memory and imagination still retain their indomitable freshness and flexibility." The recognition of the "creative" years largely explains the high standards and "toughness" of Soviet schools.

That was 1969. The experimental period is over. Now, new curricula and textbooks, worked out by the best Soviet minds, are adding a new quality to study for almost 50 million schoolchildren. Children are familiarized with the principles of operation of electronic computers as well as with the great writers of their own and other countries. I found Soviet students as familiar with Mark Twain and Jack London as our own.

One of the most heartening aspects of Soviet schools is their truly democratic character. Nowhere is special talent given more opportunity for fullest development. But the Soviet education system unequivocally rejects "elitism." It rejects the elitist approach expressed even by such an outstanding educator as James B. Conant, who, in his book *The American High School Today,* singled out the upper 20 percent of students for study of sciences, languages, and advanced mathematics. It rejects the concept of "uneducable" children (even when it comes to those with serious problems of retardation, as I shall describe). It rejects the racist concepts of "inferior people—inferior children" behind the approach to "difficult schools," which transforms teachers into custodians of classrooms and which is largely responsible for a situation where Black, Puerto Rican, Chicano and Native American Indian children lag considerably behind white children. The half-century record of Soviet schools which produced scientists and great writers from among peoples who had no alphabets, has shattered the myth of superior and inferior peoples, the logical and frightful conclusion of elitism. The Soviet educational system constitutes the greatest demonstration in history of the vast talent and ability latent in the children of workers, peasants, and of oppressed nations and nationalities that were long suppressed by previous feudal and capitalist society and given full rein only under socialism.

Visit to a Music School

This was repeatedly impressed on me but perhaps nowhere more than in Odessa's famous Stolarsky School of Music. On that same trip to the Ukraine, I met the late Duke Ellington, who was making an enormously successful tour of the Soviet Union. Duke was extremely impressed by the musical atmosphere in the Soviet Union and incidentally, the widespread familiarity and appreciation of his own compositions. "The Soviet Union," the famous Afro-American jazz musician told me, "has the climate, the proper atmosphere for music."

Stolarsky is a world of music for talented children. It's a world children enter not by chance or privilege. It's a world that seeks out the talented child. Stolarsky's teachers scour the villages and settlements of the Ukraine, visiting countless nurseries and even crèches, in a massive talent hunt. They visit crèches because that is where musical training begins in the Soviet Union. The press, radio, and TV bring the announcements of Stolarsky's auditions to the remotest Soviet villages.

Since 1961, the school has had a boarding school attached to it. About 100 of the 363 students live there; the rest, who are from Odessa, live at home. Board and tuition are free. In addition, as in all Soviet schools, the students receive stipends. The school has its own polyclinic. The 363 students are taught by 110 teachers, many of them among the Soviet Union's finest artists, since teaching is highly regarded by artists. That's about one teacher for every three students. The 11-year school included a curriculum of general secondary education in addition to intensive music courses.

The school is named after Pyotr Stolarsky, a famous music teacher. The 100th anniversary of his birth was celebrated in 1970. The school was founded in 1933, but actually started to function fully in 1939. The Nazis burned it to the ground and destroyed its instruments and library when they occupied Odessa. With Odessa's liberation in 1944, the teachers returned and helped rebuild the school with their own hands. That same year Stolarsky died in Sverdlovsk. What makes the Stolarsky school unique is that it is *not* unique in the Soviet Union. Almost every Soviet city of size has its Stolarsky.

The Pioneer Republic

The school, of course, is the Soviet child's second home, and the chief molder of his or her character. But Soviet children have a third "home"—perhaps the one they find most pleasant of all—their Pioneer organization. One of the first things we noted when we arrived in Moscow was that very few children were playing in the streets. Street life that is so much part of our city kids' existence hardly figures in the lives of Soviet children. One can romanticize the unforgettable street adventures of one's childhood and bemoan this "loss" of freedom of the streets for Soviet kids. And there are those who portray the Pioneer organization as the first stage in "Soviet regimentation."

I came to know this "regimented" life. I never met happier "prisoners." One of my most pleasurable and memorable experiences in the Soviet Union was my close four-year relationship with Moscow Pioneers, and particularly the International Club of the Pioneer Palace at Lenin Hills. Their "home," their Palace, beyond the fairy-tale dreams of any child, was practically my own. And so, as a grandfather, I saw my own childhood dreams come to life on Lenin Hills. No one is more sensitive to the secret yearnings of adults than children. My Pioneer friends readily took me to their hearts and shared with me their pride and joy in their Palace.

It was Angela Davis, particularly, who brought us together. I received a telephone call only a couple of days after news was flashed of the "capture" of Angela Davis. It was from the Moscow Pioneer Palace's Club for International Friendship. "We want to free Angela," a girl's shrill, excited voice exclaimed to me in well-taught English. "Please come to our meeting and tell us what we can do. We *must* free her," the voice rose higher. However, when I entered the packed auditorium, I saw there was little need for any direction. Tens of thousands of petitions from schools all over the Moscow area had already been collected. They were written in painstakingly neat penmanship. Many had penned their messages in English: "Dear Angela, we love you." Galya Burenkova of the 9th class in school 241, rose to recite the poem she had just written. "My heart, sound the alarm!" Galya cried out. I looked at the faces of her red-scarfed fellow Pioneers. Theirs was the irresistible outrage of the pure of heart. Thus began the movement to free Angela Davis that swept the Soviet Union.

As the Moscow correspondent of Angela's newspaper, I was frequently called upon to speak at schools, Pioneer meetings, and on TV programs. Together we welcomed Angela's sister, Fanya Davis Jordan, when she visited the Pioneer Palace. Together, we greeted Angela in a memorable victory celebration in the same auditorium where the campaign for her freedom was initiated.

I will never forget the pride with which an honor guard of Pioneer girls and boys escorted Angela around their Palace. Even more memorable was the look in Angela's eyes as she went from room to room. Angela, of course, could not see all the facilities of this 54-hectare children's paradise, which was built in 1962. It would take almost a week to visit and spend even a few minutes in the 830 circles and sections of the 14 clubs, embracing 23,000 youngsters from five to seventeen years of age. The Lenin Hills Palace is regarded by them as their Young Pioneer Republic. Beautiful and modern in construction, it has 11 buildings, workshops, a planetarium and observatory, a cosmonaut section, a stadium, closed-in swimming pool, an airdrome and landing strip for sports aircraft, a winter garden, concert hall, children's theater, film studio, art studios, ballet and folk-dance schools, and song and dance ensembles. A child coming to this Palace is guided in making his or her choice by a corps of well-trained advisers. The children are instructed by hundreds of teachers who come from Moscow State University or the USSR Academy of Pedagogical Sciences.

Angela was, of course, deeply moved by the campaign for her freedom initiated by her Pioneer hosts. But she was even more moved by what she saw. Tears in her eyes, she told the Pioneers: "This is what we are fighting for. This is what we also want for our children of Harlem, for all the children of workers."

Unforgettable Artek

The multi-hued mountains seemed to rise up from the sparkling Black Sea. Two huge craggy rocks jutted out like giants' teeth. I walked along a parklike path lined with stately cypress. Lilac and cherry blossoms dotted the landscape as in a Japanese landscape painting. All around were sun, sea, sky and song—the chirping and trilling of more than 130 varieties of birds who make Artek their resting place. A troop of boys and girls, their crimson Pioneer scarves flashing in the sunlight, sang a jaunty sailor's song as they marched by. From where I stood I could survey a panorama of streamlined buildings, their picture windows inviting the mountains, sea, sun and sky into the children's dormitories. A pretty pug-nosed Pioneer leader, with the map of Russia on her face, shook my hand vigorously. "Welcome to the Pioneer Republic," she exclaimed.

Artek is indeed a children's republic. Almost five miles long, it occupies 320 hectares (a hectare is more than two acres) of vacation land on that part of the Crimean coast once reserved for czarist nobility. More than 100 hectares make up five parks. All that a child can dream of assumes the delightful shape of reality here. Swimming in mirrorlike waters, playing in spacious fully equipped sports fields, boating, including extended excursions on the bluish-green Black Sea in Artek's own fleet, learning to soar into space in the Cosmonaut Room, a replica of the training facilities that schooled the Soviet spacemen, constructing and launching rockets, ships and planes; operating radio and TV stations; learning the songs and dances of the 70 Soviet nationalities and 40 different countries represented annually at Artek. Artek is an All-Soviet Union and international camp and it is not for nothing that the children say, "We have our own Minister of Foreign Affairs."

Artek annually plays host to 27,000 children coming from the Soviet Union's 15 Republics. The Pioneers, chosen for their exemplary study and activity by their school groups, come in eight shifts (Artek is active the year round). There are three fall and winter 60-day shifts (about 1,800 children each) and five 30-day summer shifts (4,500).

Only a socialist country, where people come first, could display such disregard for budgetary limitations when it comes to providing for its children. For 5,000 children (in summer peak) Artek has 2,000 workers. These include 900 Pioneer leaders, 28 doctors, 40 nurses and doctor's assistants. It has hundreds of kilometers of its own communications system, supplies its own electricity, heat and water and has a network of repair and maintenance shops, laundry, machines, cars, and a special park department. Artek has an annual budget of 8 million rubles. During the past 10 years, it spent 30 million rubles on a construction program designed by the famous architect Anatoly Poliansky, laureate of the Lenin prize.

Fifty percent of the children admitted to Artek are not only admitted free of charge, but their fares both ways are paid, no matter from what part of the Soviet Union they come. Of the other 50 percent, 20 percent pay half and another 20 percent pay one-third cost. Only 10 percent pay full cost—120 rubles for 30 days—about $6.00 a day.

Artek, like every organization in the Soviet Union, has a plan for its future. The camp capacity will be expanded to care for 7,600 (each shift) in the summer and 4,600 in winter shifts. A Sports City will be built which will include a 10,000-seat stadium, huge playgrounds, gymnasiums and swimming pools. Among other projects to be constructed are: a Cosmonaut City, a Science City, an underwater laboratory to study fish and sea life, a Flora and Fauna City, a movie and concert hall seating 1,600, a Pioneer City that will be a complex of school, sports and recreation facilities, and a medical complex which will provide each camp with the fullest and most up-to-date facilities.

Artek's Pioneers are surrounded by their country's glorious traditions as well as beauty. Artek itself is a great tradition. We paused at Friendship Square, a favorite gathering place for the children. Here, in the severe days of 1925, a group of 80 Pioneers assembled to mark the opening of Artek. All told, 320 children attended the camp that year. Since then about 320,000 Pioneers, including thousands of children of all lands, became Artekers. And not a few of them became the Soviet Union's heroes and martyrs. My Pioneer friends took me to one of their most sacred spots. It was a simple flower-bedecked monument to Artek heroes of the Great Patriotic War against fascism. Among those listed I read the names of Reuben Ibarruri, the son of Dolores Ibarruri (La Passionara); and Timur Frunze, the son of Mikhail Frunze, the great military leader of the Civil War against the White Guards. Artek itself was occupied and destroyed by the Nazis. For Levon Mikaelyan, then deputy editor of *Pionerskaya Pravda*, who accompanied me on the trip, every visit to Artek revived visions of the devastation. Mikaelyan fought to wrest Crimea and Artek from the Nazis. He was there on April 16, 1944, when it was liberated.

Artek is not only an ideal place for rest and recreation. It is an All-Soviet school for training the future and present leaders of the 23-million member Pioneer organization. The children who come here during the winter and fall shifts (all are from 11 to 14 years old) attend an ideal school. They have a five-day week (it is six days everywhere else in the Soviet Union) and do not get any homework. Yet all manage to keep up their high level of performance. Those who come to Artek are the best students, and the school's teachers are specially trained to get the most out of the classroom work. Maximum class size is 25; most are smaller. There are 94 teachers (including 22 who direct 8 special laboratories, teaching classes in aviation, shipbuilding, radio, TV, automobile mechanics, rocketry and driving) for about 1700 pupils. The Artek school reveals that the high level of Soviet schools is largely maintained in all the 15 Republics. Kaleria Gornastaeieva, the school director, said the school faced no serious problems in achieving uniformity of study on the part of the children and stated that only 3 to 4 days were required to overcome any individual lags.

Anyone familiar with the Soviet concern for children can understand the high qualifications demanded of Pioneer leaders. They must be graduates of institutes of pedagogy and undergo an intensive two-year special course, which includes three months of theoretical study (the rest is on-the-spot training).

In Artek "boys and girls together" in all camp activities comes naturally. All Pioneer groups are mixed, and I saw as many girl "commanders" as boys. Moreover, the boys didn't hesitate in carrying out the orders of the Natashas and Irinas. It comes naturally in Artek because the children see and live the equality of the sexes in daily life. Artek is a model Soviet camp but its real significance is that it is not the exception but only the most advanced indicator of the future ahead for Soviet children. I was told by Artek leaders that astronaut Frank Borman, who visited Artek with his wife and two sons, said he found it hard to believe anything like Artek was really in existence. Borman was surprised evidently because, like most Americans, he had been carefully "sheltered" from present-day Soviet reality.

There are some 12,000 pioneer camps servicing about 10 million children annually in the Soviet Union. Few are on the scale of Artek, but they offer similar facilities, if not on the same extensive basis. What is even more important, the children returning from their vacations do not return to a life that is in harsh contradiction to their summer experience.

The same "regimentation" that accompanies Soviet children after school and during their long summer recess, follows them on their school holidays. And, perhaps as revealing as the contrast between the U.S. and the Soviet classrooms is the attitude toward schoolchildren on holiday. Holiday season in the United States is a period of "freedom" for kids as everywhere, but it's a freedom full of worry for working-class parents, especially Black, Puerto Rican, Asian and Chicano parents in our big cities. The perils of the city streets are open to their children full time. With the exception of special children's cinemas offered by movie houses anxious to profit by the holidays and some special programs presented by church and community organizations, the children are truly "free" on their holidays.

Shortly after we arrived in Moscow, we noticed that the subways and streets were filled with groups of excited kids, escorted by parents and teachers (teachers are busy during school holidays). We had run into spring vacation. The TV, radio and press, were full of announcements of special programs. All theaters, including the famous Bolshoi, scheduled special performances, as did circuses and sports clubs. We attended an unforgettable meeting at the palatial Hall of Columns, where 1,000 children from 7 to 14 were assembled. On the richly paneled walls were signs heralding Children's Book Week. Milling around bookstalls were crowds of beribboned and braided girls and freshly scrubbed, appled-checked boys, many of them with the red Pioneer scarfs around their necks. The kids sang their favorite songs to a spirited accordion; then, led by the youngest and smallest, solemnly marched into the dazzling hall resplendent with sparkling crystal chandeliers. No one seemed to be awed by all this grandeur. It was theirs.

And what do Moscow kids do on their Christmas holidays? Well, among other things, they take over the Kremlin. The Kremlin resounds with the echo of shrill childish voices and the tapping of dancing feet. I watched as thousands of kids bundled up in their fur coats swarmed over the ancient Kremlin grounds, escorted by their *babushkas* and mothers into the magnificent modern Palace of Congresses. This goes on twice daily, from December 30 to January 10—116,000 kids sing, play games around the Yolka (like our Christmas tree), watch outstanding Soviet performers and get presents.

The Kremlin Yolka parties, initiated in 1954, are organized and financed by the Moscow City Committee of Trade Unions. The unions are responsible for winter vacation programs attended by an estimated 2.5 million kids (children attend more than one program). They also play host to the thousands of children who come to Moscow with their teachers from all over the Soviet Union. In addition to city programs, more than 40,000 kids spend twelve days at Pioneer camps in the suburbs. The twelve days of sports and fun, including three meals a day, cost their parents six rubles (about fifty cents a day).

How Soviet Teachers Are Trained

I learned *why* the "gap" between teacher and pupil, which so disturbs U.S. parents, especially parents of "disadvantaged" children, is nonexistent in Soviet schools, when I visited Moscow's Pedagogical School No. 2 which trains teachers for kindergarten and lower grades. The school has 1,020 trainees attending 35 classes in the day session and 400 trainees in 13 classes at night. The link between the theory of teaching and the actual practice is instantly in evidence. The school for children and the school for teachers coexist in the same building. There is no guesswork concerning a trainee's competence; she leaves her class on child psychology, enters a classroom of children and under the critical eyes of the regular teacher and nine of her fellow students, applies what she learned. This is followed by a critical evaluation in which all participate. I was present when one such evaluation was going on. It was lively but never destructive. The trainee took it all quite objectively.

Trainees spend a full day once a week in pupil classes during the third and fourth year (240 hours a year). During the fourth year they perform all the duties of a teacher for five weeks. In addition, they work for a month as teachers at Pioneer camps. What particularly impressed me was that the development of good relations with parents was regarded as an important part of their work. And *they are graded on this!* The trainees are intensively trained in the humanities as well as in technical matters. They must be proficient in at least one major musical instrument. They must be thoroughly familiar with photography, cameras, motion-picture projectors, audio-visual methods and equipment, plastics, the handling of tools, hothouse plants, gardening and arts and crafts, as well as child psychology, anatomy, and general academic subjects.

The training school also revealed one of the major problems of the general secondary schools—the teachers were overwhelmingly female. Only one percent of the trainees at school No. 2 were men. This lopsided composition largely applies to schools in the big cities. The trainee population is 25 percent male outside large urban centers. This one-sided composition is to a great extent the result of the attitude of young men in the Soviet Union toward the teaching profession, particularly in the general secondary schools. I came across more male teachers in specialized technical secondary schools. Teaching is largely regarded as a profession for women. It is toward the sciences and technical subjects that young men seem to gravitate. The problem has aroused considerable concern in pedagogical circles. An educational campaign stressing the decisive role played by teachers in early grades and in general secondary schools is under way.

Training Soviet Specialists

The link between theory and practice—this time between man and machine—was forcefully demonstrated to me in a specialized industrial, technological school (technicum) in Moscow. In 1971-72 these schools enrolled 4,420,000 students, including 2,841,000 in day classes, 603,000 in evening sessions and 1,176,000 studying by correspondence. The role of the technicum was summed up for me by Vladimir Tichinin, the school's director, who symbolized in person the harmony between the humanities and the sciences. "We prepare the future staffs of Moscow plants," Tichinin informed me.

There are two categories of specialized secondary schools. One, like the technicum I visited, trains specialists for industry, construction, transport and communications, agricultural workers, and economists. The second trains teachers, subsidiary medical staff, musicians, art workers, and theater personnel. In 1971, both types of secondary schools trained 1,100,000 people.

The school I visited graduates a new type of skilled worker, already part engineer. Unlike the pedagogical school, this school's composition was equally divided between men and women, with the latter apparently more attracted to plastic-chemistry courses. Of the 3,300 students, about 1,000 were in the day session and 2,300 in the evening (these attended classes three evenings a week). There were 132 teachers, about one teacher for every 25 students.

The 4 year school period includes intensive theoretical and laboratory training, followed by eight months of work at plants as workers receiving full wages. At the conclusion of this work period, the student returns to the school and embarks on an intensive 6-week preparation for final exams. This includes work on special projects and defense of their theses. I saw many of these projects. At the end of the third year the student already knows his future place of work. The assignment of each trainee is determined by considering the needs of industry, the student's qualifications and personal desires. All students are spoken to separately and exercise the right of choice. First choice, however, goes to the best students.

Soviet schools are *polytechnical*. At all levels children are taught to respect work and honor good workers, and the desire to work is instilled in them. They are made familiar with the basic elements of modern industrial production. And they themselves are involved in manual labor, not only in special classes and in plants, but in national as well as school *subbotniks*. During harvest season they participate in gathering the crops and, later as college students, during the summer they take part in labor brigades organized by the Komsomols on the major construction sites in the Soviet Union. This is known as their "third term," for which they receive the usual pay. I witnessed the warm send-offs at the college campuses and met them as they worked on the huge hydroelectric power station in Ust-Ilim in the Siberian taiga. I saw in them the embryos of the future men and women of Communist society who harmoniously combine love of labor with the highest in cultural development. I thought of Tichinin's words about the task of his technicum. "We are trying to bring up a new person—a Soviet citizen with a Communist morale and outlook. This is impossible without a broad culture."

Students in the technicum who make good grades receive a monthly stipend of 80 rubles. Those with special family problems also receive monthly allowances. In our rich country, which prides itself on its concern for the individual, especially for his full intellectual development, financial assistance is still based on the feudal concept of benevolent patronage provided in the form of scholarships for the specially talented few among the "lower classes." Furthermore, in the United States, no financial aid is given to specialized students in secondary schools. Incidentally, many U.S. college students owe their scholarships to the example set by the Soviet Union. This is indicated by Hechinger in *The New York Times Encyclopedic Almanac, 1970*, where he notes that "The turning point for modern education came in 1957, when the launching of the Soviet Sputnik provided a dramatic . . . rallying point and battlecry for all those who feared that American academic rigor has slipped to the danger point."

But the economic axe and skyrocketing school tuition have taken their toll. The November, 1972 issue of the *American Federationist*, AFL-CIO monthly, states: "College costs have risen until without some sort of aid, higher education is nearly as much beyond the means of a worker's family today as it was in 1915 when organized labor first started its goal of free state university where textbooks, tuition and laboratory work shall be free." The Soviet Union in 58 years leaped from illiteracy and schools for a privileged few to the most advanced educational system *free* to all through the university level, with stipends to make that freedom fully meaningful.

The New Leap in Soviet Schools

The level of Soviet education is taking a huge leap. This is the meaning of the decision making 10-year secondary schools compulsory throughout the Soviet Union. The two-year extension is not merely a simple addition as the new curricula make clear. It is a qualitative leap dictated by the needs of the scientific-technological revolution and Communist construction.

Millions of Soviet youth still lack the crucial 9th and 10th years of schooling. Many make up this lack later in vocational and technical schools or through correspondence courses. But this places an additional burden on the higher levels of secondary education. Some idea of the kind of leap involved in compulsory ten-year secondary education can be gathered if we think in terms of our own country. *It is as if junior college were made compulsory for every child in the United States.* A ten-year education in the Soviet Union is on a higher level than our high school. In actual school time (six days a week, six hours a day) it is the equivalent of our combined 12-year primary and high school. However, far more is packed into the Soviet school year.

By contrast, in the United States, not even the completion of high school is compulsory. Education in the Soviet Union is regarded as an all-Union responsibility. Curricula are on a national, uniformly high level. Universal education is combined with the teaching of the national cultures and languages of the particular Republics.

The uniformly high level of all schools is demonstrated in the enrollment in Moscow's higher educational establishments of all types. Their student rosters read like an all-Union roll call of Republics. From the earliest days of the Soviet Union, Russian teachers flocked to the illiterate, formerly backward national provinces to teach millions. Even today, when each Republic has its own university and Academy of Science, those who need education most are provided with the best. Today there are hardly any in the USSR who require a special approach, because there are no "backward areas."

The annual "battles over school budgets" as well as perennial school crises are also absent from the Soviet scene. The *New York Times*, June 7, 1972, for example, reported that for economy reasons the Detroit

School Board adopted a budget "that would reduce the academic year by 35 percent for Detroit's 291,000 public school children" (most of whom are Black). The idea of schools closing down or programs being curtailed or opening late because of lack of funds is inconceivable in the Soviet Union. The only times schools were disrupted there was during the Nazi invasion and then only temporarily in schools directly affected. Even in the severest days of the Civil War and World War II, education came first. The school budget is part of the Soviet Five Year Plans and is financed not through taxation but from the public consumption fund derived from the income of the national economy.

Schools for the Handicapped

The *humaneness* of Soviet schools and Soviet society is best demonstrated in the care provided children and parents who are crippled or handicapped in any way. Education is the right of every child. Those with special problems get special care. Moscow, for example, has 21 boarding schools (housing 6,000) for retarded children and those with special handicaps. The schools are specifically adapted to the particular requirements of the afflicted children. There are special schools for epileptic children, those suffering from polio and arteriosclerosis, as well as for the deaf and blind. Where parents prefer to keep the child at home, teachers are assigned (free of charge) to go to the house of the child. And, of course, all medical care is without charge. Moscow has 41 boarding schools, housing 21,000 children not afflicted by any ailment, who live and study there the year round. Such schools are attended mainly by children from large families or those without parents. These have the same curricula as the regular ten-year schools. Schools for retarded and handicapped are taught at a slower pace. Tuition is free and the upkeep of those from large families of low income is borne entirely by the government. Only parents with high earnings pay 30 to 70 percent of the cost of maintaining the child. There are even special schools in hospitals for those who have to spend extended periods in those institutions. *The entire burden for these handicapped children is borne by the Soviet government.*

In the United States not only is the backbreaking financial burden largely shifted onto the unfortunate parents, but handicapped children are among the most heartlessly neglected children in our country. Free public schooling provided to the handicapped is severely limited and does not exist at all in many states. The special schools are private and are extremely expensive—well beyond the reach of all but the most affluent parents. They run from $300 to $400 minimum per month to $800 and up per month ($10,000 yearly or more) on the average. Recently some far from adequate financial aid was provided, but it is now being cut. Michael Gorman, executive director of the National Committee Against Mental Illness (at that time), pointed out that 15 states have no facilities, public or private, for treating mentally troubled juveniles; while another 24 states have no public institutions for children of low- and middle-income groups. Our family knows all this from personal experience. A member of our family suffered from epilepsy from the time he was two and became retarded at an early age.

My wife, Gail, and I spent a day at a Moscow boarding school for retarded children. What we saw at Special School No. 103 in the Bauman district of Moscow filled us with joy for these handicapped children. But it also left us with deep anger and bitterness. Here was the life of kindness and usefulness that should have been our son's and that of hundreds of thousands of others like him in the United States. The Moscow school, which is largely for those in the early stages of retardation, is in a four-story red-brick building, the size of one of our big city public schools. Yet it houses only 150 children from 8 to 16 years of age.

This small student body is cared for by 30 teachers, a psychiatrist, nurse, two cooks, and a sizable staff of house workers. The teachers (they are paid 25 percent above the normal salary) are all specially trained. When we expressed surprise at the size of the teaching staff, Nina Serveyevna Ivanovna, the school's director, exclaimed, "But we are preparing children for *life*," with heavy emphasis on the last word. That about sums up the attitude and atmosphere of Special School No. 103.

Everything—curricula, teachers, workshops, medical and psychiatric care, four nourishing meals a day, spacious surroundings that include a well-equipped playground and, above all, human kindness—are instruments for involving the pupils in Soviet life.

Representatives of Moscow plants arrive at the school a couple of weeks before graduation to interview prospective employees. Almost all get jobs at full regular wages—in radio repair, typographical and book-binding factories; and a few, unable to work, receive a state pension. Flowers and pictures adorn the clean, spacious corridors, stairways, and dormitories. Space and sunlight enhance the atmosphere of secure calm.

Gail and I have had sufficient experience with U.S. private and state "schools," not only to appreciate the importance of atmosphere, but to detect when it is merely a facade to conceal inhumanity and indifference. But what we saw in School No. 103, from the kind and efficient Nina Ivanovna to the motherly *babushkas* (nannies) who welcomed us as they took our coats, was no facade. Why did she choose this work, we asked Nina, who had graduated from Leningrad State University as a history major. "Because it's twice the pleasure to see these children advance and to know they will find their proper place in life," she answered. As she spoke, Nina smiled at two boys waxing the corridor floor. Each had a brush attached to one leg and with evident enjoyment were dancing over the floor. "Don't they dance well?" Nina asked proudly.

Another teacher, Ivan Fomichov, presented us with the handiwork of a pupil in his carpentry class. The boy, singled out for special praise, was among the most retarded and he beamed with joy.

In every classroom there was ample cause for what Nina had described as "twice the pleasure." There were the poems the children of the third class recited with such fervor, the dresses the girls sewed with such skill, the books the boys neatly bound, the impressive wood carving and cabinetmaking displayed in the corridors, and the delightful song-and-dance comedy skit being rehearsed.

In the classrooms and workshops, the attitude adopted toward the children was one of confidence in their ability and accountability for their tasks. Rewards for work well done include special trips and public acknowledgment, and there were admonitions for failures. Neatness of appearance in dress and care of rooms were more than surface niceties. They reflected pride and self-respect, the feeling that "we, too, count."

The school curriculum was the usual one for an eight-year school but the level of work was approximately half that of the normal school. Class size was not more than 16 but we saw many that were considerably smaller. Stress is on visual education. "Children can't think in abstractions; they must see to learn," Nina emphasized to us. All around them, in their classes, workshops, corridors, rooms—the children were presented with vivid and beautiful things.

The pupils get up at 7:30 A.M., have breakfast at 8:00 and then start their classes. "Juniors," the first four grades, have classes from 9 A.M. to 12:30 P.M.; seniors until 2:30 P.M. Dinner is at 1:30 P.M.; there's a snack at 4 P.M. for juniors, and at 5 P.M. for the seniors, and supper is at 7 P.M. for the former and 8:30 P.M. for the latter. In between, there are extensive periods for rest, games and walks. Frequent excursions to all parts of the city are organized.

The children spend weekends at home with their parents; summers are spent either at Pioneer camps or on vacations with their parents. "No children remain in Moscow during the summer," Nina told us. There were 20 children without parents at the school but there is no lack of other parents to take them home on weekends, holidays or on vacations. "We make sure those who make the offer can provide our children with the proper home environment," she stressed. What do the parents pay for this schooling? More than half pay nothing, since the charge is based on many considerations: size of family, income, and special problems. But the other half do pay. "How much?" "They pay from 8 to 10 rubles a month," she told us in all seriousness. Gail and I exchanged glances and burst into laughter. It was not without bitterness.

7 / MENTAL HEALTH CARE—A TALE OF TWO SYSTEMS

A social system reveals much about itself in the way it cares for the mental and physical health of its citizens and especially of its handicapped. No one boasts more about the concern for the *individual* than the United States, a land of unrivaled wealth. Yet few countries do less for the health of their people and especially for the mentally ill and retarded. No one country does more in this respect than the one which, our propagandists charge, treats the individual as a "tool" of the state and swallows him up in a sea of collectivism.

I have chosen to begin with the Soviet approach to mental health because our family knows all this from personal experience. But perhaps no one knew this better than our son Bobby himself, who suffered from epilepsy since childhood and was affected by mental retardation.

Bobby passed away August 7, 1973, at the age of twenty-eight, in Kashenko Psychiatric Hospital in Moscow, overcome by a final shattering burst of seizures (status epilepsy) aggravated by double pneumonia and high fever. Bobby lived in the shadow of death for many years. That shadow seemed to recede in the last four years of his short life which he spent in the Soviet Union. The nightmare of state institutions and private "schools," the cruel and callous treatment—all seemed to drift into the horrible past.

Kashenko could not give Bobby a long life but it gave him four years in which he felt the simple but wonderful pleasure of being treated like a human being. It was not superior medicine or medical treatment that made the difference. Soviet mental health authorities and doctors themselves tell you that in both respects the United States and the USSR are at about the same level. The difference, above all, was reflected in the sensitive, human concern, the kindness Bobby felt from the nurses, attendants, and doctors at Kashenko. When we discussed going back to the United States with Bobby, he trembled in fear. For him, unfortunately, the United States meant state institutions and private "schools."

Bobby knew nothing about socialism (or capitalism, for that matter) but he felt the difference. What could the anti-Soviet snipers tell Bobby about "socialism with a human face"? Bobby recognized that face and embraced it like a dream he had long yearned to come true. He recognized it in the tender, warm care of the *babushkas,* in the firm but human discipline of the nurses. He recognized it in Mikhail Borisovitch Mazurski, his doctor, whom he regarded as a friend as well as physician. He recognized it in his fellow patients who gave him the comradeship he sought, who taught him Russian, who took lessons in English from him, who shared their candy and cigarettes with him. He recognized it in the parents, friends, and relatives who took Bobby into their warm hearts as they did their own.

All around him, Bobby felt deep love and concern for all who were punished by nature or adversity. Where in the past Bobby learned to shrink in fear of punishment, he suddenly felt sincere human compassion. It was not easy for him to grasp his new environment. I remember the terribly accusing look in his eyes when he first came to Kashenko. He had only known one kind of an "institution" in the United States. Why should this new place be any different? He fought and struck out at the nurses and the *babushkas* because he thought they were his new tormentors. And I remember how understandingly they took his abuse and blows and how tenderly and yet proficiently they calmed him.

Gradually Bobby began to recognize the difference. What relief and joy came with that recognition! He would recount to us every little new kindness, every new friend, every new kind word. How happy and proud he was when he participated in his first *subbotnik*, and how he escorted us to the playground to show us the flowers he had planted! For the first time in his life, he, too, counted. Bobby did not get to see much of the Soviet Union or Moscow. To him socialism and the Soviet Union was Kashenko—a hospital for the mentally ill, a hospital of excellent personnel and warm friends.

There are, of course, private places in the United States where one can *buy* more human treatment. But they are beyond the financial reach of most Americans. Like hundreds of thousands of other U.S. parents, we know what hellholes state institutions or "schools" for mentally ill or retarded are. And, like them, we were compelled to mortgage ourselves for 15 years in a vain effort to buy kindness and some semblance of concern for our son. There are numerous private schools, aware of the readiness of many such parents to pay almost any price for what they hope will be better treatment, who are in the business of selling "kindness" and "concern." Most charge a minimum of about $5,000 a year. Unless one is able to pay much more than the minimum, the private "school" is not much better than the state institution. In the main, it provides a more attractive facade that creates the comforting illusion of human care, especially on visiting days. Our son lived for many years at such a private school in upstate New York. We once happened to visit the school on a nonvisiting day, much to the embarrassment and vexation of the owners. Gone was the veneer of order and cleanliness. The scene that met us was little different from what we later encountered when we were forced to place Bobby in a state school. The "classroom" was nothing more than a custodial room, with the teacher making no pretense at anything but the most elementary teaching. Bobby and his fellow classmates were unkempt, unwashed and disheveled. We later discovered (after our son overcame his fear of reprisal) that Bobby and the other boys were quite often beaten by brutal attendants.

But the real character of this private school was revealed when the owners decided they could dump Bobby because he was too "difficult a case." The market was glutted and thus there was a "pick of cases" to be had. And they did literally dump our son. We received a call one scorching summer day to come and take him home at once. When we arrived, we found Bobby waiting for us—tied to a tree like a dog.

For months Bobby was home with us while we searched for another private school. But everywhere we met the same "requirements." Bobby's case, and this meant only his ability to control his behavior, had to meet their standards. They were totally unconcerned that much of our son's illness lay precisely in that his behavior got out of control. They, too, were guided by the market conditions which, from their point of view, were very favorable. Thus, for months we tried to be doctors as well as parents. And for weeks my wife and I had to give up our jobs, since it took the two of us at times to handle the situation. When finally we were driven to request admittance to a state school, we discovered that even these had a waiting list (with a two-year wait) and that only in a serious emergency could there be immediate admittance. It was only after such an emergency arose that Bobby was admitted to Wassaic State School, in upstate New York.

In Wassaic, Bobby lived in an extremely crowded dormitory. There was no effort to separate those who were criminally retarded from those whose condition was far less complicated. The pandemonium in this "jungle" can hardly be imagined. One doctor took "care" of about 800 patients. The poor man confessed to us he could only be aware of something wrong if a patient complained loudly enough. The personnel were so overworked and underpaid that there was a continuous turnover. The horrible conditions attracted only those poorly qualified for the demanding work.

His condition was aggravated by neglect and poor care. He had pneumonia four times in 1968 and was repeatedly in critical condition. My wife, Gail, in effect, acted as Bobby's private nurse and her constant devoted care played an important role in pulling him through. All around us we saw the difference such attention meant. Other sick patients paid with their lives for the inadequate and indifferent care they received.

The handicapped and mentally ill are "written off," shut out of view, forced to vegetate, and are treated as "things" instead of human beings. Only such an attitude can explain such institutions, which continue to exist notwithstanding the exposé some years ago by Senator Robert Kennedy and others. Only such an attitude can explain the constant economies on the minimal needs of the mentally ill.

All this is well known to the millions of parents and relatives of the mentally ill and retarded, though many Americans only become aware of this condition when it is brought to their attention through an occasional exposé or scandal. As a result of years of public pressure, some state assistance has been finally provided to families in dire need. But it is totally inadequate. Moreover, it varies greatly from state to state, with many giving no aid or very little. And as recent cuts in even this inadequate assistance reveal, it is a low priority item in the federal budget.

The Search for Kindness—an American Tragedy

Parents of retarded children in the United States have come together to try to improve conditions. One of their organizations is The National Association for Retarded Children. Nothing reveals the deplorable situation as does the list of questions presented to parents by these associations to guide them in their search for private schools or residential homes. Typical are the following questions put out by the Illinois Association for the Mentally Retarded, December, 1970. It tells the parents to note: "Are you satisfied that proper safeguards exist against hazards of fire, accidents and the like? Is there provision for regular medical care for the child? Are the potential facilities for hospitalization such as would meet with your approval if you were the one to be hospitalized? Are medical regimens available if necessary for children suffering with an associated convulsive disorder (epilepsy) or emotional disturbances? Is there a dentist associated with the school? Can they (the children) have second helpings if they desire? Is there sufficient time for the children to eat?" (And it should be remembered these are questions asked of private schools for which considerable fees are paid.) "Are you satisfied that the school does not rebate or make other unethical reimbursements for patronage?" We are very familiar with what motivates this question. The Illinois Association is referring to the commission paid an agent by the school owners for arranging the placing of a child in his school. The commission is paid for a number of years and it is usually the sum of money he receives rather than the welfare of the child that primarily concerns the agent. This traffic in misery is viewed as a "normal," lucrative business practice.

Here is how the National Association for Retarded Children, in its policy statement of October 1968, describes the conditions in U.S. mental institutions: "Living conditions in residential facilities throughout the country represent for the most part substandard conditions. Some state and private residential facilities can best be described as economically and culturally deprived areas. Often times, basic health and safety standards are not met, to say nothing of human standards."

It goes on to add: "Unfortunately, many residents in our state residential facilities are rarely seen by a physician. Drugs are prescribed and changed without a medical examination by a doctor. Abuse, neglect, and questionable deaths are not adequately investigated or reported. Appropriate measures to safeguard the health of a retarded resident through concern with such things as sanitation, availability of drinking fountains to prevent dehydration, methods of feeding and intake of food, abuse of the use of seclusion and restraints, are but a few of the medical and health concerns which contribute to *dehumanization*." [My emphasis, M.D.] Incidentally, the shocking revelations in 1975 of the callous treatment accorded the elderly in the nursing homes only underscore the inhuman treatment provided for all handicapped in our "free-enterprise" society.

Millions of American families are tormented by lifelong feelings of guilt because they were compelled to place their dear ones in such institutions. The need to preserve their own sanity compels many of them to shut their eyes to this chamber of horrors. Moreover, the social stigma that our society attaches to mental illness leads many to conceal their personal misfortune, diverts their anger from the real culprits, the indifferent government authorities, to their own family members. Thus, much of the struggle that should be directed against our inhuman society pits members of a family against each other. Many American families are torn and often shattered in their frustrated efforts to do for their afflicted ones what an indifferent society and government refuse to do. It is the poorest families, to a large extent Black, Puerto Rican and Chicano, who are most deeply affected.

Humanity—the Best Soviet "Medicine"

One of the agreements to come out of the historic Moscow Summit meeting, May, 1972, paved the way for joint U.S.-USSR cooperation in the fight against cancer, heart disease, and mental illness. Such cooperation can bring hope into the lives of millions of U.S. and Soviet families. But as much as this calamity affects Soviet people—and we have seen it in the suffering faces of mothers and fathers, sisters and brothers, as they visited their dear ones—they live with the comforting feeling that their government and society *care*. They care for their afflicted and for those who suffer with them. Medical care for mental illness (one of the most expensive ailments in the United States) is provided free of charge at every stage and for as long as is necessary. What is more, mental patients receive their stipends, if they are students; or disability pensions, if they are workers, while they are residents at psychiatric hospitals.

We were particularly impressed by the natural, healthy attitude Soviet society (and, as a result, parents and patients) takes toward mental illness. No stigma whatsoever, open or concealed, is attached to those who are so afflicted. If the sick person, after successful treatment, is able to perform the work, his previous job awaits him. If not, there is another, which takes into consideration his special needs. Thus, we were moved by the confident manner with which patients at Kashenko spoke of returning to their former jobs. They made no effort to conceal where they had worked or studied and did not at all seem to be concerned that any change in attitude would greet them on their return. This lack of worry about economic and social security is a powerful factor in treating the mentally ill.

Quite a different situation confronts our mentally ill. Few employers will reemploy or employ one who is "stigmatized" by such an illness. The knowledge of this social disapproval, as well as the difficulties of securing work and starting over again, complicate the problems of treatment and rehabilitation in the United States. All these forms of social assistance which U.S. mentally ill and their families would rejoice in, Soviet people have taken for granted as the normal attitude expected of a humane civilized society.

Some Light on a Little Known Report

The U.S. delegation of mental health experts who visited the USSR in 1967 included some of the top men in the field, as well as a prominent judge. The delegation consisted of Stanley F. Yelles, Director, National Institute of Mental Health; Dr. Walter E. Barton, Medical Director, American Psychiatric Association; Dr. Alan D. Miller, Commissioner, New York State Department of Mental Hygiene; Mike Gorman, then Executive Director, National Committee Against Mental Illness; Hon. David L. Bazelon, Chief Judge, U.S. Court of Appeals for District of Columbia Circuit; Dr. Philip Sirokin, Associate Director, National Institute of Mental Health; and Dr. Harold M. Visetsky, Director, Illinois Department of Mental Health. It published its findings in a book issued in 1969, entitled *Special Report: First U.S. Mission on Mental Health to the USSR*. Unfortunately, this revealing report, which millions of Americans directly affected by the problem would have found of great interest, was made known only to some of the medical and social work personnel in this field. The delegation stated that their sampling of Soviet mental health activities was "intensive" and "representative." It toured more than 25 mental and psychiatric facilities in Moscow, Leningrad, Kiev and the rural areas of the Ukraine, Vinnitsa and Kalinkova.

The delegation noted that Statute 120 of the Soviet Constitution stipulates: "The citizens of the USSR *have the right* to material assistance in their old age and during illness and inability to work." These are *inherent rights* which the Soviet government must and does implement with increasing resources. In our country they are programs enacted by Congress after years of considerable mass pressure. Never anything but palliatives in the first place, they are under constant attack by powerful monopoly and reactionary forces and are usually curtailed as burdensome expenditures. This is particularly the case in periods of economic decline, as was demonstrated in 1974-75.

The report of the U.S. mental health experts stresses *the continuous and comprehensive character* of Soviet mental care. It declares: "Since the basic operating principle of Soviet psychiatry is continuity of care, that care continues whether the patient remains in a specific facility, is transferred to another, or becomes an outpatient. When a patient returns to his family, he will in all likelihood be visited by a psychiatrist in his home." And they note: "In the United States such visits by a psychiatrist are still considered to be innovations, but the typical Russian psychiatrist working in a neuropsychiatric dispensary is expected to make at least 20 home visits a month." "Innovations" is hardly the word for it, what with psychiatric fees running upwards from a minimum of $30 per *office visit*. But, as the U.S. experts note, these home visits, like all medical care, are provided free of charge and are totally financed by public funds. The care, they point out, starts with the district polyclinic (there is one in each of Moscow's 30 districts, as well as in the large plants). The U.S. mental health mission observes: "From the time his mother is visited at home, during her fifth month in pregnancy, the Russian citizen has a continuing personal relationship with the polyclinic and staff. Thus mental health problems are detected at an early age and followed up and treated. Patients are referred to the appropriate hospitals. Referral has none of the amorphous quality associated with the term in the United States," the U.S. experts stress, "it includes the transfer of medical records and follow-up, the polyclinic is not a *passive agency waiting for patients to seek it out.*" The U.S. experts state, "if the patient does not respond to the card requesting him to visit the polyclinic, he will be visited at home by the nurse and, in some cases, the physician assigned to his district."

What this means in respect to *timely* assistance is only too well-known to parents of mentally ill and retarded children in the United States. No polyclinic or psychiatric dispensary opened its doors to our son, let alone sought him out at home.

The U.S. experts were quite impressed by the factory medical units which, they noted, are "of course, highly accessible to all workers." They were particularly awed by the medical unit servicing the 70,000 who work at Moscow's huge Likhachaev Automobile and Truck Plant. Try to imagine such a set-up as this at a General Motors or a Ford plant! Likhachaev's medical unit consists of a staff of 600, including 150 physicians and 250 to 275 paramedical workers handling about 2,600 patients a day. The medical services include a psychiatric unit and nine neurologists. The main task is not intensive treatment, for which patients are referred to appropriate facilities, but to help former patients on the job. The U.S. mental health mission pointedly observed that the "stigma of mental illness was not obvious either among the staff or the workers," and it added, "record cards include notes that they [the former mental patients—M.D.] are to be observed and given special support." As a result of such care and consideration, "the accident rate for former mental patients is no higher than that for other workers," and, the plant medical staff stated, "actually the reverse is true." The U.S. experts pointed out that this type of treatment and care "made it possible for the individual to work and to be accepted by his fellows and his community."

The U.S. delegation was highly impressed with Soviet stress on work. It noted that workshops are an extremely important part of all Soviet mental hospitals and facilities on every level and pointed out that the Soviet "workshop is unique in a number of respects. First, the patients are paid for their labor. . . . Work is considered to be the foundation upon which social readaptation of mental patients is based," and it goes on to state, "it would be impossible to overemphasize the importance of work in Soviet society. The workshops in psychiatric facilities are special working organizations under constant supervision of the medical staff, psychiatrists and instructors, specially trained for this assignment." The products made are not limited to the most elementary as in U.S. institutions. The U.S. delegation noted that in one of the workshops in Bekhterev Psychoneurological Institute in Leningrad, "all of the medical equipment in use at Bekhterev was made by patients." Summing up on this point, the delegation declared: *"Despite the fact that the patients had impairments of varying degrees of severity, they were being treated as people with substantial resources, able to perform meaningful activity and in many cases to learn new skills. At whatever level they were able to perform, their contribution was regarded as worthwhile, backed up with financial reward."* It puts its finger on the essence of life in this land of workers' power when it observed: "Work is a respected, indeed, exalted activity in the Soviet Union."

Apparently familiar with the disrepute in which U.S. mental hospitals are held, the delegation was particularly moved by the Soviet attitude toward mental hospitals. It declared: "It was striking to the delegation to note the vigorous enthusiasm expressed by health officials and professional personnel regarding mental hospitals. In the Soviet Union, the mental hospital occupies a particularly prestigious position," and it pointed out that they are the centers of concentration of Soviet psychiatrists. The concentration of most U.S. psychiatrists is centered upon the affluent sections of our population who can afford their fees rather than on those in most need of their services. Thus, the U.S. delegation was quite impressed by the patient-staff ratio ". . . *over all, the patient-staff ratios were virtually one to one.*" As an example, it cited Kashenko Psychiatric Hospital in Moscow. Kashenko has a staff of 200 physicians, of whom 100 are psychiatrists, 1,100 ward orderlies and 500 auxiliary and maintenance workers—a combined staff of 2,600 for 2,545 patients. Compare this to the patient-staff ratio in Willowbrook State School for Severely Retarded, which, according to the *New York Post*, December 22, 1971, had a "patient-attendant ratio that is down to 20 and in some cases of 30 to 1, in an institution where 60 percent of the patients are not toilet-trained, over 22 percent can't feed themselves and nearly 40 percent are unable to walk unassisted."

The U.S. mental health experts who paid two visits to Kashenko psychiatric hospital rated it as a "first-rate facility." They pointed out that the age of many of the hospital's buildings was deceiving since "the vigor and activity inside the hospitals quickly and decisively overshadowed the first impression of an old and shabby installation. An air of therapeutic optimism was everywhere apparent, and the abundance of professional staff made individual *patient* attention a *reality*."

Many Soviet hospitals and polyclinics present similar external appearances since the Nazi destruction, among other things, took a terrible toll of Soviet hospital facilities. Many new, modern hospitals and polyclinics have been constructed, and the 9th Five Year Plan has greatly expanded on such buildings.

The U.S. delegation noted that Kashenko's patients "were well-dressed, seemed quite self-reliant and capable of managing themselves . . . wards were spotlessly clean and newly painted" and the "patients seemed at ease; there was no tension, no disturbance, the interaction with nurses was free." In respect to the latter point, the delegation pointed out, "nursing for 65 patients totaled 28 individuals on five duty hours in a day, so that there were not less than five or six nurses on duty at one time." What the delegation observed was not just "a visiting day" appearance—we saw such scenes every week for more than four years.

I had an interesting talk with Andrei Snezhnevsky, director of the Institute of Psychiatry, Academy of Science of the USSR. The institute is located a Kashenko. Snezhnevsky, like so many top Soviet scientists I met, had little of the professional air so common among our own medical men. He had visited the United States on three occasions and appeared to be familiar with U.S. mental health facilities. His observations, I felt, were quite perceptive. "The United States has big mental hospitals, but little personnel," Snezhnevsky noted charitably, as he recalled that Eleanor Roosevelt characterized them as "buildings with no staff." He stressed that the key element in Soviet mental health practice is "timely and consistent comprehensive psychiatric aid," and pointed out this was why such emphasis is placed on the extensive network of psychiatric dispensaries. Snezhnevsky noted the United States, with no such network, has 600,000 beds occupied in its mental hospitals (this does not take into consideration the long waiting list), whereas the USSR, with a much larger population, has only 240,000 beds in its mental hospitals. The basic reason for this striking difference lies in the role played by the outpatient clinic and constant care, Snezhnevsky declared. He said U.S. psychiatrists had told him that with such clinics on a similar scale the number of beds occupied in U.S. mental hospitals would be cut 200 percent. "Our main objective is not to separate the mentally disabled from Soviet society," Snezhnevsky stressed, as he pointed out that constant care resulted in the rehabilitation of about 70 percent of those who were hospitalized.

We were impressed with the women who made up the overwhelming numbers of nurses and doctors at Kashenko. They provided a quality of tenderness. This, we pointed out, was in contrast to the overwhelmingly male composition of the staff of mental institutions in the United States who provided anything but tender care. Dr. Snezhnevsky said that Soviet experience demonstrated even in critical situations, male patients seem to restrain themselves more in the presence of women. Nurses not only undergo special training but are very much involved in the discussions on treatment of patients.

The U.S. delegation was also greatly impressed with Soviet psychiatry's stress on returning Soviet mentally ill to society and the practical steps taken by Soviet authorities to make this possible. It stated, somewhat ruefully, that this, too, could be done in our country *"when we truly decide that mentally ill people are to be brought back to society and not dismissed from society."*

The foundation of the Soviet Union's vast network of facilities rests on the psychiatric dispensary, outpatient clinic. There are twenty of them in Moscow. The U.S. delegation observed that clinics "are only ten minutes away from home by public transportation, and that service is at no cost to the patient and waiting lists do not exist."

A Visit to a Moscow Psychiatric Clinic

I visited one of the dispensary's outpatient clinics, No. 8, which serves the Kuibyshev and Sokolniki districts in Moscow. The patients, many of them middle-aged and elderly, were seated in bright attractive rooms. The doctors, mostly women, and nurses were discussing problems of treating patients. Dr. Elena Obraztsova, the chief doctor, had heard that a U.S. correspondent was interested in her clinic, and it was evident she was quite anxious to learn about our psychiatric outpatient clinics. I told her that our major problem was that we had so few of them and that psychiatric help was largely out of the reach of most Americans. Psychiatric problems, I pointed out to her, were problems that only the well-to-do could afford in our country. Obraztsova shook her graying head incredulously. "But what happens to these unfortunate people? Who helps them?" she asked.

I didn't have to ask Dr. Obraztsova a similar question. All around me were the answers. Working people of all trades, they were the kind of people you rarely see in psychiatric offices in the United States. The atmosphere was very informal, free of that intimidating professional barrier that usually separates patient and doctor in our country. One of the most pleasant differentiating characteristics of Soviet doctors, aside from the fact that more than 70 percent of them are women, is the normal, natural relationship existing between patient and doctor. Dr. Obraztsova's staff consisted of 27 doctors, 37 trained nurses and 36 other workers and attendants. This staff services about 340 people, all of whom live at home and 80 percent of whom work. Incidentally, there are six polyclinics (in addition to five children's clinics) in the area covered by the dispensary. All maintain a close and continuous relationship. The relationship between the polyclinic and the psychiatric dispensary is key to the whole system of preventive care. People in need of psychiatric care in the Soviet Union don't get "lost."

Obraztsova took us to a room in which there was a mass of records systematically arranged. "This is the medical history of the people in our district. It starts with the beginning of life.'' And here is where the link with the polyclinic is decisive. Every Soviet citizen (and foreigner living in the Soviet Union) belongs to a polyclinic from birth on. There are 30 polyclinics, one in each Moscow district. Obraztsova continued: ''Any psychiatric problem, no matter how trivial it may seem at the time, is noted by the polyclinic. We are informed immediately and consultation and care start at once *before* the problem grows. We know the families like our very own and so we know what may complicate the problem. Each doctor has assigned to her a group of families. If special care is needed, we have highly qualified professors, ready for consultation.''

The psychiatric dispensary makes use of a workshop with hothouses in beautiful Sokolniki Park. Perhaps, more than anything else, we were impressed with the dispensary's ability to *implement* its doctors' prescriptions for patients. I am referring not only to medicines and therapeutic treatment. (Medicines are provided free or at very low cost.) I am referring to necessary changes in basic living and working conditions prescribed by doctors. In the United States, the doctor's advice or ''orders to get a new job, improve one's living conditions, or go on a vacation,'' are just so many words to the average American worker. The doctor and the patient both know this. In the Soviet Union such a tragic gap between what the doctor prescribes and what the patient's financial situation dictates is nonexistent. The U.S. mental health experts noted that the Soviet rehabilitation program is backed up by the fact that *''the all pervasive government can commandeer jobs, apartments, etc., for the patient.''*

The Soviet government ''interferes'' in the personal affairs of mentally ill persons to make sure that the remedies doctors prescribe are made possible. Thus, with the cooperation of the plant or office management and union, necessary job adjustments are made to aid the patient's recovery. And even though there is still a tight housing situation, the mentally ill and their families are provided with more spacious and more comfortable apartments. Obraztsova told us that a number of apartments are annually set aside for this purpose. ''Those we recommend, receive apartments without taking their place on the waiting list,'' she said. The dispensary also has a special sanitorium to which it can send those who need such care. I asked Obraztsova what conditions would be like without such a dispensary setup. As if she were describing conditions in the United States, she replied: ''It would lead to social separation and would result in a great increase in hospital cases, chronic cases. We can't imagine life without these facilities."

The U.S. mental health experts noted that "every effort is made to ensure that all patients—even the severely impaired ones—will get as much out of life as possible." Thus, it was striking to the delegation but thoroughly in keeping with the Russian framework to find husbands and wives living together in a Home for Invalids [chronic patients, M.D.] and, indeed, "a scheduled marriage between two patients in their seventies." And the delegation concluded: "As with other elements of the care network, a major emphasis of the specialized chronic facilities lay in the preservation and maintenance of human dignity. In that regard, the Russian attempt to care for chronic patients was notable."

Child Care

The members of the U.S. Mental Health Mission were particularly moved by Soviet care for children, especially the mentally and physically handicapped. They fully bore out the picture of systematic and continuous medical care with which we were personally familiar. "In actuality, care of the child begins before he cries, on an extensive and meticulous basis with the pregnant mother. From the fifth month of pregnancy, there is the beginning of an accumulation of vast physiological data on the child yet to be born. Obstetricians and pediatricians visit the homes of all pregnant women on a regular basis. When the mother delivers the child, the children's polyclinic is immediately notified by the hospital. From that time until the child reaches the age of 16, the polyclinic is the medical hub of all health services designed to meet the special needs of children. All the families in the neighborhood know where it is located—no one has to look up the number—since there is a children's polyclinic in each district of approximately 40,000 people. There is nothing haphazard about guidelines for the care of the child in the USSR. Certain standards are established and *must be met*. For example, as soon as the mother returns from the hospital, the doctor and nurse must visit her and give her a regimen for the newborn infant. During the first months of a baby's life, the physician must call five times at the home, and the medical data on those visits must be recorded in the polyclinic files. Until a child is two or three years of age, the physician is required to see him at least once a month, and continues to see him at least every two or three months until he enters kindergarten, when the school medical unit assumes liaison responsibility with the child and the polyclinic.''

The U.S. mental health experts concluded: ''The organization of health services in Russia is complete and health services for children bears this out.'' They noted ''there are more than 70,000 pediatricians in the USSR as compared to 15,000 in the United States,'' and they correctly observed, ''with this kind of continuity of care as a base, it is usually the pediatrician who is the focal point for the professional practice of child psychiatry.'' The delegation was impressed with the comprehensive network of special schools, homes for children, and schools for the mentally retarded, neurotic children, those with speech disorders, and forest schools located in wooded areas. All provide special care at no cost or a nominal charge of 6 to 10 rubles a month.

The U.S. mental experts observed the same attentive approach in a kindergarten for the mentally retarded. Understandably, what first impressed them was the staff—147 attendants for 200 children! They made special note that ''the Russians were devoting considerable financial and manpower resources to the care of children whose financial and potential contribution to the Russian economy was at best limited.'' This, in a country usually depicted by our press as concerned solely with getting the utmost materially out of individuals! When the U.S. delegation questioned the director on this point, he replied simply: ''We think that every child, however limited, is entitled to the best that we can give him. Even if he cannot be absorbed into any educational system, *we must make his life not only endurable but somewhat joyful.*''

The delegation visited a Moscow Children's Dispensary located on the grounds of the children's hospital. For 530 children, there was staff of more than 800 people: including 83 physicians, of whom 63 were child psychiatrists, 280 nurses, 32 speech therapists, 60 teachers, 238 ward assistants, besides housekeeping and maintenance personnel. The U.S. experts were ''very impressed with the high quality of progress visible in even the most disturbed ward. Of particular note were the vases, plants and draperies in abundance, reflecting the expectation that the children would respect property and control their behavior.''

The systematic human care the Soviet Union provides for its mentally ill and retarded citizens from early childhood is an important factor contributing to the tensionless character of the city streets. In addition to poverty and racism, our government's neglect of the mentally ill and retarded helps to swell our crime rolls. Gorman, a member of the U.S.

Mental Health Mission to Moscow, stated that two-thirds of all afflicted youngsters "are quite literally lost, bounced around from training school to reformatories, to jails, and whipped through all kinds of understaffed agencies until they vanish." They don't quite "vanish." Abused and unwanted by an indifferent society and government, unable to secure employment, many are driven to strike out against both in the only way they know how—exploding into violence and bringing tragedy to their families, innocent bystanders and themselves. Often, especially if they are Black, Puerto Rican or Chicano, they are the tragic victims of police bullets.

Such tragic events are rare in Soviet life, in Soviet cities. In addition to the over-all *human* character of Soviet city life, the comprehensive care rendered to its mentally ill and retarded has done much to eliminate a potential source of crime.

8 / LIFE WITHOUT DOCTOR BILLS

When we experienced our first illness in Moscow the doctor came to our home! And she was accompanied by a nurse! Patients are not refused, or intimidated out of applying for home visits or from making frequent use of appointments with doctors. They are not only encouraged to do so but are scolded when they fail to appear for regular checkups. Despite the facilities available, many Soviet citizens are still negligent of their health. The psychological fear of "finding out" still maintains its grip on people. This is being overcome through frequent compulsory medical examinations as well as by the all pervasive preventive care. If you want to go to a rest home or sanitorium on vacation you must first get a complete checkup at the polyclinic. Behind this seemingly arbitrary procedure is care for the individual. As one Soviet doctor put it to me: "My responsibility for my patients is not limited to treating them when they are ill. On the contrary, it is to see that they do not get ill."

No one should get any idea that Soviet doctors are more proficient than ours. They are not. And like our doctors they vary in their competence. Soviet citizens, too, seek out doctors in whom they have more confidence. And some doctors give diagnoses that leave much to be desired. These are the human elements in medical practice that are not easily overcome—even in a socialist system. A struggle to raise medical proficiency is constantly going on. Polyclinic doctors have regular meetings where their work is professionally evaluated by their colleagues. The outstanding characteristic of the entire Soviet health system is the same dedicated concern that so impressed the U.S. mental health experts. Our country, of course, has many fine hospitals, with the most modern equipment. And they are staffed by highly competent doctors, nurses, attendants, and workers. The care in these U.S. hospitals is on a par with the best. But these hospitals are largely out of the reach of a very substantial part of our population. And for those Americans who are able to use these facilities, they constitute an exhausting drain on their incomes.

The *New York Times*, reporting on the city hospitals, in its issue of June 2, 1969, said: "At their worst, the hospitals betray their poor-house origins. The death rate of 6.8 per 100 discharges is nearly *twice* the rate of the 3.5 death rate of voluntary hospitals [those run by so-called nonprofit-making religious, private and charity organizations M.D.]. To some extent, this is because the city hospitals are used by poverty-stricken patients, many of whom suffer from malnutrition and have *delayed* seeking treatment." The delay as the *Times* knows well, is largely based on financial reasons. Not only the poor but people of average incomes see a doctor only when literally compelled to do so. The *Times* notes that unlike private hospitals [privately owned and run for profit.—M.D.] the city institutions are the hospitals of *last resort*—they accept any patient *sick enough* to require hospitalization. Many private hospitals refuse some patients because they do not fit their teaching and research needs. Because of this, the emergency rooms of such municipal hospitals as Bellevue, Kings County and Metropolitan continue to receive from voluntary hospitals critically ill but educationally "uninteresting" patients. "Last resort," "sick enough," and high death rate are all closely linked. They denote that in our country the very *opposite* of the Soviet approach is taken toward the health of people who can't afford the high cost of medical treatment. The cost per day for a hospital bed rose from $58.35 in 1965 to $110 in 1974. It is even higher today. In the Soviet Union you don't have to be *sick enough* to go to a hospital. The effort is *to prevent* you from getting sick enough. The *New York Times* reveals not only the class but the racially discriminatory character of the city hospitals. It quotes Dr. Steven Sharfstein, an intern at Jacobi Hospital, as saying: "As interns and residents in the city hospitals, some of us are not very different from ghetto merchants. The merchants get their profits in the ghettos and go home to the suburbs. We get our training in the ghettos and then practice in the suburbs. This kind of training breeds contempt for the patients." The Black and Puerto Rican patients are well aware of this contempt and this special treatment reserved for them. Soviet doctors are not better than ours, they are more *human*. Not because they are better human beings but because the dollar or rather the ruble doesn't figure in relations between doctor and patient.

Where Doctors Can Be Doctors

I visited Filatov Institute and Hospital for Eye Surgery, in Odessa, because I had heard of this famed hospital as the refuge of the hopeless. I saw a hospital that was the last word in eye surgery and I learned why Filatov Institute means so much to the blind and near blind of the world.

Yevdokia Budilova is the hospital's chief doctor. Budilova symbolizes the spirit of Academician Vladimir Filatov, the institute's founder—the spirit of *heart and hand*.

Budilova had been chief doctor for more than 20 years when I met her. She worked six years in that capacity under Filatov. She saw and experienced more than her share of suffering. She began her postgraduate course in a medical institute June 15, 1941, and went to the front on June 22. She was a surgeon at the front during the entire war. Budilova briefly filled me in on Filatov's statistics. "We have 168 doctors, 450 patients in eight large separate clinics. In addition 377,000 people annually visit our consultative department." She paused and added: "So you can see what grief and sadness we have here." She was silent for a moment. "I worked among the blind for many years. But no one except the sightless can fully understand the misery of blindness." Budilova's eyes sparkled: "But we have scored victories in the battle against darkness. More than 86 percent of our patients had their sight either fully or partially restored." Her eyes fixed on the wall clock which had stopped at seven. "That's when Filatov died. This was his study. He passed away at the institute—despite his age—he performed operations to the very end." Budilova continued, musing. "Filatov, you know, studied at the same gymnasium as Lenin—he was three years younger than Lenin. He had the same love and confidence in people. Filatov was a relentless enemy of pessimism. He used to say, 'there are no *hopeless* people, there are only *hopeless* doctors.' And his law was: Never say 'no' to a patient." She added: "Perhaps that's why our institute has become the last refuge of the world's hopeless." Filatov Institute services without any payment not only Soviet citizens but patients from every corner of the globe. Annually it treats patients from 50 countries and provides consultative care through a correspondence department to those fighting for their sight, from 102 countries. "We are the world's best stamp collectors," Budilova noted, with a smile. In addition, Filatov sends its highly trained specialists (fully equipped) for periods of two to four years to Vietnam, Cuba and other countries of Africa and Asia.

Filatov hospital performed, free of charge, more than 1,000 eye transplant operations. It has an eye "bank" supplied from those who died in accidents. Filatov was the father of the eye bank concept. He rejected the idea, popular among some medical people at that time, of taking eyes from the living, as "stealing the sight of others." Filatov Institute's interest in, and its relationship with its patients often lasts as long as ten years. "The fight for sight is a difficult and often a long one," Budilova pointed out. "We have no time schedule. We are not concerned with cost. We are concerned with the most precious thing—human sight. More than 87 percent of the average person's knowledge comes from sight. Successful operations do not terminate our interest in our patient's welfare."

I met the same qualities that same day in Odessa, in Rosa Kleyman, who had been for 25 years chief doctor of Chuvirena Sanitorium (founded in 1934) for children afflicted with serious heart disease. There are 500 children's sanitoriums in the Soviet Union, with half a million children annually receiving free treatment in them. Chuvirena's point of concentration is upon children's hearts. The preparation for surgery is psychological as well as physical—and, above all—imbued with affection. After the operation, the children undergo a special program that includes exercises, sports, and rest. We followed Rosa to a gym class where children were doing ballet exercises. A quotation on the wall from one of Mayakovsky's poems read: "The best clothes are our muscles and the freshness of our skin."

Drs. Budilova and Kleyman would find it hard, indeed, to practice their humanity in our dog-eat-dog society. Instead of devoting all their energy to fighting blindness and heart disease, they would have to fight for "play space for children," as at New York City's Metropolitan Hospital. The *New York Times*, June 2, 1969, noted that in hospitals children were "confined to their beds because the recreational area set aside for them has been converted into research offices by the New York Medical College." Budilova and Kleyman would be compelled to battle for the elementary right to *examine* children properly. The *Times* pointed out that "the number of health examinations—where poor vision, and hearing defects were often first detected by public health nurses—has been reduced from 90 percent of the classrooms to 50 percent.''

Soviet Morality vs. Our Sick Medical System

The entire structure of our medical health system is sick—sicker than any of the patients it treats. Charging for health is like charging for air. And what could be more inhuman than to place medical care out of the reach of those who most need it—the poor—to make them guinea pigs for doctors preparing for their rich practice?

How barbaric is a system which can spawn nursing homes that wax rich on the misery of the elderly as they hasten their end! Even the Medicare and Medicaid programs established to aid the elderly and indigent have served largely to benefit profiteers more than patients. Yet almost six years following its articles, the *New York Times*, Jan. 8, 1975, editorializes on the "sick hospitals" of New York. In 1970 the Health and Hospitals Corporation replaced the Department of Hospitals as an obvious step to stress administrative economies rather than services. The job evidently was done a bit too well, for the *Times* noted "concern over budgetary problems tends to obscure the human suffering hospitals are supposed to alleviate. . . . Lack of space, equipment and personnel in the right places at the right time has led to unwatched heart monitors and otherwise unattended patients whose lives are literally in the balance. Doctors and nurses find themselves compelled almost routinely to 'play God', determine who is a good enough risk to receive a crack at the limited life-saving stations.''

I note all this to contrast it with Soviet morality in health service. Health protection is established in the Soviet Constitution as the legal right of every citizen. *There are no privately owned hospitals or clinics in the Soviet Union*. The entire cost of financing the unmatched medical services is borne by the Soviet state. In addition to vast and ever increasing state allocations, all major enterprises finance medical and recreation facilities for their employees.

The basic unit in the system is the polyclinic, to which every Soviet citizen belongs. There are more than 40,000 clinics; their staffs work two shifts—doctors work alternately a six-hour day. The clinic is the key *preventive* unit because it is always available and operates like a huge family doctor. This explains why Academician Boris Petrovsky could report in 1973 that "80 percent of all patients *begin* and *complete* their treatment in ambulatory condition.'' The relationship between the clinic and the hospital is a very close and constant one—many clinics are attached to hospitals. The number of hospital beds, incidentally, exceeds that of the United States. It is 3,000,000 or 113 beds per 10,000. There are more than 21,000 women's consultation centers and children's clinics. Delivery and intensive pre- and post-natal care are free. Expectant mothers get 112 days maternity leave (56 days before and 56 days after childbirth). Working mothers are provided with additional privileges, including longer paid leave to nurse a sick child.

In 1913, 269 out of every 1,000 newborn infants died. In 1970, it was only 23. Incidentally, the life-span increased from age 33 in pre-revolutionary years to age 70 today.

One of the many reasons for the shortage of doctors and nurses is the high cost of a medical education in the United States. The average cost of a college education is about $14,000; it is considerably more for medical students. A medical education is generally regarded as an *investment* that must be made to pay off. And it can only *pay off* in practice among the more affluent. Soviet medical students are not guided by any need to cash in on the *investment*—all the investing is done by the Soviet government. In 1975, the number of doctors in the Soviet Union reached 830,000, one-fourth of the world's doctors. In addition, there are 2,195,000 medium-level personnel. All told, more than 5 million people are engaged in protecting the people's health.

Protection is provided particularly at the point of production. All large plants have polyclinics similar to the one at Likhachaev Auto Plant, which so impressed our U.S. mental health experts. There is one doctor for every 2,000 workers and in mining, chemical, and oil-refining industries, one per 1,000. In Odessa as I observed, the longshoreman's clinic *is located right on the docks*.

I spoke to Lou Arian, of Local 6, International Longshoremen's and Warehousemen's Union in San Pedro, California, who was part of a delegation of U.S. longshoremen who visited the Odessa docks in 1972. Arian was quite moved by the sight of that polyclinic because as a longshoreman of many years, he knows what that means to the health and safety of workers engaged in one of the most hazardous occupations.

I visited many after-work sanitoria or, as they are called, prophylacteria. More than 1,000 enterprises have set up such rest and health facilities. Here too, the concept is prevention—don't wait until you are sick enough. The mine workers of Apatit, in the Soviet Polar Region, have a rest home that in our country would be reserved for mine owners.

The workers ski and ice skate, take bobsled rides in the winter, and get special diets as well as necessary medical care.

Prevention is also promoted through a system of compulsory checkups. Particular attention is given to early cancer treatment. Cancer centers with boarding houses attached to them are being constructed out of the funds earned during recent all-Soviet *subbotniks*.

The future of Soviet medicine is exemplified by the Vishnevsky Institute in Moscow, constructed in 1971. The institute is a "city of surgery." It is 17 stories of streamlined glass and aluminum. The skilled surgeon's hand is guided by cybernetics. The computer has added speed and precision in the job of diagnosis. In 96 percent of the cases the computer has been proven correct. It has also been helpful in diagnosing early stages of lung cancer. This system enables Vishnevsky Institute to provide doctors, who are hundreds of miles away, with speedy diagnoses. The institute is directly linked with five large cities, and in the near future its network will extend to 200 cities.

Vishnevsky Institute, which has a staff of 800, is basically a scientific research center. Hence, there are only 500 beds in this vast building. Surgery is performed in six spacious operating rooms. Patients are under observation day and night through closed circuit TV.

The Right Kind of Drugs at the Right Price

The *International Herald Tribune*, October 29, 1973, quotes Dr. George J. Williams as saying: "Vitamin B-12 and Estrogen shots alone pay the doctor's rent and put his kids through college." In Moscow, I frequently had B-12 shots given to me free of charge at my polyclinic. In the Soviet Union not only are drugs extremely low-priced but in many cases the medicines are supplied free of charge.

The chief problem I found was that some prescribed drugs were not easy to get. This is annoying and time-consuming. But there is no high price to restrict use; there are no drug profiteers to push dubious drugs on the people. Before being placed on the market, all drugs go through the strictest testing and retesting.

I visited Riga's famed Institute of Organic Synthesis, headed by Academician Dr. S. Hiller. A staff of 500 scientific workers armed with the latest equipment worked here to produce "miracle" drugs in the battle against dread diseases. The institute is one of 15 that make up the Latvian Academy of Science and Riga's Science City. It is composed of 110 laboratories and scientific rooms fitted with the most modern equipment. The institute has its own experimental factory with 200 workers. Incidentally, when it was a bourgeois republic, Latvia's excellent chemists, who then only numbered 50, depended largely on "gifts" provided by Rockefeller funds and profits derived from a hotel in Rome (owned by the Latvian State University). Today Soviet Latvia has 900 to 1,000 chemists.

Hiller is a middle-aged man brimming with energy and enthusiasm. A student in the Latvian State University. Hiller was defending his diploma thesis when the Nazis invaded the Soviet Union in 1941. Like many Riga Jews, Hiller's parents were killed by the Nazis. He enlisted in the Soviet armed forces and fought in the Battle of Stalingrad. He has been the institute's director since its inception in 1957. Hiller was incredulous when I told him of the high price of drugs in the United States. "We make a profit at our low prices, so I can imagine the kind of profits your private drug companies must make," he exclaimed.

The Soviet health system already does much to ward off the ill effects of modern city life. But Soviet medical men readily admit that the problems of modern urban existence, with its rapidly increasing tempo of living, tensions, noise, and pollution, create unfavorable conditions for the physical and mental health of people. This explains why the 24th Congress of the CPSU addressed itself seriously to these problems and, among other things, proposed international cooperation in dealing with the problems of environment as well as the killer diseases of cancer and heart ailments. The agreements worked out at the historic Moscow Summit between the United States and the USSR are the first fruits of this effort to unite all mankind, regardless of social system, against the common health dangers it faces.

Polyclinic in Paradise

A Soviet sanitorium is a polyclinic in paradise! Here, nature and science unite to restore, repair, and replenish the health of a nation's workers. Here, the year-round care provided the Soviet people is combined into an extensive crash health course, usually lasting 24 days. The extensive Soviet health medical (and cultural) apparatus takes over millions of Soviet people for a month once a year and gets to work on them. It carefully checks them over, prescribes the necessary regime of exercise, treatment, diet, swimming, rest, and sun each individual must get, and follows up systematically on the implementation of their "orders." And they are just that—"orders." At first I found it a bit too organized and there are those, especially Soviet youth, who prefer a less organized rest. But the surge of vigor and freshness that replenishes your weary body makes you soon realize that it is well worth the systematic effort. Besides, you really discover there is plenty of time for your own individual brand of rest and enjoyment.

For the protection of its people's health, the Soviet Union has established the world's largest, most elaborate, most modern and luxurious facilities, natural and man-made. "Natural" should not be accepted as a matter of course. The business of health begins with nature. This is also appreciated in our country. But there's one big difference. In our country, nature's prime health and beauty space are the preserves of the very rich and rich — in that order.

One of the things that impressed me was the fact that in Sochi and Crimea I met workers from the far corners of the Soviet Union.

The first significance of the magnificent health resorts of Crimea and Sochi is that they were transformed into the property of the people from private preserves of princes. You have to visit the czar's former palace in Lyvadi in Crimea, now one of the sanitoriums run by the Soviet trade unions, to grasp the dramatic significance of that transformation. Workers, men and women, stroll along the majestic, cypress-lined paths where once the czar's family took their walks. They lunch or go to *"protzeduras"* (medical treatments) in one of the former palaces. They are so accustomed to their "royal" surroundings, they hardly take notice of visiting groups from the "free" world who stare at them. It is clear that the present occupants of the palace long ago got used to this magnificence. It was their parents and grandparents who felt the once-in-a-millenium thrill of the transformation. In 1925, Lyvadi became a sanitorium for illiterate poor peasants. Many received their first lessons in reading and writing in these palatial surroundings!

Lyvadi sanitorium, run by the Soviet trade unions (as are most sanitoriums and rest homes), today specializes in heart treatment. In addition to numerous medical personnel and elaborate facilities, a staff of 30 cardiologists provides care for 1,000 people each summer and winter. And for all this: medical treatment, idyllic beauty, luxurious surroundings, nourishing if not sumptuous meals, the cost is only 120 to 130 rubles a month. Most vacationers, however, pay only 30 percent of the cost. This then explains why I was able to meet workers from the far corners of the Soviet Union in Crimea and Sochi.

As an American, I was frequently asked: How do workers in your

country spend their vacations? The assumption of many of my questioners was that American workers also enjoy such vacation facilities. I told
them that average Americans, unlike average Soviet citizens, can't afford
such sanitoriums. My questioners were puzzled — they had considerable
illusions about U.S. wages and the American standard of living.

But the Soviet Union has gone far beyond expropriation of the czarist
pleasure palaces; it has established the largest network of resort centers
(which expands with every Five Year Plan). Walk through the center of
beautiful Yalta, shielded by the multihued mountains and bathed by the
refreshing waters of the blue-green Black Sea, and you will come across a
plaque imbedded in rock. On it is chiseled the words of the decree
adopted, at Lenin's suggestion, on May 13, 1921, proclaiming the
former palaces as sanitoriums and rest homes for the workers and peasants and establishing new ones, "to give workers and office employees
an opportunity of restoring their health and strength under the most
favorable and healthy conditions." Though wracked by civil war, intervention, blockade and economic disruption, the Socialist Republic, in
1921 to 1922, established health resorts on the coast of the Black Sea.
There was intensive construction of resorts and sanitoriums during the
years 1933-41. The country's best architects designed them. Fascist
Germany's attack on the Soviet Union halted further construction of
sanitoriums. In the occupied areas, they were largely destroyed and
plundered, particularly in Crimea and the Ukraine. Soviet troops and
partisan bands wrote some of the most courageous chapters of the war in
the struggle to liberate their "palaces." The Soviet Union regarded the
rebuilding of the health resorts as a natural part of its reconstruction and
by 1950, 2,070 sanitoriums had been established, with 255,000 beds,
more than existed before the war.

Soviet trade unions today run more than 5,000 sanitoriums (including
those for children), rest homes and tourist centers which annually play
host to 20 million workers and their children. Over 80 percent get their
accommodations free of charge or at a discount, at the expense of state
insurance funds.

Not all sanitoriums or rest homes are palatial and free from problems
and unpleasantness. Some are more luxurious than others, and cost more.
Perhaps the chief weakness—or contradiction—I encountered is one I
came across in other main aspects of Soviet life. Let me illustrate what I
mean with an experience we had at one sanitorium. The building and
surroundings were palatial. However, we were not very long in our room

(which was quite comfortable, with a breathtaking view of the Black Sea) when the bathroom ceiling began to drip. We called this to the attention of the chambermaid. "But it is a '*vihodnoi den*' (nonworking day)," she informed us. (It was Sunday.) This day off evidently included the sanitorium director, who was nowhere to be seen. And with pails in the bathroom, we waited for Monday, a "non-*vihodnoi den.*" for the repairs.

These are "little things" but they can be and are quite irritating and wasteful. And what makes them more so was the attitude toward such deficiencies. It reflects the kind of attitude toward poor-quality work that Brezhnev lashed out against in a number of speeches, and which is being combated in all aspects of work and public service.

These, then, are the "little things" that still have to be overcome by those who accomplished "big things" like turning the czar's palace into a sanitorium for workers and providing Soviet people with the world's best and cheapest vacation and health setup.

The Soviet "Secret" Weapon

The Soviet Union's "secret" weapon in the fight for health is the *collective* spirit that dominates its life. The Soviet Union has more of the *collective* spirit not only because it has practiced it longer than any other socialist country, but because that spirit was forged in the fires of unprecedented ordeals and trials. It was that *collective* spirit that met and beat off an invisible and silent enemy — cholera — when it threatened Soviet Black Sea cities in the summer of 1970.

We were vacationing at Foross, not far from Yalta, in August during the height of the cholera scare. We were amazed to find that very few cut short their vacations. What is more, new vacationers from all parts of the Soviet Union continued to arrive on schedule. The calm we witnessed was not based on ignorance or concealed information or a devil-may-care attitude. All were fully aware of the terrible danger of an epidemic. We attended regular meetings where the progress of the cholera threat was openly discussed by doctors. Behind the daily bantering, there was natural concern. The calm was based on confidence that the proper medical and organizational measures were being taken by the governmental bodies and public organizations.

It was the city of Kerch—on the Black Sea—where, incidently, one of the great battles against the Nazi invasion took place, that provided an outstanding example of the *collective* spirit I'm talking about. The 1970

Battle of Kerch was waged by an entire population as it worked, went to school, and shopped for its daily needs. None of these daily activities were interrupted. During the Great Patriotic War, Communists, putting into life the slogan, "Communists First," flung themselves into battle at the most dangerous and crucial sectors. In this emergency, too, Communists were called on to set the example. An extraordinary meeting of the Kerch Party Committee was called, followed the next day by meetings of leaders of the City Soviet, factories, and offices. The city was besieged again and the entire population had to be mobilized to beat off the new invader. An antiepidemic committee was established on a city-wide scale and in every section of Kerch. But the Battle of Kerch was also waged as a national struggle. Scientists came from Rostov, Simferopol, Saratov, Stavropol, Kiev and Moscow. Doctors and nurses on vacation along the Black Sea gave up their vacations and volunteered for the Battle of Kerch. Students of the Crimean Medical Institute joined their teachers to work with them in the areas of greatest danger.

Medical aid was brought by plane, truck, train, and ship. Ships brought water from Sevastopol. Emergency medical transports came from Gorky and Riga. Cities of the Ukraine dispatched special milk trucks and cleaning equipment. *It was an all-Soviet Union mobilization.* Food was brought to Kerch in special trucks. They halted at the city's "quarantine line." Disinfected trucks from Kerch took the food and delivered it to the city stores. All consumer goods were thoroughly disinfected before they were made available to the public. Kerch fought the enemy with cleanliness and, like all Soviet cities, *it was already well-equipped* and trained in that respect. Far more important than even the massive sanitation equipment ordinarily employed on a daily basis in Soviet cities, are the habits of civic concern and cleanliness formed in the course of more than half a century of socialist living. As a result of this all-out effort, the cholera claimed only two victims in Kerch.

The Battle of Kerch typifies the entire character of the Soviet fight to make cities livable, and all life more healthful and enjoyable.

9 / WHERE POLLUTERS CAN'T POLLUTE

Among the simple blessings that Soviet urban dwellers can still count on to a far greater extent than U.S. city residents, is the smell of clean, fresh air and the good taste of pure water. Coming from New York, I appreciate this much more than Muscovites. By their superior standards, Moscow air is not sufficiently pure. They are concerned about the considerable increase of air pollutants resulting from the notable rise in automobile traffic in the past five years. Their justified concern is shared by their city government and Soviet officials and scientists who are now devoting much attention to the problem.

Pollution, of course, is not a political phenomenon, and pollutants are oblivious to social differences. They are the by-products of massive industrialization and chemicalization, and confront all industrial countries with a serious environmental problem.

But *how* the problem has been and is being tackled and the *degree* of pollution have a great deal to do with politics and social system. The Soviet Union faces problems; we face crises. Pollution reflects the decay of our cities. Neither Moscow nor any other Soviet city has experienced a situation similar to the near disaster which threatened New Yorkers Thanksgiving Day, 1966, when the air pollution index reached 60.0 mgs. per cubic meter, five times the normal, and hastened the death of many elderly and sick people. On May 10, 1966, six months before the Thanksgiving smog crisis, the Mayor's Task Force on Air Pollution, headed by Norman Cousins, warned in the 175 page comprehensive report: "All the ingredients now exist for an air pollution disaster of major proportions.'' Noting that ''at least three times during recent years a condition of stagnant air loaded with gases and particulate matter has resulted in a sudden and detectable increase in the death rate,'' it *cautioned that under such a condition New York would resemble ''an indoor parking garage with the automobile motors running and almost no windows or doors open.''* [My emphasis, M.D.] But for its fortunate ''open topographic surroundings,'' New York City would be uninhabitable, the report noted.

The "Little Difference"

The mayor's task force of New York publicly labeled Consolidated Edison, the utility monopoly that fleeces New Yorkers, as ''the largest single producer of foul air in the City of New York!'' How did the mayor and the city government deal with this monopoly that was endangering the very lives of 8 million New Yorkers? The mayor treated the utility monopoly as if it were an independent power, a sovereign state unto itself! The mayor announced that an ''agreement'' had been reached with Consolidated Edison. (I recall this comic opera scene because I covered the ''negotiations.'') Yet, Consolidated Edison, only 19 percent of whose fuel was natural gas, which is nontoxic, balked at that time at even increasing the use of coal with a lower sulpur dioxide content because it was too expensive. The mayor's task force had ''urged'' Consolidated Edison to increase its use of natural gas to 30 percent. By contrast, the proportion of the fuel of natural gas burned in Moscow is 95 percent.

With other newsmen, I was present at a New York-New Jersey conference on air pollution, held in the Statler Hilton hotel in New York City in early January, 1967. The late Congressman William F. Ryan transformed the conference into a trial against Consolidated Edison and some of the largest corporations, particularly the oil and chemical industries, which were polluting the air breathed by 15,392,000 people. Pointing to photographs he had taken on a helicopter trip over the New York-New Jersey area, Ryan presented visual proof of the pollution poured into the atmosphere by these leading U.S. corporations. In some pictures, the smoke emitted was so dense that it was difficult to discern the stacks. Noting that local and state governments were either unwilling or unable to act decisively, Ryan called on New Yorkers to ''declare a war on Consolidated Edison.'' At one point, Ryan declared that ''no man has the right to profit at the expense of injury to others.'' But the City of New York did little to impair that ''right.''

Our irate citizenry has since compelled the enactment by Congress of laws such as the Clean Air Law in 1970 and the Water Pollution Control Act in 1972. These laws have placed some restraints on industry and heavier fines and penalties have been levied against violators of the laws. But the basic problem of how to compel the all-powerful monopolies to respect the health of the people remains. Comic opera "negotiations" have only been replaced by Alice-in-Wonderland court litigations. Cunning delaying tactics have supplanted outright defiance. The monopolies have posed a choice: employed hands or healthy lungs! This was the choice U.S. Steel gave steel workers in Gary, Indiana, in the midst of the most severe economic crisis since the 1930s when it refused to pay a $2,300 a day fine imposed by the court. Similar pressure was exerted by the auto monopolies to get the *postponement* of the installation of antipollution devices on newly produced cars, and the energy "crisis" was likewise utilized to take the heat off the utility monopolies.

The people of the Soviet Union face no such *choices* or *pressures*. The Soviet Union can face the serious pollution problems posed by massive industrialization as a united society because it has no social class whose economic interests are in contradiction to the welfare of society as a whole.

The Soviet approach to combating pollution is the same as it is in fighting disease: *prevention* is the main concentration. Before any new plant can be put into operation, it must pass a rigid inspection to insure that it has the necessary scientific antipollution equipment. This goes particularly for air and water pollution.

Soviet cities, as I indicated in an earlier chapter, live by a General Master Plan (25 years) and their shorter-range plans (5 to 10 years). One of the main problems grappled with in these plans is how to *harmonize* industry and community, plants, and people: in a word, how to make it possible for large and smaller industrial cities to produce the things people need and at the same time make it possible for them to live pleasantly and healthfully.

The huge modern plants are impressive but so are the "green belts" around these giant enterprises, the numerous little parks where workers relax during their lunch breaks, the flower pots sitting on immense automated milling machines. Trees, plants, and flowers are weapons in the fight for clean air. No tree may be cut down in a Soviet city without the approval of the local Soviet. That is why almost one-third of Moscow's total area consists of such greenery. The Soviet capital has 100 parks. Izmailovsky Park covers 1,180 hectares, almost five times the area of Central Park in New York. In addition, Moscow has 600 boulevards and gardens. There is an annual increase in greenery of 600 hectares. At the same time, Moscow is surrounded by a protective forest and belt line of 172,000 hectares, almost twice the city's size. This "protective" area is to be expanded to 275,000 hectares. These are the "lungs" of the Soviet capital. By contrast, only 18 percent of New York City land area is considered in the category of park area. The *New York Times,* June 4, 1969, noted that: "By the standard of the National Recreation Association, which says there should be one acre of park for every 160 persons, most of the city is below par."

Like Pittsburgh, Donetsk in the Ukraine is in the heart of one of the main coal mining and steel regions. But there, all resemblance between the two cities ends. Pittsburgh, for good reason, is known as the "smoky city." Yet it is hard to think of Donetsk as a coal and steel center. Nowhere is there the telltale stain of industrial smoke and grime. The air is fresh and clean. The spacious streets lined with sweet-smelling acacia trees, numerous parks, the wide artificial river, and attractive modern apartment houses make Donetsk one of the most beautiful cities in the Soviet Union. Yet Donetsk, under the czars, was a dirty, disease-ridden hellhole. And even in the early days of Soviet power, when it mushroomed as a steel and coal city, it earned the name of the "smokestack." It was occupied by the Nazis who not only murdered thousands of miners whom they buried in the pits, but destroyed the city itself.

Donetsk, now a city of one million, was transformed, as planned by its architectural institute, into one of the cleanest cities in the world.

City Planning and Pollution—Contrast Between Two Systems

In Moscow I met with Alexander Yanevsky, chief of Moscow's Planning Institute and his deputy, Yuri Sokolov. Sokolov outlined Moscow's approach to air pollution (it is similar in all Soviet cities) along three main lines: Introduction and perfection of antipollution equipment, including increased use of the least noxious fuel; moving industries or residents; and strict systematic inspection to determine where pollution norms are being exceeded. On the last point Sokolov stressed that the decision of the inspection commissions, composed of representatives of workers', scientific, and people's organizations, is law. He reported that a factory in Noguisk that violated the pollution norm was closed down for six months until the proper conditions were established. Others were also disci-

112 CITIES WITHOUT CRISIS

plined. But such violations are rare. They are *not* the result of a conflict of *interests*, as in our country, but laxity, erroneous judgment, and a one-sided approach to production. Violations are being handled with increasing sharpness. The Supreme Soviet has emphasized the urgent need to *perfect* antipollution equipment.

But Moscow faces a special problem, Sokolov admitted. Many factories were built during czarist times. A large number of them were located in the center of the city. This is a problem faced by many of our own cities. But how Moscow is meeting the problem reveals the difference in the approaches of two social systems. The Moscow City Soviet moved more than 300 such plants into industrial zone areas set up by the city. Those too old to use were demolished and replaced by new factories.

Zoning occupies a very important place in Moscow's immediate as well as long-range plans. We, too have zoning laws, but they have nowhere nearly the scope of Soviet laws, which aim at nothing less than removing inhabitants from the ill effects and unpleasant by-products of industrialism. By contrast, competition between U.S. cities to attract or retain industries is so fierce they not only extend tax privileges but "bend" antipollution laws and zoning regulations. Moscow had to grapple with a serious problem; should industries or homes be moved out of certain areas? The city administration decided to impose wider zones and to move out of the revised area those homes that were within the new borders. The new cities do not have to do any moving. They are constructed along the humanistic and efficient principles of Soviet city planning. The community areas are built for comfortable, healthy living, surrounded by parks, theaters, cinemas, sports fields nurseries, schools, and clinics. The industries where the townspeople work are on the outskirts of the city, a healthy distance from where people live. And transportation grows with the industries and homes and links the two. It's not an entirely smooth operation. Making transportation keep pace with the city's growth presents one of the most difficult problems.

Soviet Cities Do Not Inhale Their Garbage

The disposal of garbage presents modern cities with one of their most serious pollution problems. Yanovsky said most of Moscow's annual two million tons of garbage is sorted out in eight huge sanitation plants, purified, turned into compost by a special biological process and used as fertilizer. The entire process takes two to three days. Yanovsky said that the garbage which could not be disposed of this way was burned in smokeless incinerators, under strict pollution control. A network of Sanitation Central Stations keeps a watchful guard on collection and disposal of garbage. They inspect stores, restaurants, buildings and plants and have the power to enforce all aspects of the sanitary codes including the closing down of premises and the imposition of stiff fines.

By contrast, the inhabitants of our large cities *inhale* their garbage. The Report of the Mayor's Task Force condemned the New York City administration as "the worst violators of its own laws against pollution." The Sanitation Department has long used inefficient incinerators to burn up thousands of tons of refuse a day. The question is asked, "What will it do when dumping areas such as in Staten Island reach a saturation point?" The largest dumps of all are the streets of New York, and especially the streets of the Black and Puerto Rican ghettos, as a walk in Harlem, Bedford-Stuyvesant and Brownsville-East New York will reveal.

New Yorkers not only inhale their garbage, they often bathe in it. The *New York Times Encyclopedic Almanac* of 1970 (p. 500) reveals that, "the indiscriminate dumping of raw human excrement into the Hudson River has brought on a great population explosion among the maggots, eels, and harmful bacteria that thrive on a diet of such wastes. Even worse, the body products of people suffering from hepatitis, dysentery, tuberculosis and other diseases are prominently represented in the Hudson's mix." The *New York Times Almanac* acknowledges that "there are all sorts of possibilities for a fully scientific attack on the problem of garbage pollution." What then stands in the way of this "scientific attack?" The almanac answers, "Standing in the way are the *usual* [my emphasis, M.D.]obstacles—political sluggishness, reluctance of private industry (including public utilities) to make major investments for public purposes that may raise unfavorable stockholder reactions." Also "standing in the way" is the fact that the biggest polluters are the most powerful monopolies—oil refining, steel, auto, and electric power industries.

One of the first things a visiting American notices about all Soviet cities is their cleanliness. Moscow is totally devoid of New York's chief ornament, overflowing garbage cans, let alone broken bottles and empty tin cans cluttering the streets. Garbage is usually collected in the early morning hours to avoid interference with traffic. It is carted to 25 disposal points along special routes. Special care is taken to protect the health of sanitation workers and to guard them from injury. The work of U.S. sanitation workers is ranked as among the most injurious and unhealthy.

By contrast, Soviet sanitation workers do no heavy lifting and do not come in direct contact with the odorous garbage. A hydraulic lift places the garbage bins onto the truck. After being dumped, the containers are thoroughly washed with hot water and returned to the buildings.

Moscow's Mayor Promyslov (*Izvestia*, January 5, 1973) noted that although Moscow was more advanced in the handling of the garbage problem, the city was far from satisfied with its progress. Especially since, as the mayor pointed out, "the composition of refuse is changing . . . the percentage of synthetic materials, metals and glass is rising. Therefore, the problems of garbage disposal by industrial methods are becoming increasingly important." The mayor noted that garbage decontamination in Moscow is handled by a recently commissioned plant with an annual capacity of about 500,000 cubic meters, and that another garbage incinerator is to be commissioned. Promyslov declared that confronting new problems, Moscow can't "be satisfied with the traditional technology of collecting and removing utility refuse by means of replaceable containers." He noted the latter means is more expensive in manual labor and not sanitary enough. He said Moscow was working on plans to transport garbage via a piping system, and the use of large-tonnage garbage carriers equipped with compressing devices.

Another important advantage which Soviet cities have over our own in combating air pollution is *central heating*. Central heating based on heat and power plants and district boiler houses now supplies heat to the overwhelming majority of Moscow's homes and buildings. They now cover 95 to 98 percent of the city's heat requirements. In contrast, New York City has 135,000 heating furnaces and 10,000 incinerators in privately owned apartment houses and office buildings. It has 600,000 private residences. Most of these use highly noxious fuel oil or coal.

Underground Moscow

This contrast is also present in respect to the *underground* life of the cities. Let me explain. Shortly after my arrival, Konstantin Urivaev, chief engineer of Moscow's Board of Public Maintenance, took me on a tour of the city's underground system. (I'm speaking of the network of pipes — not the Metro.) "You are the first American in underground Russia," he told me with a mischievous twinkle in his eye. I informed him he could cause considerable excitement in the United States with such an announcement.

The Moscow underground I saw should arouse a great deal of interest in our large cities. Every urban center has an underground that makes modern life above ground possible. But in our country it consists of a foul-smelling web of aged, rust-eaten pipes we only become aware of when they burst into sudden floods that engulf our subways and streets, or erupt into menacing explosions. It's a hidden, grossly neglected underground.

Moscow's underground is a city *underneath* a city. It is a huge tunnel, almost ten feet high and equally wide that parallels the main city streets for a distance of 87 miles. In it, neatly arranged, as if in a vast modern industrial plant, are the pipes and wires that provide Moscow's life lines. On one side are the whitewashed asbestos-covered pipes that carry Moscow's central heating to all the apartment houses; on the other, the sturdy water pipes. The pipes are washed and painted three times a year. The tunnel is fed steady streams of fresh air by a powerful ventilating system and is lit up like a thoroughfare. Every 300 meters there are street signs to show exactly what part of Moscow is above. Telephones are everywhere, so that the locations of workers inspecting, cleaning or making repairs are always known at the station. All repairs are carried out in this factorylike underground. Moscow's streets are rarely torn up to repair a worn-out water main. Gas mains are in their own underground network, since they represent a special problem and danger. Safety measures are taken to guard against possible gas leaks. Inspectors equipped with meters similar to those used in Soviet mines, daily check the tunnel.

It has been quite a few years since Moscow experienced a serious gas explosion. Water breaks are also rare, for similar reasons. The station, incidentally, is on a 24-hour alert. Moscow's underground never sleeps.

Fighting Automobile and Water Pollution

The Soviet Union is now manufacturing more than two million vehicles a year. This is still far below our own vehicle level but more than twice the Soviet 1970 level. From what I have observed, the problem of pollution, traffic congestion and accidents is getting to be more acute. Automobile exhaust everywhere contains harmful substances. Regulation is enforced quite simply — service stations, which are all state-owned, sell only the least noxious gasoline in cities.

Soviet engineers have developed a device called the neutralizer, which, when installed in the exhaust pipe of a vehicle, renders the exhaust gases harmless and reduces the toxic content to a minimum. They have also developed a liquid gas automotive engine that cuts toxic exhaust by nearly 50 percent. Liquid gas fuel is obtained through oil and gas processing and is much cheaper than gasoline. Moscow also curtails the noxious effects of automobile pollution through its unrivaled network of underground passageways. Contact between pedestrian and exhaust fumes, which reach their highest peak at crossings, are kept to a minimum. The pedestrian underpasses, which provide a safe and comfortable passageway under most of Moscow's main streets, decrease by 10 to 15 times the amount of noxious fumes inhaled by Muscovites. They have also decreased accidents and helped speed up traffic. But the problem of fumes is far from solved, and the accident death rate of 500 a year reveals the seriousness of traffic problems.

Moscow transport also uses nonpolluting electric power. Trolleybuses and streetcars, which are electric-powered, form a large part of the transportation of Soviet cities. The USSR Research Center for Electric Transport is working on an electrically driven truck and passenger electromobile but many problems yet have to be solved before they can be mass produced.

At the height of the public outcry in the United States against the pollution of our rivers, lakes, and ocean shores, Bernard Gwertzman, then Moscow correspondent for the *New York Times,* wrote an article which presented a grim picture of water pollution in the USSR. Reading Gwertzman's article, Americans could conclude that nowhere is the situation any better, even in the leading land of socialism. Thus, they would reason, water pollution has nothing to do with social systems, nothing to do with the giant monopolies which own our industries and abuse our natural resources, nothing to do with our government which for decades has permitted them to pollute our water and air. That obviously was the intent of the owners of the class-conscious *New York Times.* All that is necessary for an enterprising correspondent, out to portray Soviet deficiencies, is to read self-critical comments and fashion them into what seems to be an "authoritative" piece. This is exactly what Gwertzman did in his article on Soviet water pollution, which was based on a critical article in the Soviet journal *Agricultural Economy,* by Boris N. Bogdanov, chief of the Ministry of Agriculture's Department of Nature Conservation, Reserves and Hunting.

I asked Bogdanov to comment on Gwertzman's article. Bogdanov, a bluff and hearty man, chuckled as his interpreter translated Gwertzman's piece. "That's for your disturbed Americans," he exclaimed. "Of course, my article contained critical comments. Its aim was to focus on a number of weaknesses," Bogdanov pointed out. "And now I will give you the picture with which the *New York Times* does not deal."

The story begins with the October Revolution. One of the first decrees issued by the young Soviet Republic was drafted by V.I. Lenin — the famous Decree on Land which expropriated and nationalized the land of Russian feudal nobility and capitalists and gave it to the land-starved peasants. Soviet water legislation is based on and proceeds from that decree. In February, 1919, a Central Committee for Protection of Water Resources was established. Incidentally, the decrees on water played a decisive role, particularly in the Central Asian republics, where it was used to break the age-old stranglehold of the feudal beys on the extremely limited water supply. Water was life in these parched lands, and the control of this precious liquid meant domination over the lives of the people.

Not only was water taken out of the hands of the czarist spoilers, but the natural resources, for the first time in man's history, were treated as a common treasure of the people. And, as such treasures, they were protected as never before. Poor as it was, and suffering from the ravages of a cruel Civil War and intervention, the young Soviet state spent considerable funds to construct water supply systems, provide sanitation, filtering and protecting sources from pollution. Czarism left little of a heritage in this respect, and its sanitation was on an abysmal medieval level, resulting in frequent epidemics of typhus and dysentery. Soviet expenditures to protect water from pollution rose steadily, and during the recent period increased at a yearly rate of more than 100 percent.

The devastating war on Soviet soil set back the fight against pollution. Not only were countless reservoirs and water systems destroyed but thousands of factories had to be transported from Moscow and Leningrad, and many other threatened cities to the Urals and Siberia. Thus, many postwar pollution problems were "inherited" from the inevitable neglect during the period of the Nazi invasion. "The factories operated without roofs. The issue was existence, not pollution," Bogdanov told me. He paused and added: "Our inherited difficulties can be explained and justified. But can those in your country?"

A high point in the renewed fight against pollution was reached when a plenary meeting of the Central Committee of the Communist Party of the Soviet Union discussed the need for up-to-date all-Soviet Fundamentals of Water Legislation. The Fundamentals were published in all newspapers and throughout the land. Tens of thousands of proposals were considered and in December, 1970, the Fundamentals were enacted into law by the USSR Supreme Soviet. The law *forbids* putting any industries into operation that have not been properly outfitted with filtering sewage and antipollution installations. This was in effect for some time, even before it was enacted in the Fundamentals. All new Soviet plants must pass careful inspection *before* they begin operating to insure they have the necessary equipment. The Fundamentals also forbid the commissioning of irrigation, watering and drainage systems, and other hydrotechnical installations unless they have been properly equipped with antipollution devices. The Fundamentals prohibit the floating of timber in bundles and rafts without ship propulsion, not only in navigable rivers, but also in rivers, canals, lakes, and reservoirs enumerated in a long list. Sewage may be disposed of only by permission of the authorities concerned, and only if it does not increase the content of pollution in the reservoir above the permissible level or if the user has purified the sewage to the degree required by law. It is forbidden to use water objects for the disposal of industrial, household, and other waste. These requirements are strictly enforced by state inspection and with penalties for violation. Bogdanov pointed out the severe penalties include stiff fines and imprisonment.

Bogdanov's information was confirmed in my meeting with Academician Andrei Voznesensky, who is in charge of water pollution problems for the Soviet Academy of Science. This academician is the father óf the famous Soviet poet Voznesensky. Andrei Voznesensky pointed out that many industries spend considerable sums on water anti-pollution equipment. He noted that in the case of chemical and paper plants, it comes to about 14 percent of the total cost of construction, and also stated that stress is being placed on reusing the same water for industrial purposes. The noxious wastes, incidentally, are put to profitable use.

Voznesensky noted that the Soviet Union, which has 11 percent of the world's water resources, nevertheless confronts serious water problems. About 75 to 80 percent of its water resources are concentrated in Siberia and the north, areas which are sparsely settled. Some 15 percent of the rivers flow into internal seas (Caspian and Aral) which do not find their outlet into oceans. Water taken from such rivers can reduce the level of the seas and increase the amount of salt deposits, thus diminishing the food supply for fish. This is what happened in the Caspian and other waters until the Soviet Union put a stop to such practices.

The Soviet Union has performed engineering miracles to redistribute artificially its vast water resources, taking water from well-supplied areas and feeding it to places in need of water. For example, the great Kara Kum Canal carries water some 500 miles from its source, the Irtysh River. (The construction of the Kara Kum Canal which has turned a desert, the size of some of the largest states in Europe, into an industrial and agricultural paradise, is another one of those fabulous *human* stories that fill socialist life.)

In contrast to New York City's handling of the water pollution problem, Mayor Promyslov reported (*Izvestia,* January 5, 1975) that the quality of water in Moscow's river is "improving year after year, due to the increasing capacities and perfection of the purification setups." He pointed out that "the Moscow River is now sanitarily and technologically controlled over a 500 kilometer distance from its source all the way down to the mouth. Control for microelemental compositon of the water, for carcinogenic substances and viruses has been intensified." Here, too, Promyslov was anything but smug about Moscow's progress. There are parts of the Moscow River which are still polluted. He stressed, "A great deal of work is yet to be done with the sewage discharge of both industrial and utility origin." He was able to state that "in 1975, new purification and decontamination setups will be built at 500 enterprises in Moscow. Work is now in progress to clean up the bed of the Moscow River."

The True Story of Lake Baikal

A good deal of the hullabaloo raised by some U.S. correspondents on Soviet pollution centered, strangely enough, on the "situation" in Lake Baikal. They portrayed a picture of ruthless Soviet "industrialists" willfully and defiantly polluting the waters of Baikal. They obviously counted on the sad experience Americans have with U.S. industries and their ignorance about the Soviet Union's social system to sustain their distortions. I decided to visit Lake Baikal and see for myself.

First of all, it should be pointed out that the outcry about the threat of pollution faced by Baikal came from every section of Soviet society— scientists, trade unionists, the Communist Party and government officials and the Soviet press, especially *Komsomolskaya Pravda* and *Literaturnaya Gazetta.* The picture of an outraged Soviet citizenry fighting the "establishment" is a mechanical carry-over of conditions of our own society, dominated by the Consolidated Edisons. In the Soviet Union, the people have been the "establishment" for more than half a century. More than 30 million Soviet citizens are members of volunteer conservation societies. Enforcement is really based on "community control" here. Area inspection and control committees include members of peoples' organizations, shop workers, trade union leaders, Party secretaries, Komsomol leaders, and scientists.

There was some difference of opinion between those who one-sidedly emphasized industrial production and those who insisted that the basic balanced approach laid down in Lenin's decree had to be adhered to. By U.S. standards, Baikal's shores are almost untouched by industry. One of the large enterprises is the huge cellulose plant. I discussed the problem with the plant's director, who assured me his plant would not be permitted to operate one day if it didn't have the proper purification equipment. As I looked at Baikal's untamed beauty and sparkling waters I thought: What would our Rockefellers and General Motors do if they had a Baikal in their hands? One can get a good idea from this description by Norman Cousins, in the *New York Times Encyclopedic Almanac*, 1970, p. 449. He reports: "Every major river in the United States is grossly polluted. Even the lesser streams have been made slimy and foul by factories that freely sluice their noxious wastes downstream away from the scene of the crime. Once beautiful Lake Erie, which receives many such streams, is a prize exhibit: today the lake reminds one of Coleridge's 'Silent Sea,' its waters are now a nephritic brew, millions of its fish have been killed off. . . ."

Baikal did confront the problem of pollution. Scientists at the Institute of Lake Studies on Baikal as well as scientists in Moscow discussed the problems with me honestly and objectively. Baikal first faced such problems almost 200 years ago when its shores were settled and crop farming and cattle breeding developed, and timber was felled. The floating of loose timber polluted its water. The pollution problems grew, especially after the war, because of the accelerated development of industry and the rise of cities in Siberia. The question was posed: Did the answer lie in shutting down all existing enterprises and all production in Baikal's vicinity? Was it necessary that Baikal's vast treasure of forest, its power resources, mineral deposits and fertile soil lie untapped to protect its purity? Soviet scientists reject the approach of some Western conservationists who contend that only by leaving nature untouched can environment be protected and pollution controlled. After considerable scientific study and debate, the conclusion was that Baikal's beauty and purity could be maintained at the same time that its rich resources were tapped. Baikal could provide *both* material wealth and beauty to the country. The answer lies in the *rational* use of Baikal resources, in guaranteeing its protection from pollution and despoliation. This approach was summed up in a special resolution on Baikal accepted in 1971 by the USSR Council of Ministers and the Central Committee of the Communist Party of the Soviet Union. How to protect Baikal was the subject of widespread debate and gave birth to the film *By the Lake*, one of the best recently produced by Soviet filmmakers. The film used the issue to go deeply into the whole meaning of Soviet society, in which the goal in all progress is based on the slogan, "everything in the name of humanity and for humanity." The very outcry on Baikal distinguishes Soviet society from our own.

The measures to protect Baikal include the following: No loose timber floating (it was stopped at the end of 1973); a vast program of construction of purification systems; improved forestry management and forest amelioration; strict control over the protection and reproduction of fish reserves. A special ship, which is a floating laboratory built in Lan Ude, the capital of the Buryat Autonomous Republic, is now regularly taking samples in Baikal of air and water to determine their pollution level.

I spoke to Pete Seeger, the famous folksinger and fighter against water pollution, when he visited the Soviet Union in 1973. Pete, who sings and sails on our beautiful but polluted Hudson River to awaken the conscience of America, made a special trip to Baikal. He was greatly impressed with what he saw and brought back a bottle of Baikal water. "I'm going to drink this on television," he told me, "to answer those in our country who are equating pollution in the United States and the USSR." Baikal is being transformed into a vast rest and recreational zone. A highway around its extensive shoreline is planned, as well as improved rail and air communication.

It would be hard to find a comparable equivalent to this Soviet program in our country because we have nothing like Lake Baikal, which holds 20 percent of the world's fresh water supply. It would be as if the U.S. government took over one of the Great Lakes, rid it of its industrial pollution and turned it into a beautiful recreational area for the working people.

The "Secret" of Soviet Civic Pride

Soviet cities are strangers to a special kind of pollution that transforms the city streets and even the parks of our large cities—especially New York—into garbage dumps. Take, for example, this typical scene in New

York's Central Park after a concert attended by 135,000, as described by the *New York Times,* June 4, 1969: "But after they departed, the meadow resembled a huge garbage dump. Obliterating the grass was a prodigious rug of chicken bones, half-eaten sandwiches, cartons, bottles, and paper." Such a scene would be unthinkable in the Soviet Union. Moscow and all Soviet cities are among the cleanest in the world. And this goes especially for their beautiful parks, which are properly called "Parks of Culture and Rest." The cigarette butts and matchsticks around bus stops in Moscow, particularly, mar an otherwise perfect scene. But, by any standards, Soviet cities literally sparkle. No streets in the world get the kind of constant scrubbing they receive daily.

It begins with early morning. An army of about 20,000 sweepers scrape the sidewalks with picturesque and surprisingly effective birch brooms. Each apartment building and store front has its own contingent. The sweepers are usually mothers who find it easier to work near home and their pay compares favorably with the average wage. The cleaners are usually helped by their sons and daughters of school age. They are supported by the most up-to-date cleaning equipment.

But their most effective assistants are Soviet citizens. One of the most appealing qualities of Soviet citizens is their civic consciousness. They regard the streets as they do the floors of their homes. I've come across those who don't have this attitude, especially among some rude, would-be tough youngsters, who think it a sign of their independence to throw cigarette butts and spit on the streets. But these are hardly the rule, and I have seen some get a public dressing-down from irate Soviet citizens that made them squirm.

The overwhelming majority, including the mass of youth, have been brought up to respect their homes, their streets, their parks, the Metro — all public conveyances and services as socialist property. More than half a century of such living has made this a natural characteristic of most Soviet people.

It showed every day in early March, 1969, shortly after our arrival here. Each night I would look out of the window and wonder what would happen to the city in the morning. I had good reason to wonder because I knew what had happened in the city I had left only a few weeks before. New York was not only paralyzed for days by a snowstorm Muscovites would laugh at, but 50,000 tons of garbage turned the city into a kind of garbage dump. The city officials refused to put to work the thousands of sanitation workers who had reported as soon as the snowstorm struck.

The city turned them away because it was Sunday, a day for which it would have to pay double-time.

I found that Moscow sanitation and maintenance leaders knew the remedies for a difficult problem and applied them promptly. Thus, each morning I discovered the snow was cleared when I got up. The night snowfall was piled up at the edge of the street in huge piles. Snow machines, looking like something that descended from Mars, were lifting the frozen heaps into trucks.

The key to the victorious battle waged by Soviet society against pollution lies in precisely this: *It is a struggle waged by a united society which has eliminated antagonistic classes, a society which has eliminated those who not only obstruct the battle against pollution, but are themselves the chief promoters of pollution.* In the Soviet Union polluters can't pollute!

10 / TRANSPORTATION FOR PEOPLE OR PROFITS?

A ride in the Moscow Metro is one of the most unforgettable experiences for every American I met in Moscow. When I spoke to New York City Council President, Paul O'Dwyer, and Manhattan Borough President, Percy Sutton, in Moscow's Hotel Russia in December, 1973, they talked of the Moscow Metro with the same enthusiasm as did all long-suffering New York straphangers. They had the opportunity to learn firsthand that a subway ride need not necessarily be a grim experience and can even be enjoyable.

Urban transportation, especially with the development of the scientific-technological revolution, constitutes one of the most complex problems of city living. Soviet cities are hardly immune to these problems and have far from fully resolved them, notwithstanding their beautiful and efficient metros that have now spread to six major cities in five republics. But Soviet cities point the way to solving the difficult problems of mass transportation. More than 5 million passengers ride the Moscow Metro daily and the figure is steadily rising. In intensity of traffic and number of passengers, Moscow Metro holds first place in the world. On the other hand the number of riders on New York City subways and elevated lines declined to the lowest level since 1918. [The city then had 2.5 million less population.] Rising fare, crime and deteriorating conditions are responsible for this drastic decline. The Moscow Metro (I should say the Soviet subway) ideally combines efficiency and beauty.

The Moscow Metro, which is air-conditioned in summer and winter, is one of the favorite meeting places. Air pumps change the air three times every hour. A special staff regularly checks the atmosphere to see if it conforms to the norm, 1.5 milligrams of dust particles per cubic meter of air. It always registers below the norm. Each station is an individual art gallery, depicting in bronze and frescoes some chapter of the October Revolution or of the history of the Soviet people. "Ploshad Revolutsia" is the story of the makers of the October Revolution in sculpture. Kiev station is a history of the Ukraine in frescoes. The metros of Tbilisi and Baku, likewise are living histories of the cultures of the peoples of Georgia and Azerbaidjan. Trains and station walls in New York subways are covered with nightmarish scribbling and designs smeared in paint. It is as if the inmates of an insane asylum had been turned loose with paint and brushes to portray their hallucinations.

The Moscow Metro is also the epitome of efficiency. You ride with literally clocklike precision. A huge clock on each station wall clicks off the seconds. Trains usually come at intervals of 90 seconds in rush hours and about two minutes at other times and keep to schedule.

Every New York subway rider is familiar with the numerous break-downs that cause uncomfortable delays and often lead to accidents. These mishaps reflect the steady deterioration of an aging subway system that has been badly neglected. I never came across a serious breakdown, or even a nonworking door for that matter, in my years of riding the Moscow subway. It can be explained quite simply: constant, meticulous care. Incidentally, this makes for an understandable pride in their metro on the part of the workers that is reflected in their high labor discipline.

Here is what is behind the Moscow Metro's precision timing. The 7,500 trains go to a depot for a checkup and a quick cleanup after every 6 to 7 hour run. Every two days they are taken to a sanitary station where they are washed inside and out and carefully inspected. First, the dust is sucked up by air compression tubes. Then, the roof, doors, floors and windows are scoured with mechanized brushes and dried with hot air. In addition, all cars undergo a system of thorough repair every few days. It is here that defects which could lead to train breakdowns are discovered and taken care of. Each station gets a similar daily going over. Escalators are dusted every four hours. Tunnels are given regular showers with high-pressure hoses. Each station is dusted and swept during lull periods. But all this would still not make the Soviet subways the cleanest in the world, if not for the cooperation of Muscovites. It is they who by their conscientious attitude do the greatest cleanup job of all. It is a rare sight, indeed, to come across someone who would litter the spotless Soviet subways.

The Moscow Metro runs from 6 a.m. to 1 a.m. and has a working force of 17,000. Each train has a motorman (or woman) and an assistant who calls out the station and other directions and supervises the precision operation of the train schedule There is a stationmaster at each station (usually a woman) in uniform who aids aged, disabled or any other passengers in need of help in getting on and off the train.

Escalators play an important role in maintaining the rigorous schedule. They are swift moving and kept safe by good care. The escalators are under the care of responsible supervisors, usually middle-aged women seated at the end of the escalator line. Many are pensioners who add to their income by this employment. They have a microphone at one hand and a brake lever at the other. Calm instructions accompanied by the proper action usually correct a mishap quickly.

My wife and I experienced a strange sensation during our first week in the metro. Something seemed to be missing. Then it came to us: no police patrol the cars. In the New York subway, police armed with bulging revolvers and walkie-talkies are constrant traveling companions. Few places in our crime-ridden cities are as unsafe as our subways. The motherly woman who changes your rubles into 5-kopeck pieces in Moscow Metro's change booths would regard you as some escapee from a lunatic asylum if you told her she had a "dangerous job." Yet, in New York the pay booths are sealed off from passengers by glass, bulletproof enclosures.

Surface Travel—the Bus and Minibus

When I told a Moscow bus driver that in many U.S. cities passengers will not be accepted without having the exact fare (to minimize the danger of holdups), he regarded me incredulously. In Moscow's buses, trolleybuses, and trams (there are 6,200 buses, 2,500 trolleybuses and 1,500 trams) the driver, often a woman, sells you booklets of ten-fare coupons, announces the stops, and answers your questions concerning directions.

Few jobs are as nerve-wracking as driving buses in the streets of modern great cities, whether in New York or in Moscow. But I met few Moscow bus drivers who responded to requests for information with irritability, or regarded their passengers with hostility. It's because they are not exposed to all the tensions our bus drivers drive with: fear of holdups and assaults, responsibility for collecting fares, overload of work resulting from economizing on service, fear of loss of jobs—all of which make the driver the butt of the resentment of passengers. Soviet bus drivers are not only free from all these tensions but like all workers, they know their labor is respected and exemplary work is honored. Some are deputies to the USSR and republic, district, and city Soviets. Their pictures grace the front pages of Soviet newspapers and magazines, and together with all other men and women of labor, they are the leading stars of Soviet television. The problems they face are the object of scientific study. Everything is done to try to eliminate or lessen the hazards of driving.

Our winters are like springs compared to Soviet winters. Anyone familiar with the efficient Soviet system of instant snow removal can well appreciate the nerve-wracking tensions and dangers from which Soviet drivers are relieved. All this goes to explain why Soviet bus drivers can afford to be more pleasant and patient than our abused, overworked, and unappreciated bus drivers.

The nearly free fare has been a constant factor in transportation costs for Soviet citizens. (It is 5 kopecks for the metro, 4 for trolleybus, and 3 for trams.) The 5-kopeck fare has not been raised since the Moscow Metro went into operation on May 15, 1935, and the fare for the surface lines has not been changed since 1948. In that same period the fare for the New York subway has risen 1000 percent (from 5 to 50 cents) and the end is hardly in sight. In Chicago, it is 55 cents. Moreover, the soaring fares are accompanied by deterioration in services. Millions of Americans who depend on public transportation are caught in the ever tightening noose of the "transportation crisis," deteriorating conditions, skyrocketing costs, and curtailment of services.

The very opposite road has been traveled by public transportation in the Soviet Union. Soviet cities, which have grown rapidly as a result of the tremendous pace of industrialization, still face serious transportation problems. This is particularly the case in respect to transporting freight across a vast land. Poor passenger transportation service is sharply exposed in the Soviet media. Typical of this gadfly role played by the press is a lengthy article in *Pravda* on January 30, 1974, which detailed the sad state of public transit in Novosibirsk, a city of 1,200,000 population in Siberia. The greatest problems in respect to public transportation understandably exist in those areas facing particularly rigorous weather conditions. But *Pravda* does not let Novosibirsk off the hook, despite its weather difficulties. It points out the reasons for the weaknesses — bad organization and failure to carry out plans. *Pravda's* critical article was in response to numerous letters it received from Novosibirskers complaining that poor transit resulted in their getting to work late and staying home nights instead of going to the theater. But our weaknesses in the United States are the result of a policy of years of neglect of public transit, whereas in the Soviet Union they flow largely from poor organization. This is a problem that still plagues the Soviet Union in many aspects of Soviet life, and it is on this that the sharpest fire is concentrated.

The metro, the chief and best means of transportation, is spreading to cities throughout the Soviet Union. But the other means of transportation play an important and a constantly improving role. Surface lines— trolleybus, autobus and tram—are not only cheap but, on the whole, efficiently run though hardly comparable to the metro. Of course, much of the reason for this gap lies in the fact that movement underground does not encounter the difficulties confronted on the surface. Thus, the main emphasis in Soviet public transportation is on the metro. And it is steadily expanding, not only in relation to the number of cities with metros but, in the extension of the Moscow Metro itself. In five years, Moscow added 12 new stations to the metro. Each new microarea with its cluster of high-rise apartment houses, has a relatively short wait before a new trunk of the metro stretches out to its environs.

The situation on the surface lines is as follows: The service is quite good on the main thoroughfares and adequate for most parts of the city. Americans who are familiar with long waits would be delighted with the rapid service on the surface lines covering Gorky Street (the main street) and most other main arteries. In all, except late hours, I rarely had to wait more than a couple of minutes for a bus or trolleybus. The movement of traffic is not bad though Moscow is beginning to come up with some of our well-known bottlenecks during rush hours, because of the considerable increase in vehicles in the past five years. The ride is usually comfortable but less so in winter, because the buses and trolleybuses are insufficiently heated to withstand the severe Russian winters. This hardly seems to faze most passengers, who are not only well bundled up but have a different concept of what constitutes ''cold'' than we do. Service is generally good (extremely good by our standards) but in some areas the schedule left much to be desired. There are also lines where the buses are so packed during rush hours that it is difficult to close the doors. Here is where the patient but firm authority of the bus driver as well as the collective discipline of Soviet citizens comes into play. But there is still enough "individualism" surviving among some Soviet citizens to result in a stubborn tug-of-war between the determined Soviet citizen with one foot outside the door and the bus driver who has to halt the bus for a moment or two.

One of the big problems is how to make it more convenient for the Soviet passenger to pay his fare. The complaints one hears are largely confined to those areas where the surface service has not yet attained the general good level. And they are loud and clear and given prominent notice in the Soviet press.

Mass protests against Soviet authority are not necessary because the Soviet citizen, based on 58 years of experience, knows that the Soviet power, which undertook to build the Moscow Metro when it was just getting on its industrial feet, and has greatly expanded it in the cecades since then, is moving heaven and earth to improve all aspects of Soviet life. More, the Soviet citizens know that through the press, the local Soviet deputy who must regularly meet with and account to his or her constituents and through the vast network of committees of people's control, they can not only *complain* but *correct*. Thus, for example, *Pravda* does not limit itself to letting off steam, especially when it comes to the needs of working people. *Pravda* followed up its sharp criticism of transportation weaknesses in Vladivostok and Samarkand on November 28, 1973, with a detailed report in its March 3, 1974 issue on what these had done to correct the shortcomings. *Pravda* has a daily column entitled "After Criticism" which reports on what was done to overcome deficiencies exposed in the paper. But Soviet citizens know this from the steady improvement in all aspects of life. These are often not as prompt as they could be. This explains the constant prodding by the press. But what makes for corrections and improvement is that everything, including the service on line "X" on Avenue "Z" is all based on fulfilling yearly and Five Year Plans. Soviet plans are public committments for improvements and all the forces of Soviet society led by the Soviet government and the Communist Party are brought to bear to guarantee the improvement. Soviet citizens know this as they know their ABC's, because they are the *chief* instrument in guaranteeing all the improvements in their lives.

The minibus offers one of the most convenient modes of transportation. It is hardly a profit maker. But, what a public convenience! Here's how it works: You pick up the minibus at a designated point (they usually run along the main thoroughfares and have a fixed route). You travel in greater comfort than in the bus, though not yet with the comfort provided by a cab. You are taken right up to your destination if it is along the route. And you pay only 10 kopecks for the ride. However, there are problems connected with this convenient mode of transportation. Often, there's a long line during rush hours and since the minibus is more limited in space than buses, there is a correspondingly longer wait.

The low cost of Soviet taxis, if applied in our great cities, would make this the most popular mode of transportation. Workers would ride to work by taxi in New York if they could do it at Moscow prices.

Taxis in Moscow

The taxi fare (uniform throughout the Soviet Union) is stabilized at 10 kopecks for a kilometer (⅔ of a mile). The meter is registered at 10 kopecks when you enter the cab. You can ride from one end of Moscow to the other for about 3 rubles. The average Muscovite uses taxis far more extensively than the average New Yorker, for whom this is a very expensive means of transportation. There are more than 14,000 cabs in operation in Moscow, carrying nearly 500,000 passengers daily. At least twice as many cabs could well be used. By comparison, if one takes New York cab fares as an example, the meter starts running at 65 cents and it ticks off 10 cents for each one-sixth of a mile. You can hardly get very far on $3.00 in New York. Taxis are therefore employed as a common means of transportation only by the more affluent. They are used for special occasions, holidays, or emergencies by average Americans. And for that other purpose—as a sort of personal night security escort for the growing number of U.S. city dwellers who are fearful of walking our crime-ridden streets after nightfall. (Sovet taxis would go out of business if they had to depend on this kind of trade!) There are additional important differences between Soviet and U.S. cities in respect to taxis. Nowhere have I come across a Soviet cabbie who refused admittance to a would-be passenger because of nationality or the color of skin. In our country, Black and Puerto Rican Americans, Chicanos, Asian and Native American Indians urgently in need of a taxi are ignored by empty cabs which stop to pick up white customers. Nor is there that barrier of distrust and fear, now symbolized in the closed off compartment that physically separates the cab driver from his fare. Driving a cab in Moscow is a hard job as it is anywhere, but it is not the dangerous one it is in our great cities.

Yet there are some problems and unpleasant features. First, the demand for taxis greatly exceeds the supply. This often makes it quite difficult to get a cab during the peak hours. There are taxi stations but the *ochered* (lines) at peak hours are, indeed, long ones. Then, too, there are some cab drivers, a small minority, who take advantage of the great demand (especially in late hours) to charge their passengers more than the legal price of the fare, and some, a very few, even make their special price with their customers without running the meter. These are all serious violations and violators are severely punished when they are caught. But the very private character of this means of transportation makes such infractions possible. Tipping, too, has unfortunately become part of the fare for many Soviet passengers. There is hardly an atmosphere of compulsion, for, by law, the cab driver is entitled only to his fixed share of the fare. (Soviet cab drivers are among the best paid workers.) I've come across quite a few cabbies who refuse a tip. But the practice is widespread enough and I consider that it does exert some sort of a corrupting influence—though this should not be exaggerated. Tipping is hard to eliminate. It is a hangover from the bourgeois past that tenaciously clings in certain branches of service like restaurants and barber shops, where it has traditional roots.

The Soviet approach to public transportation is based on the principle motivating socialist society: the utilization of material and human resources to improve living conditions steadily in every respect. This explains why at a time when it was still far behind the United States and most leading capitalist countries, it built the palatial Moscow Metro. Construction of the metro started in 1931 during the depth of our Great Depression and the world capitalist economic crisis. Even when the Nazis were at Moscow's gates, construction continued. Three new stations were opened in 1943.

The Soviet Union regards public transportation as an essential public service and not as a commercial enterprise. The motivating principle guiding it is to make transportation adequate, comfortable, convenient and as pleasant as possible. This does not mean that Soviet public transportation is run at a loss. On the whole, even with the extremely low fares, passenger transportation in the Soviet Union is run on a profitable basis. The Moscow Metro is a profitable venture, notwithstanding the fact that it has maintained a very low fare since 1935.

The basic reason for this steady growth and improvement is that public transportation in the Soviet Union is not milked dry by high profits and exorbitant salaries for top officials or by the graft that lines the pockets of those who award lush construction contracts. Nor is it saddled with the ever mounting debt on the interest payments on loans provided by the banks.

Construction and equipment for public transportation are provided for in the Five Year Plans as well as in the Twenty-five Year Master Plans of Soviet cities. The construction costs are paid for by the Soviet government, Soviet republics and the city Soviets. But I was told by Vassily A. Shogin, deputy engineer of the Moscow Metro: "We pay back for all this out of our yearly surpluses. We have already paid back for more than 50 kilometers." This was told to me in 1969. One of the reasons for the "yearly surpluses" is that the metro is being used by more passengers and more frequently.

The sad plight of our public transportation system is the result of quite a different approach. Transportation, whether of freight or of people, is primarily a business. And like all businesses, the basic concern is with maximum profits, not people's welfare. Perhaps nothing better characterizes this approach than the plight of our railroad system. Many of the multimillion dollar family fortunes in our country were founded on the profits milked out of the railroads when that industy was justly regarded by America's "robber barons" as the most fertile field for profits. Here is how Professor Jean Gettmann described this "lush" period of our railroads (*Megalopolis, the Urbanized Northeastern Seaboard of the United States, A Twentieth Century Fund Study,* the M.I.T. Press, Cambridge, Mass., 1965, p. 656): "From the 1880s to about 1920 the railroads were, with banking, the more select sector of business; the securities of the railroads were considered an excellent investment 'blue chips' and 'growth stocks.' " And as long as the "blue chips" kept pouring in, the U.S. money kings were prepared to invest their capital in the railroads. But when the profit stream no longer seemed to flow in the direction of the railroads, it shifted to other outlets; the men who had been hailed as the "builders" of our nation's railroads shifted their capital investments into new and more profitable ventures. Professor Gettmann (p. 656) notes that after the 1920s, the railroad industry was "replaced by other industries" as "growth sectors" of the American economy, among them the automobile manufacturers and the large petroleum concerns. These became "blue chips." Thus, without the slightest concern for the public interests, the railroads servicing passengers were literally run into the ground.

The folding up of one of the largest railroad lines in the United States, the Pennsylvania Railroad, the curtailment and elimination of passenger railroad service throughout the country, demonstrate this. Railroad passenger service was consciously permitted to deteriorate, and everything was done to discourage people from patronizing this means of transportation. Today we are largely left with AMTRAK (National Railroad Passenger Service), which, despite constant large federal subsidies, steadily increases fares while it reduces services notwithstanding bitter public protests. The railroad magnates concluded that "passenger traffic brings them only deficit, *while, in private corporations, they must make profits so as to pay dividends to their shareholders and interest to their bondholders. Staying in the business of passenger transportation, it is said, would make them lose too much money."* (Prof. Gettmann). This explains the critical condition of our railroads and our urban public transportation.

The very opposite is the picture in respect to Soviet railroads. From one of the most backward railroad systems of any major country during czarist days, this means of transportation has been built so fast that "The USSR now ranks first in the world in the length of electrified railways, having left all other countries far behind. As much as 95 percent of all the country's traffic is driven by electrical and oil engines. . . . On the whole, the railway transport system of the USSR ranks *first in the world* in volume of both freight and passenger traffic and is far ahead of the United States of America. . . The cost of freight and passenger traffic on Soviet railways is the *lowest* in the *world* and is *one-third* of what it is in the U.S.A." (Planned Development of Transport in the USSR, L. Chertkov, Director Complex Transportation Problems Institute, under USSR State Planning Committee, Planovoye Khozhayastov #21971.]

The very atmosphere on Soviet trains reflects pride and progress. Pride as well as proficiency in running the Soviet Union's vast, ever expanding, ever modernizing railroad system starts with childhood. I observed the Pioneers of Volgograd run their three-mile railroad. The universal interest and love of children for railroads are not confined in the Soviet Union to the floor of a playroom. Many are given the opportunity to learn how to manage and execute every operation in this complex means of transportation. There is a Pioneer railroad in every Soviet city of size.

One of the chief shortcomings is in the dining cars, which I found are frequently poor in preparation of meals as well as in service. Soviet passengers take all this philosophically; they usually bring large supplies of food with them. Then, too, one can pick up anything from an apple to a boiled chicken before boarding.

No spot is more colorful than the Soviet railroad stations and nowhere does one get a more intimate and friendly introduction to the warm and hospitable Soviet people than on the passenger train.

The "Menace" of Public Transportation

The same basic reason that determined the rise and decline of our railroads lies beyond our long standing and deepening urban transit crises. Before our money kings shifted their capital investments to greener pastures provided by the mass production of automobiles and the vast auxiliary industries, the privately owned and run city transit systems were highly regarded as "blue chip" and "growth" stocks. Theodore Dreiser, the great American progressive and humanist writer, gives a profound and unforgettable picture in his *The Financier* of the fierce rivalry among the rising money kings in Philadelphia for this lucrative field of profit. The House Committee on Banking and Currency, in its report to Congress on July 3, 1962, noted that "94 percent of the mass-transit systems in the country are privately owned and privately operated." *(Metropolis: Values in Conflict,* Wadsworth Publishing Co., Inc., Belmont, California, 1965, p. 170.) The owners of our mass transit systems dumped or neglected their "private" property when profits ceased to be lush and beckoned elsewhere.

Public mass transportation was and is viewed by the powerful auto, oil and highway construction monopolies as a threat to their profits. And General Motors dealt with this "threat" in the typical fashion reserved for eliminating competitors. It crushed the "menace." To what lengths the auto monopoly went, was revealed in an extensive study by Bradford C. Snell *(International Herald Tribune,* February 26, 1974), who testified before the Senate Anti-Trust Subcommittee. Snell's study disclosed, according to the *International Herald Tribune,* that "General Motors played a dominant role in *destroying* more than 100 electric surface rail transit systems in 45 cities, including Baltimore, Philadelphia, New York, St. Louis and Los Angeles—between 1932 and 1956." (In the same period the Moscow Metro was constructed and vastly extended.) Snell cites Southern California and Los Angeles (which today has probably the worst system of public transportation of any large city in the United States) as particular object lessons of GM's campaign of ruination. Southern California, he notes, was served 35 years ago by a smog-free electric railroad system, the world's largest (Pacific Electric), which had 3,000 trains and annually carried 80 million passengers through 56 cities, towns and communities. A holding company, the National City Lines, was set up in 1930 by GM, Standard Oil of California and Firestone Tire Company. They gave NCL more than $9 million by 1950 to convert 16 states to GM buses. The buses were sold to operators who were required to sign a contract forbidding purchases of new equipment "using any fuel or means of propulsion but gas." The study shows how General Motors bought up and scrapped electric rail systems in order to make the people completely dependent on private automobiles for transportation. Snell states that the noisy, foul-smelling buses turned earlier patrons of the high-speed rail system away from public transit and, in effect, *sold millions of private automobiles*. The result was not only the destruction of public transportation but "this city [Los Angeles] is today an ecological wasteland: the palm trees are dying of petrochemical smog; the orange groves have been paved over by 300 miles of freeways; the air is a septic tank into which 4 million cars, half of them built by General Motors, pump 13,000 tons of pollutants daily." Snell points out the critical predicament in which this has placed the inhabitants of Southern California as a result of the "energy crisis." He notes that "a shortage of motor vehicle fuel and an absence of adequate public transport now threaten to disrupt the entire auto-dependent region." The study shows that the "Big Three" of the auto industry, General Motors, Ford and Chrysler "reshaped U.S. ground transportation by eliminating competition among themselves and getting control over rival bus and rail industries, and maximized profits by substituting large, gas-guzzling cars and trucks for trains, streetcars and subways and buses."

Testifying before a Senate Anti-Trust Committee, Los Angeles Mayor Thomas Bradley, Afro-American head of the third largest city in the United States, fully backed up the charges made by Snell's study *(Daily World,* February 28, 1974). Bradley told the U.S. senators: "As you can see from these series of historical events, the destruction of a system in Los Angeles with over 1,000 miles of tracks took place in a very calculated fashion." And how were General Motors, Ford and Chrysler punished for this "calculated" crime against millions of Americans? Bradley noted that the conviction of the three giant corporations on criminal conspiracy and monopoly charges resulted only in a $5,000 fine for G.M. The court did not stop the elimination of the electric-powered systems.

The greedy public-be-damned approach is further demonstrated by the auto industry's stubborn refusal for many years to produce the more economical and less space-consuming compact cars. The oil monopolies, closely allied with the auto magnates, viewed with great concern the rising public demand for compact cars because "such preferences may cause some decline in the quantities of gasoline used by motorists; such decline in consumption would not only mean less revenue for all the gasoline producing and distributing industries, but it could also have serious consequences for the program of highway building, for it would decrease the collection of state and federal taxes on gasoline." *(Megalopolis,* p. 682.) Professor Gettman also noted *"surplus consumption was built into the American automobiles together with accelerated obsolescence."*

Today millions of Americans are stuck with oversized gas-guzzling cars which consume vast quantities of gasoline at skyrocketing prices. The automobile has revolutionized modern life and, in the main, this has been a positive development. But in the hands of greedy monopolies like General Motors, Ford and Chrysler, it has, particularly in our cities, become a Frankenstein. It has taken over our city streets so that this instrument of mobility today paralyzes the movement of urban traffic. The disregard by the oil and auto magnates of the harmful effects of the noxious fumes emanating from their products has been one of the chief contributing causes to the pollution that is choking our cities. But perhaps the most significant social abuse of the automobile lies in the way it has been used to undermine public transportation in our cities. In addition to the calculated destruction of public transportation described by Snell, the powerful lobbies, representing the allied auto, oil, and highway financial interests, repeatedly pushed through federal and state legislatures vast appropriations for highway construction while they blocked all measures designed to help provide urban public transportation. The result is that the United States has, perhaps, the greatest and most modern highway system in the world and one of the most backward urban transportation systems among all of the major countries.

There is nothing wrong with creating the finest and most modern highways. What is wrong is the way this has been consciously *counterposed* to mass transit because of the profits to be gained from the former.

What is wrong is that profits and profiteers determine whether we have good roads *or* good subways and buses.

The automobile long ago ceased to be a luxury in the United States (as it still is in most parts of the world). The auto monopolies (and the finance companies) saw to that. In many of our large cities, not to speak of the suburbs and outlying areas, the automobile is the primary and often sole means of getting to and from work, or getting anywhere. The two-car family is not quite the symbol of United States affluence it has been ballyhooed to be by Madison Avenue—it is more a symbol of the expensive burden of transportation placed on the American people. In most cases, the two cars are dictated by the need for two or more working members of a family to get to work in different parts of the city. And in the suburbs, where shopping centers often can only be reached by auto, one car in the family is hardly enough. Some of my Soviet friends who were just beginning to experience private car ownership on a relatively mass scale do not fully understand this aspect of the problem facing Americans. After all, photographs of happy, prosperous American families driving in their flashy cars are familiar the world over. They are quite prominent in the United States official periodicals circulated in socialist countries. But what the *Voice of America* and the overseas propaganda machine are silent about is that the ownership of the cars has hardly made Americans either happy or prosperous. They ignore the fact that many Americans who own automobiles can hardly afford them. They make no mention of the fact that the mass scale of cars has been used to shift the burden of transportation onto the backs of the mass of the American people. The burden is a twofold one: the high cost of buying and maintaining these cars, and the scarcity of transportation and high fares for those without them. Former Secretary of Transportation Volpe noted that "The word I am getting from around the country and from my talks with leaders in the Black community is that being physically stuck in the slums—unable to get out to where the jobs are—is one of the leading causes of urban violence and unrest."

Like Los Angeles, Detroit, the heart of the auto industry, provides another example of how our great cities have been brought to this condition by General Motors, Ford and Chrysler Corporations. Some 25 to 30 years ago Detroit had a good urban transit system and a 6-cent fare. But steady undermining of the Detroit Street Railways (one of the few publicly owned transportation systems) by the auto monopolies dominating the "city of cars," reduced it to a state of crisis and decay. Here is how William Allan, veteran correspondent in the auto city for the *Daily World,* February 7, 1973,describes the process: "The game, of course, was to sabotage the operations of the Detroit Street Railways (DSR) so that Detroit's huge working class, who traveled back and forth to work on street cars, would be forced to buy automobiles for transportation." And Allan points out: "Today the majority of the riders are Black workers— lowest paid, first fired or laid off, longest unemployed. Few can afford to own and operate an automobile. But to travel to and from work, *in view of the DSR's inefficiency and atrocious service, they are compelled to go into debt."*

Much of the expense of the auto today is the price Americans pay for the absence of convenient, cheap transportation. Under present conditions, the automobile is used, on the one hand, to shift the burden of transportation costs from the government and society to the individual and, on the other, as a justification for the lack of good urban transit systems. The current energy and fuel rip-off, which has tremendously boosted the cost of running a car, only indicates the prospect facing U.S. car owners. By contrast, the price of gasoline in the Soviet Union, which is much cheaper than ours, has remained the same.

The deepening transportation crisis in the United States is compelling many cities to give greater consideration to public transportation. Even Washington has been finally forced to come up with a mass transit program, inadequate though it is. For the first time, Congress is beginning to appropriate funds for public transportation. But this had hardly started when it was jeopardized by "economies" as a result of the depresssion in 1975. And such considerations are all based on the all-important profit motive. Since, in contrast to the early days, the profits to be made here are not great, and the transportation systems have long ago been milked dry, many private corporations have dumped them on the cities. The Senate Committee on Banking and Currency reported *(Metropolis Values in Conflict,* p. 167) that the committee was informed that since the beginning of 1954, a total of 214 transit companies have been sold and an additional 152 *have been abandoned.* "Free enterprise" abandons transit lines as well as buildings when it no longer can make a suitable profit out of either. The Senate committee noted that "the American Transit Association estimates that there are *60 cities* of 25,000 population or more which have no public transportation service at all." (p. 100.) When private enterprise is ready to "dump" its transit lines (always for a good profit, it should be added), the city government is always ready to oblige. Thus, inhabitants of our cities are not only deprived of adequate public transportation, for which they pay outrageous fares, but they are made to bear the cost of bailing out the private owners when they are prepared to turn the bankrupt lines over to the city. In place of private ownership, the deteriorating urban transit system is usually turned over to an "authority," that monstrous anonymous device for putting the back-breaking financial burden on the people, and placing this vital service beyond their control or influence. The "authority," whose main function is to make the transit system profitable, makes the payment of interest on the loans and bonds (controlled by the big banks) its primary consideration.

From 1904 to the 1940s, the New York subway was milked dry by the powerful private interests who owned it. Then, when it was unloaded onto the city and taken over by the New York City Transit Authority, the law under which the "Authority" operates provided that there must be a "self-sustaining fare." This meant, in simple words, that the subway rider must bear the cost of wages, materials and all other operating expenses plus debt service for the bond holders.

Czarism bequeathed a real horse-and-buggy transportation system to the makers of the socialist revolution. By comparison, at that time our cities were in a flourishing state in respect to transportation, with elevated lines, trolleys, buses as well as the beginnings of mass production of automobiles.

The Nazi invasion took a terrible toll in destruction of railroads, roads, and all kinds of vehicles in the Soviet Union. Overcoming its backward heritage, the ravages of civil war and intervention, the incalculable devastation of World War II, the Soviet Union has today the cheapest, most efficient, and certainly the most pleasant transportation in the world. We had no such obstacles to overcome; we, in fact, were way ahead in this respect as well as in most other aspects of modern urban life. Yet, never has our public transportation system been in a greater mess than it is today.

11 / CITIES OF BROTHERHOOD

The Soviet solution to the problem of nations and nationalities living together has never been more important for the people of the United States than today. In no major capitalist country is the crisis in the relations between various nationalities more starkly revealed than in the United States. And nowhere is it more nakedly exposed than in our great cities. For our crisis in "race relations" has merged with the crisis of our cities. The combination has produced a *crisis in living*. This is a uniquely U.S. phenomenon that has made our urban existence one of the world's most horrible examples of capitalist living. Millions of Americans are finding such a life unbearable. No one more so than the Black, Puerto Rican, Chicano, Asian and Native American Indian peoples confined in tight, segregated pockets. The "pockets" have since expanded so that during the past decade, for example, Blacks have come to form a majority, or a near-majority, or at least very substantial sections of most major U.S. cities, far out of proportion to the 11.2 percent they constitute of the nation's total population. According to the 1970 census, these include: Washington, the nation's capital, 71.1 percent; Gary, 52.8 percent; Newark, 54.2 percent; Detroit, 43.7; Baltimore, 40.4; Birmingham, 42 percent; Philadelphia, 33.6; Chicago, 32.7; Cleveland, 38.3; New Orleans, 45; Atlanta, 51.3, and New York, 21.2. The impact of this twofold crisis is underscored by the fact that 73.5 percent of the population of our country live in urban areas on 1.5 percent of the land.

The ghetto outbursts of the past decades have made it abundantly clear that life in our great cities can never become livable until it is livable for

140

these oppressed minorities. The crisis of our cities is demonstrating the bankruptcy of the capitalist solution to the question of ethnic relations.

Americans would benefit by taking an objective look at Soviet experience in solving the national problem of the coexistence of nationalities and nations. Few countries in the world faced it in a more complex form or are as multinational as the Soviet Union. And few had inherited more discrimination from the former land of pogroms and the prison house of nations. Soviet experience can be helpful in combating reactionary forces in our country who are playing on deeply imbedded racist prejudices and fears. Having made the cities unlivable, these forces propose to turn them into armed camps. They would enforce institutionalized second-class citizenship.

Soviet experience demonstrates that urban centers can only become cities without crisis if they are, among other things, also *cities of brotherhood. Most important, Soviet experience shows how this can be done.* One week every year, our country celebrates "Brotherhood Week." The Soviet Union does not proclaim Brotherhood Weeks. It *lives* brotherhood *every day.* December 30, 1972, marked half a century of the fraternity of its more than 100 nations and nationalities as the Union of Soviet Socialist Republics. The difference between the two countries is expressed by much more than the vast span separating one week from 52 weeks a year. It is the difference between word and deed, promise and performance. Nowhere in the world is there a more awesome gap between pious words and ignoble deeds on "brotherhood" than in the United States. And nowhere are words and deeds in greater harmony than in the Soviet Union. In five years of living in, and visiting, dozens of cities in 14 Republics, never one did I come across a single clash between peoples of different races and nationalities. Not once did I witness the use of police or military force against any of its 100 peoples such as I had observed in the brutal "occupation" of Harlem by an overwhelmingly white police army during the ghetto outburst of 1964.

During my five years in the Soviet Union, new shameful chapters were added to the U.S. "solution" to the national question. They are symbolized by names familiar to the entire world: Attica, Baton Rouge, Angela Davis, Bobby Seale, the Soledad Brothers, George Jackson, Wounded Knee. The Soviet Union has given the world quite different symbols. One of the most meaningful of them was provided during the mid-1960s, when the "dirty war" unleashed against the Black ghettos was in full force. I'm referring to Tashkent, capital of Soviet Uzbekistan, which had constituted one of the oppressed sectors living in the czarist prison of nations. Tashkent was nearly devastated by an earthquake April 26, 1966. I visited the city in 1969.

The Reconstruction of Tashkent

The defense of Stalingrad demonstrated the unity of the multi-national Soviet peoples as it confronted the mightiest and most barbaric war machine in history. Tashkent revealed the unity of the Soviet people in the face of natural disaster.

Americans are familiar with, and prize, the helping hand good neighbors extend to each other in times of calamity. The rebuilding of Tashkent was a *helping hand applied on an unprecedented national scale*. A few hours after the earthquake, Leonid Brezhnev, General Secretary of the Central Committee of the Communist Party of the Soviet Union and Premier Aleksei Kosygin arrived in Tashkent.

In the United States, also, it is not uncommon for the President and other leading public figures to visit scenes of natural disasters. In the spring of 1972, large areas in Pennsylvania and other states were devastated by floods. President Nixon made his appearance at the scene of disaster. But the President, who did not hesitate to spend billions of dollars to destroy Vietnam cities, villages and dikes, was so parsimonious to Pennsylvania's destitute citizens that the state's Governor Shapp publicly protested the government's heartlessness.

Tashkent provides a stark contrast. By train, plane, truck, and bus, the working people of every Soviet Republic poured into Tashkent. It was as if the entire nation were moving to the *front*. Construction workers from Moscow, Leningrad and other parts of the Russian Soviet Federated Socialist Republic, from the Ukraine, Azerbaidjan, Georgia, Kazakhstan, Turkmenia, Byelorussia and the Baltic republics unloaded their huge cranes and excavators. All came with their own equipment and materials. The people of Tashkent—men, women and children—greeted them like liberators, with flowers, music and tears.

Thirty-five percent of Tashkent was destroyed; 96,000 residents lost their apartments; 35,000 their homes; 41 percent of the enterprises were severely damaged; 181 schools and 600 food shops and many restaurants were demolished. The army of builders (joined by tens of thousands of soldiers and students who gave up their vacations), lived in makeshift barracks—many for two and three years. By September 1—three months after the earthquake—the schools were opened. To make up for the destruction, 20,000 apartments (twice the previous number) were and are being constructed annually.

Tashkent, a city of 1,460,000 people, suffered no loss in population since many who came to help remained to live. (About 10 percent left the city after the earthquake.) Thus, Tashkent today is even more multinational. It suffered no panics or epidemics. About 30,000 children were "adopted" temporarily by families and Pioneer camps and rest homes all over the Soviet Union. New lifelong friendships were born in the throes of Tashkent's tragedy. The spirit of national unity sustained Tashkent as it once did Stalingrad.

Kara Kum and Wounded Knee

It would be great if the courageous and militant liberation fighters of Wounded Knee, of the many ghettos and barrios in our land, had the means to visit Turkmenia. Let them see with their own eyes what was accomplished by the entire Soviet people to transform the Kara Kum desert into a near paradise. Let them meet with the Turkmen Academy of Science, which is largely composed of the sons and daughters of nomads. Let them hear the story of how Bibi Palvanova, whose mother wore the hated *yashmak* (a hood covering the face completely), and who was herself sold at the age of 14 to her husband, became Minister of Education of Turkmenia. Let them walk through the beautiful green city of Ashkabad, a desert military outpost under the czars in 1881 and now a modern, industrial, cultural and scientific center (253,000 population). Let them visit the central library of 1,500,000 volumes, in a land where less than one percent could read or write in 1914-15.

The courage of today's fighters for freedom has exposed to the world the U.S. monopolists' "solution" of the question of the Native American Indian people's rights. It is a "solution" that decimated them by wars of extermination in countless Wounded Knees; that robbed them of good lands and shunted them into ever smaller barren reservations. The genocidal character of this extermination is revealed in the size of the Native American Indian people's population, which is smaller today than it was 500 years ago.

Fifty thousand Indian families live in unsanitary, dilapidated dwellings; in huts, shanties, and even dilapidated automobiles. Their unemployment rate is more than 5 times the national average. Forty-two percent of Native American Indian schoolchildren—almost double the national average—drop out before completing high school. Literacy rates are among the lowest in the nation; sickness and poverty rates are among the highest. Ten percent of Native American Indians age 14 have had no schooling at all. Nearly 60 percent have less than an eighth-grade education. Their infant mortality rate is 32 per 1,000 births—10 points above the national average. The incidence of new active cases of tuberculosis among Native American Indians and Alaskan peoples outstrips the national average *seven times*. More than half the Indians obtain water from contaminated sources, and use waste disposal facilities that are grossly inadequate. Virus infections, pneumonia and malnutrition—all of which contribute to chronic ill health and mental retardation—are common among Indian children. Fifty percent of Indian families have cash incomes below $2,000 a year; 75 percent below $3,000. The Native American Indian peoples were not only decimated physically but their culture, traditions, and languages are treated with contempt. In a word—genocide!

Turkmenia tells quite a different story. In 50 years of socialism the population of Turkmenia doubled, 2,988,000 as of 1972. Fifty years ago only .07 percent of the population were literate. Today not only has illiteracy been completely wiped out, but some 60,000 students are enrolled in the impressive University of Turkmenia, in Ashkabad, and in other pedagogical, medical, agricultural, and polytechnical institutes. Turkmenia has more than 3,700 research associates working in scientific institutions, more than half of whom are Turkmen. It has an Academy of Science of 646 members, 249 of whom are women, 56 Turkmen women. All of them were the offsprings of illiterate parents or grandparents. Turkmenia has 25 doctors per 10,000 population, a *higher rate than in the United States*. Cholera, smallpox, malaria and trachoma, which once plagued and decimated the population, have all been eliminated. The average lifespan was less than 35 years before the Revolution; it is now over 70.

Friedrich Engels pointed out that under communism "the whole sphere of the conditions of life which environ men, and which hitherto ruled men, now come under the domination and control of man, who for the first time becomes the real conscious lord of nature because he has now become master of his own social organization." Engels' prediction is dramatically demonstrated in the huge Kara Kum canal. The Kara Kum desert covers an area of approximately 230,000 square miles, which is larger than France. When, almost 50 years ago, in February, 1925, the

Turkmen Soviet Socialist Republic was established, "the masters of their social organization" were largely nomads living in a feudal society. Life in this desert land was dominated by an eternal, roving search for water. The search was expressed in an ancient Turkmen saying: "A drop of water is a drop of gold and at the same time a teardrop." The fight for these "drops of gold" constituted one of the decisive battles to bring Turkmenia in step with the all-Soviet march toward communism. The October Revolution catapulted Turkmenia from feudalism into socialism—skipping the stage of capitalism.

The wounds of the Great Patriotic War, which took 20 million lives and ravished more than one-third of its territory, had hardly healed when, in 1954, the Soviet government turned to the construction of one of the world's greatest canals across one of the largest deserts. The battle with Kara Kum was waged by a Soviet "international brigade" representing every Republic, under intense heat (about 114 degrees Fahrenheit in the shade) and with very little water to wash with or to drink. It was a battle against heat, moving sands, and the notoriously wild Darya River whose waters were harnessed to feed the man-made river. The struggle was led by a worker-scientist alliance in which the Turkmen Academy of Science, formed only three years before—in 1954, played a particularly important role. The battle with Kara Kum forged probably the world's greatest collection of desert scientists. The conquering of Kara Kum, like the conquest of Siberia's taiga and the Far North's tundra, opened up an incalculable treasure chest that has enriched Turkmenia and the entire Soviet Union. Its gas, the cheapest in the Soviet Union, is now being piped to the central cities; its oil has made Turkmenia the Soviet Union's fourth largest producer of "black gold." It also produces quite a good deal of "white gold," cotton. But it was the transformation I saw on the Nine Commissars State Farm (named after nine Communist commissars killed by the British and Basmachi counterrevolutionaries), and in Ashkabad that particularly hit home to me the meaning of the battle of Kara Kum. My guides proudly escorted me along rows of newly constructed brick single-family homes sitting on the edge of paved streets. Nearby were dozens of similar homes in various stages of construction. The rent paid for these four-room homes was 4 to 5 rubles a month.

I saw mounds of cotton covered with canvas awaiting transportation. Lined up in a vast motor park and housed in large repair shops, were 150 tractors. The state farm also has 1,000 cows and 2,000 pigs. In the near future, supplying Ashkabad with meat not cotton will be its main task. In operation were: two 10 year middle schools, a nursery and kindergarten, dining room, clubhouse, summer theater, and medical station. Under construction were a hospital, bathhouse, a Palace of Culture, stores and a sports stadium. Not far from this modern urbanlike oasis, were signs of the old nomadic life. A herd of camels driven by a youth, his shaggy Turkman sheepskin hat cocked jauntily on his head, moved lazily along the well-paved road. Nearby were a few primitive clay huts hugging patches of desert sand. As everywhere in the Soviet Union, the old recedes before the rising new.

I recalled this scene as I read the article in the *New York Times* magazine, March 18, 1973, by Alvin M. Josephy, Jr., describing the plundering of the pitiful land still left to the Native American Indian peoples. "Grabs for Indian resources have reached the dimensions of a massive assault by all sorts of conglomerates and huge industrial combinations. Tribe after tribe has become split into factions; the government has encouraged and aided coal companies to strip-mine Indian lands, much of them held sacred by the traditionalist Indians. . . . Power companies to build monster, polluting generating plants, transmission lines, railroad spurs and truck highways on reservations; and real estate and industrial development syndicates to erect large projects among the Indian settlements for the use of non-Indians."

Ashkabad—The City That Blooms in a Desert

The Soviet government also mobilized the nation's resources to reconstruct Ashkabad, while its war wounds were still bleeding. Ashkabad, a tiny village at the end of the 19th century, had become a thriving city of 100,000 after the October Revolution. It was completely destroyed by an earthquake in 1948. Ashkabad, a city of unobstructed desert skies, fought the desert for trees, grass, and flowers as well as cotton. And it wears its deep, many-hued green with the pride of a victor; it is a city of wide streets enveloped by endless archways and dotted with numerous parks.

Ashkabad glories in its man-made river; it is now a thriving river port; its new lake sits on its outskirts. A nomadic desert people have now become not only prosperous farmers, skilled workers, scientists and artists, but also seamen, fishermen, and gardeners. It is a city of Turkmen symmetry. You see the beautiful, ancient, geometric, stylized patterns of its famed carpets everywhere.

The Turkmen people have leaped into the approaching 21st century. But they took with them their ancient culture and art, which is experiencing an unprecedented renaissance. Like all Soviet cities, Ashkabad is also a city of expanding microhousing areas, with the new areas retaining a distinctive Turkmen flavor. Much of the city still consists of solidly built clay, single family homes enclosed by walls of white, pale blue, and pink.

The city is an important industrial center. I visited its highly mechanized glass factory that exports fine quality products to many countries. Above all, what impressed me was the plant's Palace of Culture. Constructed with the voluntary labor of its workers, like the Kara Kum Canal, this palace was a monument to Soviet triumph over the desert. Turkmenia had only four small towns before the Revolution. All its many new cities have been constructed in the fifty years of Soviet power.

Ashkabad's Turkmen Institute of Agriculture is a seat of learning that would be the envy of any country. Ninety percent of the students come from and return to Turkmen villages. In its 40 years of existence, the institute has trained an army of agronomists, botanists, and geologists for the battle with the Kara Kum. But the institute is concerned not only with producing agricultural experts. A. Rustamov, its rector, emphasized to me: "Our students are returning to their farms and villages. They must not only be good specialists; they must be village cultural leaders. The construction of communism means narrowing and eliminating the gap between country and city." About 40 percent of Turkmen Institute graduates work for and receive two diplomas—in a cultural as well as an agricultural specialty.

The institute was completely destroyed in the 1948 earthquake. "But look at us now!" Rustamov exclaimed. We had come to the institute's beautiful, sunlit cultural center that houses its large library, a 900-seat theater and innumerable recreation rooms.

Rustamov was born in Turkmenia and, like most Russians we met in Central Asian Republics, he was deeply attached to his Republic. His father was one of Turkmenia's few teachers in czarist days.

"The history of our institute and Turkmenia," Rustamov said, "is in these statistics: In 1930 when we were founded, we had 200 students — now we have 5,500; we had 30 professors and teachers, now we have 300; we had 10,000 books in our libraries, now we have 250,000; we didn't have a single Turkmen scientist, now we have an Academy of Science and 100 candidates of sciences."

Compare these achievements of a once nomadic people to the struggle

Indians in our country have to conduct for even rudimentary education. The *International Herald Tribune,* March 27, 1973, in an article appropriately titled "Struggling for Life," gives this description of Navajo Community College, a two-year college proclaimed as "America's first Indian-organized and operated institution of higher learning." That this was a "token" concession on the part of the Bureau of Indian Affairs, a white-dominated government agency that runs all "Indian Affairs," is indicated in this account of the "state of affairs" at Navajo College. "Of 3,421 students who enrolled at Navajo Community College since it opened, including 1,828 full-time students, *only 46 have been graduated.* . . .Navajo Community College shares facilities with a high school run by the Bureau of Indian Affairs in the tiny community of Many Farms, Arizona. The high school is a series of ugly green buildings. *Not a blade of grass, nor a bush grows on the campus,* which turns into a sea of mud in winter, rain, and snow. There is little for students to do. No town to visit; movies once a week. *Some of the bored students turn to drink — others to drugs."* [My emphasis, M.D.]

Front Line Fighters of Kara Kum

The battle with the desert is led by the chairman of the village Soviet. It is a struggle not only to overcome a hostile nature but to narrow the gap between village and city. This struggle is largely directed by women in most Republics in Central Asia. Eight of the nine "chairmen" of the village Soviets in the Ashkabad area are women. They are leading the fight with fervor, firmness and calm wisdom.

The village Soviet (like city Soviets) is a collection of experts, all of whom have specific responsibilities. There is no gap between discussion and performance, and the chairman of the Soviet must not only be the overall expert, but the chief checker upper. The village Soviet, like the city and supreme Soviets, combines executive and legislative power; it *implements* its decisions.

The village has its own subsidized dramatic group and is regularly entertained by Ashkabad's Turkmen academic dramatic theater and the ballet and opera theater. Ashkabad's theaters have mobile song and dance groups which bring the stage to lonely shepherds tending their flocks. The village Soviet has a youth committee which concentrates on encouraging young people, especially girls, to qualify themselves for higher institutions of learning. Where once they were reluctant, the young women are now in hot competition for entrance into colleges and technicums.

One of Bagir's most exciting and important committees is the "Women's Soviet," consisting of nine members. It deals with all problems confronting the women of the village, including cases that arise when the old habits of male supremacy crop up. It is through the work of such committees in the villages that many gifted artists, doctors, and engineers were produced.

Ogulgozel Taganova, chairman of the Bagir village Soviet, typifies the new socialist woman of Turkmenia. Her mother, who was illiterate, was married off at the age of 12, and when her husband died she was promptly sold to another husband. O. Taganova finished school and became the first tractor driver in the Ashkabad area. Then it was discovered that she had an exceptional voice and she entered the Moscow Conservatory of Music. Despite the pleas of the Conservatory's director, Taganova, upon learning that her mother was quite ill, returned to the village — to stay.

I asked if she experienced difficulties with the men of the village in being accepted as village leader. She smiled. "In the beginning, yes. But I know my people very well. Everyone is now used to the idea," she said, as male members of the Soviet served us tea and cakes.

In the Land of the Pamirs

There are many areas in the Soviet Union where urban life actually only came into existence with socialism. The Soviet Tajik Socialist Republic, the home of the Pamir Mountains, "the roof of the world," is one such region.

In Turkmenia, the enemy was the desert. In Tajikistan, the foe was the mountains, which occupy 93 percent of its territory. Like Turkmenia, before Tajikistan could master nature, it had to overcome the legacy of its past. I spoke with Hamid Godoyev, a candidate of science. Godoyev, a charming, youngish man with graying temples, ceremoniously poured out tea, a delightful ritual which precedes every discussion in Central Asian Republics.

"There are those who say a land which never experienced capitalism cannot provide the best example of socialism." Godoyev noted, "But our history shows otherwise. Tajikistan skipped the stage of capitalism — we went from feudalism into socialism. We had very little land, as you can see. And there was very little water. The primitive agriculture was controlled by the beys (feudal landlords). The beys had the water and took half the harvest for any water they supplied to water-hungry peasants. All-consuming taxes accompanied dire poverty. If a daughter got married, there was a tax — if a son was born, another tax. That was feudalism. So you may ask how could a land so burdened by its backward past avoid capitalism and advance toward socialism? The answer is: only by receiving the wholehearted, selfless help that would enable us to catch up with the more advanced Russian people. And we received much help! Up to 1935, 85 to 90 percent of our budget was financed by the Soviet government. Our Revolution had not only historic backwardness to contend with but internal enemies. The armed struggle with the Basmachi, feudalist counterrevolutionary bands who were aided by the British, continued until 1932.

"Now, we are working to build a Communist society. It's a very complicated question and it will take a lot of time. First, to build a Communist society, a firm material basis is needed. That's the significance of the Nurek hydroelectric power station, which has an 11 million kilowatt-hour annual capacity. Fifty years ago Tajikistan had a total capacity of 100 kilowatt hours. Now we have 370 large plants — among them electrical, chemical, aluminum, machine-tool, and refrigerator. Our mountains are yielding their vast mineral treasures. Our agriculture is well on the road to mechanization. In the past 50 years 50,000 hectares of arid land have been made fertile through irrigation and amelioration."

He stopped to emphasize another point.

"But building communism means more than industrial and agricultural advancement. It means molding a new person; highly educated, cultured, hard workers with high moral and ethical principles. That is the most difficult and most complicated task of all. The past — especially religious past — still lingers on. There are still cases where very young girls, too young, get married. We still have petty thieves and petty speculators. But the main thing is that a firm foundation has been laid. From a land of illiteracy, we have become a country of scientists. We have 16 permanent repertory theaters. We have 1,200 libraries, including branches on *every* collective and state farm and in *every* plant.

"Communism also means eliminating the gap between city and village. We had quite a gap! We had no cities. Even Dushambe was a kishlak (village). It now has a population of 350,000. We live in harmony with our Russian, Uzbek, Georgian, Tartar, Ukrainian brothers and sisters and the many other peoples who make up our Republic. What is it

that unites or disunites a people? From our history we know: private ownership disunites. Before the Revolution a brother killed a brother for 5 meters of land. Today, our people are united on the basis of public and collective ownership." He smiled confidently. "That's a firm foundation for building communism."

A Helping Hand in Kishinev

The Soviet government's helping hand to Kishinev, capital of the Moldavian Soviet Socialist Republic, demonstrates the special assistance given to those Republics which initially formed part of the young Soviet state but were compelled to take a detour from the path of socialism. Thus, the peoples of these Republics have had almost a quarter of a century less of socialist life, of socialist planning and construction. One of the most remarkable chapters in Soviet history is how this quarter of a century gap was made up. The Baltic Republics and Moldavia, in all spheres of life, are now on a par with the rest of the Soviet Union.

In 1971, the USSR Council of Ministers outlined a comprehensive plan for the reconstruction of Kishinev, a city comparable in size to Newark, New Jersey. Since, during the decade I covered urban affairs for my paper, I never heard of a similar law enacted by our Congress for any U.S. city, I was particularly intrigued to see what this meant for Kishinev.

Dynamic Mayor Ivan Kushkevitch was in on the project from the beginning. Talking quite frankly about the city's problems, he strongly suggested that I make an on-the-spot check on how decisions were being fulfilled.

The point of concentration was new housing. From 1971 through 1975, 35,000 new apartments were constructed with schools, nurseries, polyclinics, stores and plenty of greenery shaping up the typical Soviet micro-areas. A new, modern Moldavian Opera and Ballet Theatre burgeoned Kishinev's cultural pride. Leningrad architects had designed a new 16 story hotel, a press and publishing complex and new cinemas. Architects and designers from Kiev were helping erect a new dramatic theatre, while creators from Tbilisi aided the building of a new central library.

Kishinev was one massive construction site: 40 miles of new sewer conduits, 60 miles of gas mains, 66 miles of modern highway; hospitals adding 1770 beds; a 2000-seat circus; Pioneer palaces, and a new Palace of Culture for Kishinev's railway workers (20 percent of the city's work force). The face-lifting was breathtaking, as breathtaking as hearing the heavenly singing of nightingales in Pushkin Park, the center of the city.

The Soviet government's aid, financial and otherwise, was concrete. But the most important result of the Soviet government aid was the spirit it had stimulated among Kishinev's citizens. Tens of thousands pledged to donate 100 hours of labor each to reconstruct their city. Saturday's and Sundays, thousands participate in weekly *subbotniks*. Deputies to the City Soviet, led by Mayor Kushkevitch, were demonstrating leadership by example (there are 400 city deputies, 238 men, 162 women, more than half of whom are workers). None are professional politicians, since deputies are not paid and work at other jobs for a living. Many are engineers and technicians.

"Kishinev is 500 years old, but it is a young city," Mayor Kushkevitch exclaimed. It is young in the same sense as the many ancient cities which have been reborn in the years of socialist society, of workers' power.

From the Ghetto into the Mainstream

The real story of Soviet Jews the Zionist anti-Soviet campaign is attempting to conceal lies in the transformation of the ghetto Jew, excluded from the mainstream of Russian life under the czars, into the Soviet Jew, an integral part of Soviet life on all, including the highest, levels. This is a subject for another book. This is the story the *New York Times* and our big business press generally refuse to tell — and for good reason — it would shatter their effort to portray Soviet Jews as suffering from anti-Semitism, eager to flee to Israel.

Like many American Jews, I know of the flight from the pogroms of the czarist past, not from general but from personal history. It explains how I came to be an American. My father preceded the rest of the family to New York in 1912 (just before I was born) from the ghetto town Volkovisk in Byelorussia. He deeply loved Russia and the Russian people but he couldn't bear the idea of his children living under the threat of pogroms. The hard life of the *shtetel* Jews that Sholom Aleichem described in his immortal stories was also the life of my family! My grandfather, a poverty-stricken boy of 11 was picked up on the dirt road of his village by Czar Nicholas I's recruiting officers. It seems that a rich family had "bought out" their son, and my grandfather was chosen at random to replace him. After all, who would miss this barefoot boy of a poor Jewish family? And so my grandfather became a *"Nikolaevsky soldat''* — 25 years of his life were spent under the most brutal and brutalizing conditions.

In one form or another this was the story of many, if not most Jews, under the czars. It explains the massive flights and emigrations. It explains why New York City and other cities became the home of hundreds of thousands of Russian Jews. The real story of the Soviet Jews is that Jews stopped running away from their country, that instead of flocking to U.S. cities they flocked to Soviet cities. Efforts to portray the desire of a small fraction of Soviet Jews to go to Israel as a flight from persecution are ludicrous to anyone familiar with the position of Soviet Jews.

Nothing reveals the transformation and the liberation from ghetto existence more than the fact that Soviet Jews are natural and integral parts of all major Soviet cities. I say natural and integral advisedly because one would search in vain for "Jewish neighborhoods" like those in our country. Soviet Jews, with the ending of the ghettos, poured into the big cities. This process was accelerated after the war. Many were evacuated from the areas overrun by the Nazis to the large cities, in more secure positions. Two million Soviet Jews were thus evacuated and saved from certain annihilation. Today they form substantial proportions of the main cities. In Moscow, they are about 5 percent of the population (250,000), and there is a similar percentage in Leningrad. In Odessa and Kishinev they constitue 12 to 19 percent of the population.

The *luftmensch* (one who makes a living out of air, without any real trade or profession) had long disappeared together with the ghetto (together with small shopkeepers they made up 54.4 percent of the Jewish population of czarist Russia). Soviet Jews are in all professions and industries. I met Jewish academicians, scientists, artists, writers, directors of industries and farms, university professors, government and Party leaders, workers in factories and collective farmers. Everywhere I met the living statistics of liberation. They fully confirmed the figures given by Premier Alexei Kosygin, Chairman of the USSR Council of Ministers, in answer to a *New York Times* correspondent in October, 1971, during a visit to Canada. "Jewish people constitute 8 percent of the entire scientific personnel in the country, 20 percent of the writers and journalists, 8 percent of the people in arts, and 6 percent in medicine, even though they account for less than 1 percent of the population. In respect to this percent of the population there are 9 times more Jewish people in higher education than Russians."

Birobidjan, embracing only a tiny fragment of the Soviet Jewish population, nevertheless constitutes an important chapter in the history of the transition from the ghetto to the mainstream.

Before my journey to Birobidjan, I met with Aron Vergelis, a poet widely read in Russian as well as Yiddish and editor of the Soviet Yiddish monthly cultural magazine *Sovietische Heimland*. Incidentally, *Sovietische Heimland*, with a readership of more than 25,000, has a circulation far exceeding that of any Yiddish-language magazine in the United States. As a paratrooper, Vergelis fought from Brest-Litovsk to Berlin. His mother, sister and her children were killed by the Nazis in cold blood.

Two million Jews participated in the war; a half million in the ranks of the Soviet Army; 340,000 received awards and medals, of which 117 were as Heroes of the Soviet Union. Lieutenant-General David Dragunsky was twice winner of the Hero of the Soviet Union medal. A bust of Dragunsky was erected on the very spot where his mother was killed by the Nazis.

Vergelis's story is the story of the transformation of rootless, ghettoized Jews into Soviet citizens fully integrated into the life of their country. It is the hard rock of Soviet reality on which present distortions will be shattered. "The main thing is to become honestly acquainted with our life, to understand the transformation of the ghetto Jew into the Soviet Jew. We do not want to idealize our life. We had bad as well as good times, but the truth is sufficient."

In August, 1970, I visited Birobidjan, where *shtetel* Jews like the Vergelis family had come many years before without trades or professions, products of forced *"luftmensch* existence." Above all, the land-starved Jews came to make things grow. In Zavety Ilyicha, a collective farm in Waldheim Village, near the city of Birobidjan, I saw how they made things grow.

Like the city, Waldheim was wrested from the taiga. In the farm's museum I saw pictures of the 20 pioneer families. Many of them are today alive and occupy a special place of honor there. The children of many have understandably made their own lives in other parts of the Soviet Union, as engineers, scientists, musicians, writers, soldiers, and workers. But enough remained to make the Zavety Ilyicha one of the most prosperous collective farms in the Soviet Union. The chairman, Vladimir Peller, a hero of World War II, is a Deputy to the USSR Supreme Soviet.

The farm's school has the same high-level comprehensive curriculum and facilities as any ten-year school in Moscow. In line with its special needs, agricultural sciences come in for special stress. And the collective farm itself provides the students with their natural laboratory and practice. The school revealed more eloquently than any statistics how the gap between country and city in the Soviet Union is being narrowed. Among the students in the last 30 years, 62 have become engineers, 85 technicians, 81 agricultural specialists, 54 teachers, 14 doctors, 9 cultural workers, 10 tractor drivers, 12 bookkeepers, 255 skilled workers and 160 employees of government and public institutions.

Sholom Aleichem in Birobidjan

In Birobidjan one may walk along Sholom Aleichem Street and the spirit of the immortal Jewish bard is everywhere. Those who long for the narrowness of ghetto existence and think of Jewish life in terms of exclusiveness, may bewail the fate of the Jews in Birobidjan. But the Jews of Birobidjan are proud of the international character of the city and the Jewish Autonomous Region.

In Birobidjan, Sholem Aleichem's descendants live in peace and harmony with 14 nationalities, including Russians, Ukrainians, Tartars, Chuvash, and Nanei. Almost 30 percent of the city's population of 56,000 are Jewish and an equal amount are Russian. The Jewish Autonomous District, part of which borders on the Chinese People's Republic, is about 24,000 square miles in area and is part of the Far East Region and the Russian Federation. It is today an agriculturally rich area and abounds in valuable minerals and fine marble. The beautiful marble in the Byelorussian Station in Moscow's famous metro comes from the Jewish Autonomous District. Birobidjan is a lively city and its role as the district's administrative and cultural center is expanding. I slept in the modern, attractive 170-room hotel built in 1969, and had my meals in its fine restaurant, which specializes in Jewish delicacies.

My first train stop in the Jewish Autonomous District was the village "IN," whose name appeared on the station platform in Yiddish and Russian, which are the official languages of the district. On the street I heard Yiddish but it was spoken mostly by those of the older generation. The district radio station service carries nightly programs of news and culture in Yiddish, and features Yiddish concerts, songs and sketches on Saturdays and literary translations on Sundays. The Sholom Aleichem Library has an impressive collection of 140,000 books. On a visit there I saw a Tartar boy reading one of Sholem Aleichem's books in Russian. Six volumes of Sholom Aleichem's works were published in Russian in an edition of 225,000 copies. The library, of course, contains his complete works in Yiddish. It regularly sponsors dramatic readings of his stories and the writings of contemporary Soviet Jewish writers in Yiddish and Russian.

The Jewish Autonomous District publishes a Yiddish newspaper, the *Birobidjaner Stern* and its Russian counterpart, the *Birobidjaner Zvezda* (the *Birobidjan Star*). The *Stern's* editor, Naum Korchinsky, said interest in the newspaper was greatly increased as a result of the spirited response of the Soviet Jews to the Zionest-directed anti-Soviet campaign. "We received hundreds of letters from Jews all over the Soviet Union asking for copies of our paper," Korchinsky told me. The letters condemned Israel's war against the Arab peoples and supported the *Stern's* denunciation of the Zionist leaders. The *Stern*, which has a staff of 25, is published 5 times a week and is read throughout the Soviet Union, as well as abroad. Its circulation increased 200 percent in the past three years. But perhaps the chief cultural pride of Birobidjan and the Jewish Autonomous Region is its Jewish Peoples Theater. The dramatic group won first prize in the Russian Federation's 1967 amateur theater competition. I discussed the work of the Jewish People's Theater and Yiddish cultural life in Birobidjan at a meeting that ended up with an unforgettable spontaneous concert at the Palace of Culture. Mikhail Bengelsdorf, director of the Jewish Peoples Theater, stressed the popularity of the Jewish Peoples Theater not only among Jews but also Russians and peoples of all nationalities.

"We print a resume of all our plays' plots in Russian but few bother to read it. They understand what goes on without any explanation—the theater speaks for itself." The drama group's repertoire consists of dramatizations of works by Sholom Aleichem and other Yiddish classicists; a play by Gerhonsov, the Soviet Yiddish writer killed in the Great Patriotic War, and works by other contemporary Soviet Jewish writers. The Jewish Peoples Theater has attracted a small group of Jewish youth but Bengelsdorf noted it was not easy to get youth interested in Yiddish. I pointed out that Yiddish drama groups in the United States had a similar problem. The *Sovietische Heimland*, all agreed, was stimulating interest in Yiddish culture and the language. Under consideration was a proposal to form a combined Russian-Yiddish professional theater that would broaden its repertoire and perform plays in both languages.

Survival of National Prejudices

Are there survivals of national prejudices in the Soviet Union? Of course there are. It would be utopian to expect that half a century can cleanse Soviet man and woman of one of the most tenacious "heritages" nourished by centuries of national discord and strife. I have come across some cases reflecting the survival of national prejudices. All were connected with intimate personal, and especially family, relations. The weeds of prejudice have largely been uprooted in the Soviet Union. According to the 1959 census, there were 102 mixed marriages per 1,000 families. The ratio is undoubtedly higher now. One rarely thinks in terms of "mixed marriages" in the Soviet Union—they are so common.

I remember the simple but unforgettable words that summed up this natural process by Yakov Kul, the trade union director of the Dalselkhomash tractor plant in Birobidjan. Kul, a Soviet Jew who never forgot his childhood years in the Ukraine under Nazi occupation, was responding to the Zionist "Save the Soviet Jews" campaign. I put down his words as they poured forth from his heart. "After so much suffering, we Soviet people are living in peace; every year our life gets better. You saw how we live in Birobidjan, peoples of all nations, like one family. *That's the life we know, that's the life our children understand*. They fall in love and they get married. They don't ask: are you a Jew, Russian or a Tartar? Our relations were tested in life—and in the war years under the severest trials. So we know the life we want. Tell me, what is it these people want from us? Why do our peaceful pleasures stick in their throats? Why?"

There are some (a small minority) who are against Kul's, against the Soviet approach, to "love and marriage," who still cling to national prejudices. The Soviet Union is a country of 250 million people with the histories, traditions, and cultures of 100 nations and nationalities. Much of their history under czarism and before was based on relations of prejudice and conflict. When one considers the transformation achieved in such a brief historical period, one can well agree with Brezhnev that the great brotherhood that now characterizes the Union of Soviet Socialist Republics has no equal in history. But Soviet leaders are well aware that the march to communism requires the uprooting of the remnants of national prejudices and they recognize this demands persistent ideological as well as other forms of struggle. Thus, Brezhnev declared: "It should be remembered that nationalistic prejudices, exaggerated or distorted national feelings are extremely tenacious and deeply imbedded in the psychology of politically immature people. These prejudices survive even when the objective premises for any antagonisms have ceased to exist. It should also be borne in mind that nationalistic tendencies often interweave with parochial attitudes, which it turns out, are akin to nationalism.'' This struggle to uproot these survivals of national prejudices is complicated by the ceaseless efforts by anti-Soviet propaganda agencies to stoke the dying embers of these prejudices. Take the unprecedented world-wide Zionist ''save the Soviet Jews'' campaign, mounted chiefly from Israel and the United States. This is a subject requiring more treatment than I can devote to it here, but let me make this observation. Those taken in by the ''save Soviet Jews'' campaign, including some who should know better, underestimate the tenacity of national prejudices which can and do survive among a formerly oppressed people *long after* all forms of oppression and discrimination are removed. Our big business press has been able to exploit the ignorance of most Americans on this point. The overwhelming majority of Soviet Jews are represented by the Yakov Kuls, who have been fully integrated into all aspects of Soviet life. They are an integral part of the process that is molding a new historical community—the Soviet people.

U.S.-USSR—Two Paths to Urban Development

Soviet urban centers, whether ancient cities like Moscow, Kiev, Baku, and Samarkand, or villages that grew into cities under socialism, are cities of brotherhood because the 100 peoples who flocked to them, built them, work in their plants and enterprises and now inhabit them, living and working as *equals*. ''Joint labor and struggle have forged the Soviet people's common traditions,'' Leonid Brezhnev noted in his summation of a half-century of the Soviet family of socialist nations, on the occasion of the 50th anniversary of the establishment of the Union of Soviet Socialist Republics.

I saw what amounted to a muster of the 100 peoples who make up the Soviet Union on every construction project. They came to build and to live in the ancient and new cities. But nowhere were they herded into filthy rat and roach-ridden slum ghettos. Nowhere were they brought to do the dirtiest and hardest work at the lowest pay. Nowhere were they the first to be fired and the last to be hired. Nowhere were their children shunted off into second-class schools to be given just enough schooling to continue the menial occupations of their parents. Nowhere were they the special targets of brutalized racist police. They constructed the great projects and worked in the modern plants and farms as equals, as engineers, technicians, architects, economists, agronomists, skilled workers as well as laborers. They lived as neighbors in the same newly constructed homes or waited their turn for them to be built like all other Soviet citizens. Their children had the doors of education wide open to them for any profession, trade or calling they were able to earn by devoted study. This was the half-century path to cities of brotherhood traversed by the entire Soviet people. This is the meaning behind the conclusion of the 24th Congress of the CPSU that a "new historical community, the Soviet people" had emerged and was in the process of formation. The Soviet people is being formed and molded in the process of reconstructing together their Tashkents, Ashkabads and Kishinevs; in building *together* Kara Kum canals, Ust-Ulim, Nurek, Krasnoyarsk's hydroelectric power station. And before that they were forged in the fires of *united* struggle against the Nazi invaders. They were cemented in *joint reconstruction of their destroyed cities and villages.*

A View from the Top

The 50th anniversary of the establishment of the USSR offered the world an opportunity to compare two roads to solving the problem of national harmony, American and Soviet. For example, leaders of the Black liberation movement in the United States justly raised the demand for some compensation, some special assistance and allowances by the U.S. government to make up for more than three centuries of slavery, serfdom, persecution and discrimination—not to mention lynching. The gist of their request was this: Long oppression and endless wrongs have not only brought us great suffering; they have penalized us by denying us equal rights to education and development, which places us in an economically, socially and politically disadvantageous status. Thus, to achieve real equality, we need not just equal treatment but special help to overcome the handicaps forced on us.

These legitimate demands of an oppressed people were not only disregarded, they were denounced as demands for "Black privileges." The U.S. government never seriously considered them but responded with *token concessions.* Even where "affirmative action" made possible some increased minority representation, these have been short-lived and under constant attack. There were *great promises, the enactment of new*

160 CITIES WITHOUT CRISIS

laws and the handing down of some judicial decisions. All have since been considerably eroded by Washington's application of "southern strategy" policies.

The contradiction between word and deed, promise and performance, reached its peak in the 1960s. It was this taunting contradiction which played a major role in triggering off the ghetto uprisings. The Report of the National Advisory Commission on Civil Disorders appointed by President Johnson, July 27, 1967, to explain the causes for the ghetto rebellions in 1964-67, declared: "The expectations aroused by the great judicial and legislative victories have led to frustration, hostility and cynicism in the face of the persistent *gap between promise and fulfillment.*" It warned: "Our nation is moving toward two societies, one black, one white, separate and unequal."

The very opposite has been the case in the more than half-century history of the USSR. The very point rejected out of hand by our "free-enterprise" society and its government—the need to make up for past oppression and the backwardness inflicted on oppressed peoples—was the *starting point* of the approach by socialist society and the Soviet government to solving the national question.

In the Union of Soviet Socialist Republics, the more backward Republics were accorded a status of *special equality.* More equality for those penalized by history and czarist oppression meant sacrifices by those who, in a backward, war-torn country, still occupied a more advanced position—the Russian people. Few people in history have accepted and carried out with greater honor such sacrifices.

12 / CITIES OF 100 FLAVORS

The Soviet Union is a tourist's dream. Few countries offer such a variety of sights, sounds and smells, such a feast of cultures, such intimate contact with the glories of the ancient past, and such a sense of the even more glorious future. It is a future you can see in the process of construction. Soviet cities, whether they are more than 2,500 years old like Samarkand, the seat of Tamerlane's sprawling empire, or as young as Ust-Ilim, which is being carved out of the Siberian taiga, are unfinished cities. The new look is daily fashioned before your very eyes and literally raised up from the ground by an immense battery of sky-piercing cranes. The Soviet Union has more young and youthful cities than any other country. In little more than half a century of socialism, more than 1,000 cities and towns have come into being.

But a tour of Soviet cities can be a painful as well as a pleasurable experience. A walk through the streets of many of its cities is a journey through the calvary of their unprecedented ordeals. The Soviet Union is a land of martyred, hero cities that bled from countless wounds. It is a land of brotherhood graves where millions lie together as they fought and died together.

I can never forget (nor do I want to) my first visit, May 9, 1961, to its largest and most agonizing brotherhood grave, Piskarevskaya Memorial, in Leningrad, where 600,000 of the hero city's 900,000 dead, lie together.

In Volgograd, Kiev, Odessa, Donetsk, Lvov, Riga, Vilnius, and martyred Minsk, tragedy and triumph are all indissolubly bound together. That is why Soviet celebrations of V-E Day, as joyful as they are, will always be sad. Only a people who paid such a price could so treasure every street, every building, every ancient monument.

It would require a separate book to describe the distinctive charm of Soviet cities. Leningrad and Kiev are justly known throughout the world for their beauty. Let me start with lesser known cities, built and populated by the Soviet youth.

Shock Troops in the Construction of Communism

What do youth do in a society where the socialist revolution triumphed more than half a century ago? What "new worlds" have they left to conquer? There are some in our country who view revolution solely as a process of upheaval. They bemoan the "debilitating effects of soft living." that come with years of peaceful socialist successes. They say: revolution defeats itself as soon as it begins to move closer to its goals, as it increasingly provides the mass of the people with the comforts and joys of living. The logic of such thinking is to regard revolution as the end as well as the means.

The Soviet Union also has its youth problems. How could it avoid them when the very process of maturing presupposes the resolution of problems such as charting an outlook toward life, and finding one's place in life. I met a number of Soviet youth who were not satisfied and who were groping. But what is most characteristic of Soviet youth is their purposefulness, their sense of confidence in the future.

The battle for communism is, above all, a battle of construction. And construction is a way of life here; for no one more than the young and, first of all, for members of the Komsomol. On university campuses in Moscow at the close of the school term in June the scene resembles the army staging areas in preparation for attack. The battles these student recruits were going off to fight were being waged on 107 decisive construction sites: in the tundras of Siberia, in the wide expanses of Central Asia, the far reaches of Primorye and Sakhalin Island. And in the spring of 1974, they marched off from the 17th Congress of the Komsomols to build the Amur-Baikal Railroad. The Komsomols are the shock troops in the construction of the hundreds of new Soviet cities. This army, led by Komsomols, moves from construction site to construction site, from city to city. Numbering tens of thousands, it composes the youngest, most enthusiastic, and one of the most experienced construction forces in the world.

The giant Soviet construction effort is the main task of the Komsomols, and it is efficiently organized, with responsibility for each project fixed on a particular city and area of the Komsomol organization.

The job, first of all, entails large-scale but selective recruiting. Experience has shown "volunteering" is hardly enough to go on for the long pull under difficult working conditions, often in subzero weather, for extended periods of primitive living. About 42 projects are in the most rigorous regions of Siberia and the Far East.

Komsomol builders bring with them not only their youthful zeal but also pride in their great tradition. It goes back 42 years to the generation of the 1930s which built Komsomolsk on the Amur, today a major industrial city. The Komsomol who directed its construction was Alexei Marytesov, a hero of the Great Patriotic War against fascism, who lost both his legs in battle. The Komsomols are the first to come and the last to leave a construction site. In addition to youthful "city fathers" and "mothers," the construction process has created a sizable force of permanent builders with their own high *esprit de corps*. They are the most valuable of all the volunteer builders, particularly in Siberia where every construction site starts from scratch. Siberia has been the school of engineering for thousands of young workers. The rigorous climate and primitive living conditions provide unique on-the-job training.

Not only their skills but their characters as well are being molded in construction. The "new worlds" these Soviet youth are conquering, place particular demands on collectivity as well as individual initiative. Their triumphs over Siberia's forbidding frosts call for the brand of courage their fathers demonstrated in the historic "ten days that shook the world." I saw all this in the unforgettable days I spent in Ust-Ilim, Siberia, in 1970.

Ust-Ilim — Electric City in the Taiga

Our small 12-seater Antonov plane seemed flimsy as it fluttered over the endless stretches of taiga. Below were Siberia's wondrous virgin forests that seemed to shut out all human existence. Below, too, snaking its way along this wilderness of riches was the prime target of Komsomol construction in Eastern Siberia — the Angara River. Suddenly tiny patches of civilization loomed into view: rooftops of wooden homes and concrete prefabricated apartment houses, the outlines of a hydroelectric power station in its first stages of construction. Cranes with a lifting capacity of 80 tons looked like toys from a child's erector set. Antlike figures stood or crawled about.

We had arrived at Ust-Ilim, where the mighty Angara was being harnessed to create another 4,500,000-kilowatt hydroelectric power station and a modern city of 200,000 was being built. Three of the residents rushed over to greet me. They were Anatol Frolev, Komsomol First Secretary of the Ust-Ilim area; Valery Dokuchaev, Komsomol secretary of the construction project; and Boris Yanisov, deputy editor-in-chief of the *Ust-Ilim Pravda*. I was, as they told me, the first correspondent from a capitalist country to visit Ust-Ilim.

Ust-Ilim is a roughly hewn frontier city, one of the latest socialist outposts in the Komsomol-led offensive to tame the taiga. Only a winding ribbonlike road, called the "Road to Life," connects it with civilization — Bratsk. Big brother Bratsk, its chief supplier of material and equipment and many of its most experienced workers, had itself been wrested from the taiga only 15 years earlier. Ust-Ilim was born an electric city (power supplied by Brother Bratsk) and, like all other Siberian cities, it will be among the most electrified in the world. Not a single chimney stack will be permitted to pollute the fragrance Ust-Ilimers breathe in from the taiga.

Material incentives are an important and necessary element in stimulating the construction of the Ust-Ilims. Bonuses and other benefits provided are based on climatic and other arduous conditions of labor. The average wage in Ust-Ilim is a good deal higher than the Soviet average. Bonuses go up to as high as 40 percent of the wage. There are additional bonuses for economizing on material. Workers receive 36-day vacations yearly (the average in the Soviet Union is 24 days). Once every two years they can travel home, free of charge. Men retire at 55 and women at 50 years of age, but they can retire earlier in some cases, depending on length of service. Every year's service in the zone is counted as a year and a half. But bonuses and benefits, important as they are, hardly account for the outpouring of youth and the tenacity with which they stick to their rigorous jobs. Forty and fifty degrees below zero centigrade is not at all unusual here. Work is usually halted only when it hits 45 or more below. Moreover, many give up other jobs, often in nonphysical categories, to join in the construction. There are, of course, those who can't take the hardships.

In Soviet life, hydroelectric power stations and cities — modern comfortable homes, nurseries, schools, theaters, cultural clubs, and stores just go together. And Ust-Ilim already has all of these. I visited one of the nurseries (Ust-Ilim is a city of young mothers) where 250 children were cared for by a staff of 90, fed three meals a day at a charge of 10 to 12 rubles a month.

Few in Ust-Ilim thought of what they were doing in ideological terms. When I asked the young builders at construction sites and in their dormitories to describe how their life was helping mold Communist man, the response was blank stares and an awkward silence. The fault was not theirs but the questioner's. The answer was *before* me, in their collective struggle with the Angara and the taiga, in their warm comradeship. It was in the sacrifices and struggle, in half a century of socialist living, in what brought them to Ust-Ilim.

In Ust-Ilim, one breathes the spirit of comradeship as one inhales the fragrant taiga air. Comradeship is welded in struggle. But Ust-Ilim points the way to the comradeship that can come when people can at last stand united in the battle to master the environment. Siberia's wealth lies, above all, not only in its incalculable resources but also in the youthful builders of Ust-Ilim and Bratsk. Siberia, the land of exile and forbidding frost under the czars, is today not only one of the prize sources of the sinews of Soviet industry, it is a vast school for communism. And its "classroom" projects are hydroelectric power stations, huge timber complexes, aluminum plants, railroads, airports and cities in the taiga like Ust-Ilim.

As everywhere, women play an equal role in all phases of the construction of Ust-Ilim. They are engineers; from the cabins of huge cranes they direct the movement of 80-ton loads; they are political leaders. They are engineers as well as political leaders because both functions are essential.

Where will the builders of Ust-Ilim go from there? Many will follow the Angara River where there are six hydroelectric stations and, of course, cities to be constructed. But many of the builders will settle in Ust-Ilim.

The path to communism is long and difficult, as Lenin long ago pointed out. The lingering habits of individualism and self-seeking are far more difficult to conquer than the Siberian frosts. Ust-Ilim is just one of the glimpses of the future.

Academic City Novosibirsk — Siberia

Novosibirsk was my last stop in a 14,000-mile journey in July, 1970, in Siberia and the Far East. Actually, Academic City is not a city at all. It is part of the Sovietski District of Novosibirsk. In Academic City, science and beauty, man and nature blend in natural harmony — it is a city built into birch and pine forests. Here you not only inhale but *taste* the fragrance of the forests around you. In Moscow, Academician Nikolai Nekrassov put Siberia's challenge this way: Siberia and the Far East contain the Soviet Union's main material resources but they have only one-tenth of its population. Eastern Siberia (2,500,000 square kilometers in area) is about five times the size of France. Much of the area is gripped by bitter winter for seven months, and in the north for ten months a year, with a temperature of 40 to 50 and even 60 degrees below zero centigrade. Yet Eastern Siberia in 1970 was annually yielding 30 million tons of oil, and by 1980 this will reach 230 to 240 million tons yearly. The key to tapping this treasure is the *alliance of science and worker at the point of production.* Siberia and the Far East are not to be taken by mass assault or by mass migration. Such an approach to the most severe parts of this vast area is considered neither practical nor necessary. Rather, the outlook is that of harnessing rivers, piping gas, the extraction of oil and minerals, the construction of cities and great industrial plants, all with the mass mobilization of scientists and technicians at both the point of production and that of the planning board. And living and working conditions for those who come to construct and stay are to be made as comfortable and as beautiful as possible. Hence, Academic City, Ust-Ilim, Bratsk, Amursk, and Komsomolsk-on-the-Amur.

Communist party leaders informed me that the need for manpower in these areas still outstrips the supply, and there are those who leave the forbidding regions to migrate to less severe parts of the Soviet Union. However the characteristic feature is both *quantitative and qualitative growth in active population.* Academic City demonstrates this growth. Founded in 1957, it had a population of 54,000 in 1970, of which 15,000 work in 22 scientific research institutes. Of the latter, 5,000 have scientific degrees. There are 53 Academicians among them. Thus, Siberia's city of science has probably the greatest single concentration of scientific workers in the world. Only 12 years ago there was only one Academician beyond the Urals. The greatest increase in Academic City's population — 50,000 — took place in the years 1967-70. The nuclear and social analysis institutes are mainly manned by former Muscovites. An entire institute of electronics and automation came from Lvov. Similarly, a mathematics school came from Ivanovo. The most *socially active sections of the population are coming to Siberia.*

The scientific workers of Academic City work closely with 300 industrial enterprises — though not exclusively in Siberia. Academic City also trains cadre for other new scientific centers and is an *incubator* of future scientists. It has a special school for talented youth that gives them a three year preparatory course for the "city's" university. From 60 to 80 percent qualify for the science university; all others are admitted to other universities. Academic City University teachers scour the country's schools in a nation-wide talent hunt. The best students come to Academic City (all expenses paid), where they attend lectures for a month and are tested again for the special preparatory school. The university attracts many youth from minority peoples. Of the student enrollment there were 50 Jewish; 22 Ukrainian; 14 Yakuts; 12 Tartars; 12 Kazakh; 3 Bashkirs; 4 Koreans; 6 Buryats. Jews, who are little more than one percent of the population make up almost 7 percent of the enrollment.

Donetsk and Makeevka—Cities of Labor Safety

Nature, which buried one of the world's richest deposits of black gold in the Ukrainian earth, also made this treasure one of the most difficult and dangerous to extract. Gas, the miners' main enemy, is plentiful in the bowels of Donbas, and sudden explosions present a far greater menace than in the U.S. mines. The mines are among the deepest in the world, burrowing as far as 4,000 feet underground. At that depth the temperature can reach 100 degrees Fahrenheit. No wonder Anatoli Suhorukov, Director of the Bazharov mine in Makeevka, who is familiar with the problems confronted by U.S. mines, told me: "God was more considerate to your miners. They face far less difficulty and dangers than we." But as the huge army of black lung victims, limbless men and numerous casualties of mine catastrophes testify, the greedy U.S. coal operators and indifferent Washington more than make up for the Lord's mercy. A research study, conducted by the U.S. Consumers Protection and Environmental Health Service has revealed that more than 100,000 U.S. miners are affected by coal miners' pneumoconiosis or black lung.

No other coal miners in the world are backed up by so formidable a safety and health force as I saw in the Soviet Union, at the Makeevka State Mining Safety Scientific Research Institute and the Donetsk Coal Miners Emergency Rescue headquarters. I observed them in operation 1,000 meters below the earth's surface in the Bazharov mine in Makeevka. The Makeevka scientific institute, set up in 1927, consists of 1,350 scientific and research workers (600 of them scientists) working in 25 of the most up-to-date laboratory buildings spread over 23 hectares of parklike surroundings. Makeevka scientists concentrate on the control of four main mining hazards: gas, sudden explosions, high temperature and dust particles (silicosis). Danger from methane gas and sudden explosions has been reduced to a minimum by a comprehensive system of scientific detection and safety mechanisms.

A graph on an automatic control chart shows the percentage of methane gas in the deep mines. At 1.3 percent, a mechanism automatically shuts off all the mine electricity, thus immediately suspending all work in the danger area. All miners immediately leave the area.

The mine also has a safety mechanism which automatically sounds an alarm when it detects methane gas. But Makeevka scientists are not satisfied with it because the mechanism depends too much on subjective factors. And so the scientists have come up with a miner's lamp which contains an element so sensitive only to methane gas that it blinks, warning the miner of the danger. The danger from sudden explosions has been vastly reduced by a most intensive scientific study of coal layers and seams. The hazardous areas are all carefully charted and saturated with safety measures. I saw row on row of water basins sitting on beams overhead. The tremors of a nearby explosion unleashes them like automatic fire hoses to drench the danger zone.

Dust particles are combatted with water. Donbas coal is washed, like clothes, with a chemical detergent. The fight against dust particles extends from extraction to conveying the coal out of the mine. Holes are drilled into seams every four meters — water holes to give the coal an internal bath. From 50 to 80 percent of the dust particles are eliminated this way. The water process removes 95 to 97 percent of the dust particles. The result is that to a very great extent the battle against silicosis and pneumoconiosis has already been won. In 1970 there was only one case of silicosis among the 3,000 (1,800 of whom work underground) in this mine, and it involved a digger who had labored 20 years in the mines.

Cables are the life lines of miners, and they are guarded accordingly. The elevators transporting miners to and from the depths are doubly protected by emergency brakes that act like parachutes in case of faulty cables. A mobile cable meter provides on-the-spot checkups of "tired" cables. Temperature is controlled by a vast ventilation system that pumps cool pure air into the mine. When we were 1,000 meters below the earth, the temperature was about 75 degrees Fahrenheit and a gentle breeze was blowing. Without "God's consideration," the Donbas mines have been made among the safest in the world. The accident rate is decreasing 20 percent a year. "About 40 percent of our cost of production goes for providing safety and health measures," Suhorukov noted. "The cost of our coal is greater than yours," he added quietly.

All this could not help impress a U.S. delegation of coal experts who visited the Makeevka Institute on June 4, 1970, and wrote: "The U.S.A. delegation of coal experts (the first to officially visit the USSR) had the honor to visit the State Safety Mines Institute in Makeevka today. The work being done here must be an inspiration in coal mine safety advancement all over the world. We salute you on the excellency of your achievement."

The visit of Tom Druax, an Ohio miner, to Donetsk and Makeevka in 1973 on an exchange basis, to see mine safety methods, had a profound impact on him and the United Mine Workers Union. The *UMWA Journal* (November 1 to 15, 1973) carried a two-page interview with Druax. Asked if he considered his trip fruitful Druax replied: "Well, first, I think anything the union can learn about how to make the mines safer is important. I don't care where the idea comes from — if it's going to save lives for our own men, then we ought to try it. I'm not advocating socialism or communism, but I was greatly impressed on the trip by Russian emphasis on safety." And for good reason! George Morris, veteran progressive labor journalist (*Daily World* November 20, 1973) estimates "on the basis of government statistics that as many miners were killed since the UMWA was formed in 1898 as are working in the mines today." What the normalization of USSR-U.S. relations can mean for U.S. miners is clear — among the most important, it can save many lives.

There is an elaborate setup to *rescue* miners when disaster strikes. This highly efficient, *permanent organization* contrasts with the haphazard "volunteer" rescue operations that are mobilized to meet mine catastrophes in the United States. Great emphasis is placed by the Donetsk emergency headquarters on *preventing accidents*. An army of inspectors regularly checks for the slightest violations. If the amount of dust particles is above the norm, work is immediately stopped. The emergency headquarters is a city in itself. It houses 2,000 workers, of whom 1,000 are techincians, 250 coal mining engineers and 40 are candidates of science. All work in an impressive building containing 22 huge laboratories. They have their own school and dormitory for the 200 students and a special medical group consisting of 120 doctors and assistants. I saw a fleet of special emergency trucks on the alert, ready to respond in 90 seconds. "We have relatively few accidents," Director Ivan Belik told us, "but we have to be ready when they happen." The emergency force services the coal mines in Donetsk areas but will respond to calls for assistance anywhere, including other countries. The emergency headquarters makes its own safety and rescue equipment, which it exports to 18 countries. The emergency "city" is like a resort area. The workers, who can go on pension at 50, live in private homes surrounded by gardens. Parks and orchards cover the grounds. Backed by these cities of safety, Soviet coal miners work at their hazardous occupation with a sense of security no other coal miners in the world have. And their wives and children share their assurance. Everything possible is done to reward the miners for their heroic and hazardous labor. Their pay is *three times* the average Soviet wage. They can retire at 50 (ten years earlier than ordinary Soviet working men), and if they choose to continue work, their pension raises their pay to *four* times the average Soviet wage.

They get up to 45 days of fully paid vacation a year. The miners union has an unparalleled network of sanitoriums, rest homes and weekend sanitoriums at all the best vacation spots in the Soviet Union. They have nurseries and summer camps for their children at minimal cost. Miners who want to study (one-third take after-work courses) are given two additional "vacations" (with pay) to prepare for exams, 20 days in spring and 20 days in autumn. The homes of the miners we saw are a far cry from those in typical U.S. mining patches. They are neat, solidly built brick private homes—each with a lovely garden. And miners have more cars on the average than most sections of the Soviet population.

Soviet miners do not live in drab, dirty, dull mining towns, far removed from the cultural life of the country. They live in or on the edge of beautiful, clean culturally alive cities like Donetsk and Makeevka. Only the somber silhouettes of prerevolutionary mines that dot the horizon remind one of coal in Donetsk. In fact, it was difficult to think that we were entering a coal mine. A beautiful, modern, spacious building sits on top of the coal pits. Besides the union, Party and administrative offices, it contains an attractive clubhouse, large auditorium, game and lecture rooms, and a lunchroom which boasts of tasty Ukrainian dishes.

But perhaps what impressed me most was the *honor* paid to coal miners. Donetsk's chief monument is a coal miner who stands proudly in the center of the city—the real master of his realm.

Oil Without Rockefeller

Oil without Rockefeller, oil with 57 years of socialism, transformed a once backward, oppressed country of veiled women into an advanced industrial nation with a flourishing science and culture, a land in which women play a leading role in every sphere of life. Oil without Rockefeller not only wiped out illiteracy, it made it possible for socialist Azerbaidjan to teach more students than the combined totals of Iran, Iraq and Turkey; to train students from 38 countries, mostly from Asia, Africa and Latin America; to send specialists to Yemen; to build a power station for the Democratic Republic of Vietnam; to aid in prospecting for oil in Syria, India and Pakistan; and to study the earth in socialist Cuba.

In 1920, the life expectancy of Azerbaidjan's oil workers was 28 years; today it is 72 years. The pictures I saw in Baku's Azerbaidjan Museum of History explained why Maxim Gorky described the conditions of Baku oil workers as the closest thing to hell on earth.

Baku is a city sitting on an oil well. Here the oil derrick has joined the crane as the symbol of Soviet power. But despite its phenomenal industrial growth, it is hard to think of Baku as a sweating industrial giant. Baku is a giant dressed in green, adorned with shaded trees, parks, squares and pavilions. Baku is an extraordinarily beautiful city; its thriving, dynamic, socialist present blends harmoniously with the charm of its ancient past (Baku is 1,300 years old). Wide boulevards lined with towering, sleek, streamlined structures are only a stone's throw away from narrow, winding, 12th-century streets that breathe history at every step.

A city little larger than Cleveland, Baku has a rich cultural life that includes six professional repertory theaters, operas, ballet, and puppet theaters. All are well patronized by oil workers.

Oil extraction on the Caspian also brings with it serious problems. These were frankly discussed with us by Baku's city leaders and the heads of the Academy of Science. The Caspian is the main source of the Soviet Union's most prized fish export, black caviar. Stringent protective measures are strictly enforced. An extensive network of purification systems is in constant operation to minimize the harmful effects of oil extraction. The damage has not been fully eliminated but it has been considerably diminished by these measures.

Samarkand, Socialist Rome of Central Asia

This city, which celebrated its 2,500th birthday in 1970, is a living museum of ancient Uzbek culture. It is the Rome of Central Asia. Samarkand is additional proof that no society exhibits greater respect for the treasures of the past than socialism, the society of the future. It again demonstrated that no government lavishes more care (and money) on restoring and maintaining religious works of art than the Soviet government. Samarkand and Bukhara reveal this is true for the artistic heritage of the Moslem faith as it is of the Christian. The Shakh-I-Zinda (Living King, a 14th-century complex of mosques, medrassahs (religious schools) and tombs, is a sacred visiting place for Moslems of the world. It is doubtful whether ancient Central Asian culture has been anywhere more fully and faithfully preserved than in the cities of Samarkand, Bukhara and Khiva in Soviet Uzbekistan.

In Samarkand one has the sense of being immersed in history. The sheer quantity of its architectural beauty produces a qualitative effect on the viewer, particularly experienced in walking through the Shahk-I-Zinda with the labyrinth of magnificent creations, many of them constructed during the reign of Tamerlane, the Conquerer, in the mid-14th century. Ancient Uzbekistan was not only a center of artistic beauty, it was a seat of great scientific learning. This was especially demonstrated in the reign of Ulughbek, Tamerlane's grandson, statesman-scholar-scientist of the 15th century. Ulughbek's 100-foot observatory with its huge sextant still stands as living testimony to the genius of that early explorer of the cosmos. By means of that extent, Ulughbek calculated the calendar year as: 365 days, 6 hours, 10 minutes and 8 seconds. Present calculations are: 365 days, 6 hours, 9 minutes and 6 seconds.

Uzbekistan also is the home of one of the oldest Jewish communities. The Jews of Bukhara, who have lived in that city (which is 2,000 years old) since the 6th century, constitute 10 percent of the population. Bukhara has a population of 120,000. There are active synagogues in Bukhara and Samarkand.

In Samarkand one grasps the excitement and color of an oriental bazaar. It is not only a marketplace; it is the center of local life. The bazaar is an extraordinary mixture of sights, sounds and smells, which combine to produce a powerful appeal to the senses. It is a place not only of outdoor selling but of open-air eating. It is one huge oriental picnic: mouth-watering *shashlik,* lamb barbecues, tantalizing fish frys, steaming caldrons bubbling with plov (rice, lamb, and vegetables), fresh flat breads and huge chunks of dinye, luscious Central Asian melon. The bountiful displays of fruits, vegetables, meats, spices, and colorful textiles testify to Uzbekistan's abundance. A visit to Samarkand and Bukhara reminds one how much the Soviet Union is culturally as well as geographically a part of Asia. It makes one realize how ludicrous is the effort of some to exclude the Soviet Union from Asian affairs. My trip made it easier to understand the reasons for the increasingly important role Uzbekistan and other Soviet Central Republics are playing in the Arab, Asian, and African world. Tashkent and Samarkand have been hosts to numerous conferences on problems confronted in these newly liberated and developing parts of the world. Tashkent's Oriental Studies Institute, one of the most complete in the world, is a fount of information, research and creative work on Asian culture and history.

Samarkand is far more than a living museum. Its proud inhabitants have the best of two worlds. Like the Romans, they daily live and relive their ancient glories. But Samarkanders live with the spirit of Lenin as well as that of Uzbekistan's Navei (14th-15th century poet) and Ulughbek. Turbaned, brightly robed riders astride donkeys, plod its winding streets in the old quarters, as huge trucks, excavators and Gargantuan tractors headed for the cotton fields zoom by. Overhead sleek Ilyushin-18's and 24's pierce the skies. Elderly, white-robed women still instinctively shield their faces as they encounter a male passerby. But their smartly dressed daughters (the adaptations of Uzbekistan's famous symmetrical patterns adding distinctive charm to their attire) march off to their classes at Samarkand's 30,000 student university. Much of the city is still composed of walled mud huts. They are picturesque (particularly for photo-seeking tourists), but they constitute a reminder of the immense reconstruction job that still lies ahead for many areas of the Soviet Union. Samarkand's pride, its newly built Gagarin district of 40,000 apartments surrounded by complexes of stores, schools and crèches, points to its nondistant future. Uzbek city plans are concentrating on the elimination of the mud huts by 1980. Samarkand, a city of 300,000 (second in size in Uzbekistan) is also one of the most industrially developed.

Minsk's Tender Trees

Byelorussia's tender birch and poplar trees swayed and bent with the stern autumn wind as our Moscow train approached Minsk. They reminded me of the supple bamboo trees I saw in heroic Vietnam in 1970. The bamboo, too, bent but bounced back. The tender birches are as old as New Minsk and the hundreds of reborn towns and villages in Byelorussia. Only the executioners of trees and towns of Vietnam and Byelorussia bear different names.

New Minsk is a city of joyous pride and unforgettable sorrows. Our hosts spoke of each new complex of beautiful homes, each new factory, school and sport palace—as a monument to their heroic dead. Minsk and Byelorussia died twice in half a century. As border areas they felt the first fury of two German invasions—1914 and 1941. The Soviet people speak with particular pain and pride of Minsk and Byelorussia. The statistics of Byelorussia's ordeal are staggering: 2,360,000 killed (one-fourth of Byelorussia's population); 380,000 transported to Germany as slave laborers; 209 cities, 720 villages, 80 percent of Byelorussia, was reduced to ashes. This is the equivalent of 50 million Americans killed and our entire country destroyed with the exception of the East Coast. Byelorussia fought the Nazis to the last man, woman and child, 1,100,000 as Soviet soldiers, 375,000 as partisans, and 70,000 in the underground. One hundred sixty-two underground newspapers were published in Nazi-occupied Byelorussia.

The veteran partisans spoke with warm affection of their Jewish comrades, many of whom commanded detachments. Maria Ossipova described how the partisans, aided by the people, forged passports, hid children and transported entire Jewish families to safety. The underground Communist Party organized a special ghetto detachment, led by the Feldman brothers, to aid and defend Soviet Jews whom the Nazis herded into ghettos.

From my meeting with Minsk's partisans, I went to Khatyn, Byelorussia's Lidice. It was in the name of Khatyn's martyred dead that the people of Minsk and Byelorussia condemned the murderers of My Lai. Khatyn's 26 bells were tolling as we approached, summoning the world "never to forget." Each bell stands on the spot where a home and a family once lived in this peaceful village. On March 22, 1943, the Nazis placed in a hut its 152 villagers (76 of them children, the rest women and old men) and turned them into a funeral pyre. All who tried to escape were gunned down. Three miraculously escaped—Yusef Kaminsky, then 56, who now lives near Khatyn, and two boys. A huge statue of a gaunt man with haunting accusing eyes, bearing a boy in his arms, stands guard over the "village." It tells Kaminsky's story.

Byelorussia had 135 Khatyns. They are marked by 135 graves, each containing soil in a flower pot from the extinguished village. Nearby are three baby birch trees and an eternal flame. The three birches represent Byelorussia's living; the flame, its dead. A Wall of Remembrance lists the 260 Nazi concentration camps in Byelorussia. Each camp is marked by a prisonlike niche, listing its location and the number of victims. It was a roll call of Byelorussian villages and towns, familiar to Sholem Aleichem's landsmen in the United States who still belong to *landsman-shaften* bearing these names: Mogilev, 40,000; Grodno, 25,000; Brest, 27,000; Minsk, 20,000; Polotsk, 50,000; Slutzk, 14,000; Orsha, 10,000; Gomel, 100,000. I came upon a name I had heard my parents speak of with nostalgia. It was Volkovisk, my birthplace and the home of a generation of my father's family. Twenty thousand perished in Volkovisk's concentration camp.

We came to Khatyn's last appeal to humanity. It read: "Good people—remember! We loved our motherland and you, dear people, and we were set afire, alive. We appeal to you: let grief be transformed into courage and strength so that life will not have died forever."

The partisan veterans I met resembled Minsk's man and woman in the street. And well they should. Maria Borisovna Ossipova looked like the *babushka* (grandmother) she is. She was a librarian when the Nazis invaded her country. She became a Hero of the Soviet Union by the time it was liberated. This gentle librarian helped blow up Kube, the fiendish gauleiter of Minsk, as he slept in his bed. Victor Leventsev, a teacher, commanded a partisan detachment and became a Hero of the Soviet Union. These "Heroes" returned to their peaceful occupations to transform grief into "courage and strength."

Reduced from 270,000 in 1940 to 50,000 in 1944 when it was liberated, Minsk today has a population of 860,000. Only 8.5 percent are over 60. It is a city of young people and young trees. Red and green, the colors of life, are the colors of Minsk. They envelope everything: the impressive Academy of Science building, the Polytechnical School and the burgeoning industrial complexes. Minsk's auto plant and its highly regarded computer symbolize Byelorussia's resurrection and its leap from skins and straw (its chief products under the czars) to 120-ton trucks and thinking machines under socialism. In 1968, industrial output was ten times the 1940 level and 81 times that of 1913. But Minsk's and Byelorussia's glory is its gigantic housing construction. Many of its people were homeless and compelled to live in underground hovels as a result of the terrible devastation. During the last few years, 100,000 apartments were annually constructed in Byelorussia, 16,500 in Minsk alone.

New, gleaming, reborn Minsk is more alive and thriving than ever. It has outlived the Nazis as well as the czars.

13 / CITIES OF MANY CULTURES

A nthony Lewis, correspondent of the *New York Times,* visited the Soviet Union in April, 1973. Here is what he had to say about the cultural life of Tallinn, ancient capital of Soviet Estonia. "The cultural activity in Tallinn is staggering by our standards. The week I was there the opera house played Verdi's 'Trovatore,' Mozart's 'Seraglio,' Tchaikovsky's 'Eugene Onegin,' and a number of ballets. Musicals showing were 'Man of La Mancha' and a local version of 'Love Story.' The Moscow Chamber Orchestra played Bach and Vivaldi, and there was a performance of Verdi's 'Requiem' that could have graced New York or London, by the Estonian Radio Orchestra and chorus. All that when the whole Republic's population is 1.3 million." *(International Herald Tribune,* April 7-8, 1973) Lewis added: "There are Estonian and Russian theaters. The ballet repertory in the last few years has included modern works to the music of Bartok, Stravinsky and Barber as well as the classics. The opera has done six Verdi operas, five Puccini, Strauss' 'Der Rosenkavalier,' Gershwin's 'Porgy and Bess.' " I can add that this small country, about equal in population to Philadelphia, also has nine top professional permanent repertory theaters, a state Philharmonic Society and eleven People's theaters (amateur theaters very close to professional standards). Tallinn has a population of about 400,000. Compare any U.S. city of that size culturally with Tallinn.

I lived a couple of years in Akron, Ohio, which is a little smaller in population than Tallinn. But culturally there is no comparison. Akron didn't have a single professional dramatic, opera or ballet theater. Like the overwhelming majority of our cities, Akron was a cultural desert. Once in a while a few drops of culture dropped on its parched soil when a theatrical, musical, or dance group passed through on a nationwide tour.

Lewis's article is appropriately titled "Some Surprises in Estonia." Among the surprises he notes is that Estonian "remains the common language. . . . Children are taught in the language of their parents, which means that 70 percent of the schools are in Estonian, from day-care through university."

For more than half a century, the Soviet Union has been the scene of an unprecedented renaissance of 100 national cultures. Yet, to this day, Soviet culture is falsely presented as only Russian culture—more as an instrument of "Russification." This blackout on the multinational character of Soviet culture is reflected even in the constant news reference to the Soviet Union as "Russia."

Russian culture and the Russian language have, of course, played very significant roles in the multinational renaissance. And no one appreciates this more than the artists from the other republics who were trained in the conservatories, theaters, ballet, opera and cinema schools of Moscow and Leningrad, and their offspring in the 15 Republics.

I spent a delighful day in Tartu, Estonia's ancient city, with the famous Vanemuine Theater and its extremely imaginative director, Kaarel Ird.

Tartu has a population of only 80,000, but 250,000 attend Vanemuine's 550 performances every year. Theater lovers come from every part of the Soviet Union not only to enjoy the theater's original productions but to learn from its experiences. Vanemuine, which in 1970 celebrated its 100th anniversary is a unique theater; it is drama, ballet and opera, all rolled into one. It is also singularly versatile; its actors, directors, and producers participate in productions in all three genres. Versatility and Vanemuine just naturally go together. Vanemuine practiced total theater long before that concept became popular in the United States.

Tartu's audience is a small-town audience. Ird showed me a statistical study of Vanemuine's audience, which revealed: 33.2 percent are workers; 31.2 percent, students; 17.7 percent, intelligentsia; 11.3 percent, school children; and 6.8 percent, pensioners. More than 35 percent are newcomers from the collective farms of neighboring areas. "Tartu is not Moscow, with its multitude of theaters for all tastes. Vanemuine has to meet the demands of the entire people. It has truly to be a people's theater," Ird stressed.

From its imaginative director to the modernistic stages and auditoriums, Vanemuine breathes the spirit of innovation and originality. It was the first in Estonia to stage Shakespeare's *Coriolanus* and *The Merchant of Venice;* Prokofiev's opera, *The Player;* and a number of operas by Mozart, as well as *Orpheus and Euridyce* (Gluck). Its repertoire includes: Brecht's *Three-Penny Opera* and *Galileo* (it was one of the first to stage the latter in the entire Soviet Union); Shaw's *Saint Joan;* classical Russian and contemporary Soviet plays, and, of course, works by Estonian writers and composers, past and present.

Vanemuine was born in a national resurgence against the domination of the Baltic German barons. It suffered when Estonia, after a brief period as a socialist state, was compelled to take its 20-year bourgeois detour. For 20 years Estonia enjoyed the "blessings" of the "free world." Its native bourgeois rulers, obsessed with anti-Sovietism and anticommunism, sold their country's independence first to a number of imperialist states, and in 1934, they made Estonia a dependency of Hitler's Third Reich. Vanemuine and Estonian culture paid dearly for this betrayal.

There was a brief revival in 1940, when Estonia rejoined the Soviet Union. Then came the Nazis. Vanemuine, in the autumn of 1944, after the retreating Nazis had set fire to it, became a mass of ashes.

Today Vanemuine is housed in a Palace of Culture that would be the envy of any major U.S. city. The palace has three beautiful auditoriums, one seating 840, another 700, and the third, 500. It also has a large open-air theater. Its revolving stage can compare with the best of Broadway. It has a well-stocked library, an attractive lunchroom and numerous work, study and make-up rooms. There is a staff of 400, which includes: a drama group of 35; ballet, 33; opera, 20; chorus, 50; orchestra, 50.

Many of Vanemuine's best actors and directors work in factories or are budding scientists and university students. It has three schools: drama, ballet, and vocal. Ird, Vanemuine's director since 1941, also heads the drama school. Vanemuine, of course, has its own national tradition and unique form, but in its own way each Republic has its Vanemuine.

Latvia's Cultural Renaissance

I visited Riga in July 1972. A campaign on the "Baltic problem" was moving into high gear in the United States as part of our official annual observance of "Captive Nations Day." The campaign likewise seemed to be timed with the world-wide celebration of the 50th anniversary of the establishment of the Union of Soviet Socialist Republics. Our press was then making the most of the self-immolation of a mentally disturbed Lithuanian youth and the hooligan actions of a group of anti-Soviet youth. Disregarded, of course, was the fact that Lithuania increased the volume of its production 50 times over that of 1940, when it joined the Soviet Union, as did Estonia and Latvia. One can cite statistics on the cultural renaissance in the Baltic countries but two examples will better serve the point.

I visited the Palace of Culture of Riga's VEF plant, which is especially noted for its high-quality transistor radio. VEF can be compared to our RCA or Philco in terms of size. But try to imagine RCA or Philco building a Palace of Culture like this for its workers. The VEF "club house," an imposing structure with Grecian columns has a full-time staff of 44 to service 44 groups, comprising 1,800 participants, ranging from children to pensioners. The palace has two theaters, one Lettish, the other Russian. Both have at their disposal a 900-seat theater and a modern revolving stage. There is a people's chorus of 105, conducted by a prominent musician from the Riga Conservatory; a national folk instruments orchestra; an ensemble of 20 violins, film, radio, technical, and "inventors" groups—as well as numerous sports groups. In 1971 the ensembles gave 285 concerts, attracting audiences of 300,000. They frequently appear on Soviet TV and thus are known to millions.

The cultural renaissance is also flourishing in Latvia's countryside. I saw this at the Festival of Song and Labor in the city of Ogre, an agricultural and garment center not far from Riga. More than 25 collective farms took part in a pageant of Latvia's ancient songs and dances. In colorful costumes that meticulously recreated each particular period in history, collective farmers danced and sang their joy of labor on a huge, open-air stage in a pine-tree theater. The audience was largely the region's farmers but it included many shop workers, students, and professionals. It was a festival of all generations. None were too young nor too old to thump or twirl in the lusty Latvian folk dance.

This is how Soviet Latvia not only preserves its ancient heritage but keeps it as green as the ivy Janus crowns worn at the festival.

Turkmen Tea in Ashkabad

I spent a delightful evening in Ashkabad's attractive Opera and Ballet Theater. Hader Allamurov, the theater's director and chief conductor of its orchestra, ceremoniously poured the Turkmen tea as he related the story of his country's cultural rebirth and his own life.

They are really one. Until the Revolution, no choruses, not to speak of opera, symphony or drama, exisited in Turkmenia. Only Bakhshi, roving troubadours, preserved the ancient folksongs and poems. The Republic now has, besides the Opera and Ballet Theater, six theaters, and a symphony orchestra. The night before I left Ashkabad, a dramatization of Ernest Hemingway's *Farewell to Arms* was being performed in the Turkmen language in a packed house. From what I saw and heard at the Opera and Ballet Theater, talented artists have come into bloom. Prominent Russian writers, composers, artists, actors and musicians gave unsparingly of their time to teach them. Russian writers learned the Turkmen language to be able to translate into Russian the works of Turkmen poets, dramatists and writers.

In 1937, Allamurov was admitted to the famous Moscow Conservatory of Music from which he graduated in 1948. He has been chief conductor for 26 years and the director of the Ashkabad Opera and Ballet Theater for ten years. Allamurov drew on the rich store of Turkmen melodies to compose many songs and orchestral pieces.

The three young Nuriev brothers, all recognized composers, symbolize Turkmenia's cultural renaissance. Durdi Nuriev's melodic musical comedy deals with the conflict between the old and the new as it affects two young people in love. It was fresh and original, a skillful blend of ancient folk with contemporary themes.

A Journey to Lvov

I visited Lvov, when the trial of a handful of Ukrainian nationalists who were working with the former Nazi collaborators living abroad was big news in the U.S. press. Now the hostile newspapers made it appear it was Ukrainian culture that was being destroyed and the Ukraine itself that was being erased as a nation.

In Lvov I met with Ukrainian cultural leaders, among them Yaroslav Vitoshinsky, head of the city Soviet's cultural department. I read them clippings from our press. Vitoshinsky's father had lived in the United States and Canada before returning to his homeland and so he was more familiar with this slander. "Let me answer with facts," he stated simply, and added: "Then I'll show you the facts." But first about the city— *Lviv,* in Ukrainian. Lvov, as we call it, is the Kiev of the Western Ukraine but with a West European flavor. Sitting on the crossroads of the East and the Baltic, this ancient city (founded in 1256) absorbed the finest in the architectural art of medieval Europe but still clung to its own national character. The spirit of Ivan Franko, Ukraine's immortal poet, patriot and internationalist, hovers over the city he lived in for 40 years.

Lvov is a city of Old World and Slavic charm, with the vigor and optimistic purposefulness of Soviet cities. It is in a way the symbol of a united Ukraine. History detached Lvov and detoured the Western Ukraine from the Ukraine's main historical path. It was occupied until 1772 when, after the first partition of Poland, it was ruled by Austria. From 1919 to 1939, Lvov and the Western Ukraine were occupied by reactionary bourgeois Poland. In all these many years, Ukrainian culture and the Ukrainian language were stifled and suppressed.

In September, 1939, when Soviet troops moved into the Western Ukraine to check Nazi expansion, the Western Ukraine voted for Soviet rule and reunification with the Soviet Ukraine. In the two years of Soviet life before Nazi occupation, a veritable cultural revolution began to sweep Lvov and the Western Ukraine. On the eve of the war, there were in the Western Ukraine, 3,614 clubs, 2,169 libraries, 23 museums, and 13 theaters. Only 30 miles from the border, Lvov was overrun in ten days. Incidentally, Cardinal Josef Slipiyi, head of the Ukrainian Uniate (Catholic Church) whose charges of Soviet persecution of Ukrainian Catholics, made from his home in Vatican City are regularly featured in the (U.S.) press, helped the Nazis organize an SS division of Ukrainian nationalists. In the first days of occupation, the Nazis, aided by Ukrainian fascist nationalists, slaughtered almost the entire Jewish population and massacred thousands of Communists and those who had welcomed Soviet power, including many of the finest scientists and cultural leaders of Lvov.

Isak Pein, Peoples Artist of the Ukrainian Republic, and director-conductor of the renowned Lvov Philharmonic Orchestra, was its first conductor when it was organized in 1939. Most orchestra members were killed by the Nazi and Ukrainian fascists when the city was occupied.

Lvov region has a population of 2,500,000, of which 86 percent is Ukrainian. The city of Lvov has a population of 600,000. This would compare roughly to northern up-state New York and Buffalo, respectively. This should be borne in mind in considering the following statistics. The Lvov region has 1,600 cultural clubs, 1,800 libraries, 11 state museums, 5 scientific museums and 220 people's museums, which trace the cultural as well as the social history of towns and villages. Most impressive is the fact that Lvov Region has 20 symphony orchestras! Many of them are in the villages and on collective farms. The city is a highly regarded Soviet musical center, demonstrating the role played by Soviet cities in narrowing the cultural gap between town and country. The village and farm symphony orchestras are the fruit of concentrated effort on the part of the famed Lvov Conservatory of Music and Philharmonic Society.

In classes at the conservatory, students from villages as well as towns were being taught Russian, Ukrainian and world classics, as well as ancient Ukrainian instruments, like the *bandura,* which are now taking their proper place in the world of music. One of the Lvov Region Soviet's major concentrations is the construction of a network of village and cultural complexes. These include palaces of culture, 12 to 15 rooms for amateur groups, dance halls, libraries, outdoor auditoriums, stadiums, parks, and recreational centers. The region has 10,000 amateur groups involving 200,000 participants. The Ukraine has 26,000 clubs, 106 amateur theaters, and 150,000 amateur art circles. The vast quantity of amateurs and the intensive training they receive from the best Soviet artists *is producing a qualitative effect. It is narrowing the gap between amateur and professional.* This is true, for example, of the Ynost Ukrainian Dance Ensemble, directed by Yaroslav Ventukh. It is made up of 80 young men and women who attend technical schools. Their teachers are skilled machine workers and technicians. Their dance ensemble is an after-school activity. But watching them, we could understand why some who saw them perform in Italy had questioned their amateur status. "One of our boys had to go to a plant and work one of their machines to prove he was a student-worker," Ventukh recalled, with amusement. The Trembita Choir is known the world over as is the Verkhovina Song and Dance Ensemble.

No U.S. Steel Hours

Television is one of the most effective instruments for bringing the cultures of 100 peoples into the homes of 250 million Soviet citizens. As I became familiar with the language, I became an avid Soviet TV fan, first, because of what one does not see on Soviet TV. Absent is the world of crime and depraving sensationalism. Absent are the television commercials that plague the U.S. TV screen. The air waves under socialism are truly free. They don't belong to any Soviet equivalent of General Motors or U.S. Steel corporation. There are no U.S. Steel hours or General

Motors programs. There are no CBS, NBC or ABC corporations to cash in on every minute of TV time.

In the Soviet Union there is not only no pliant government to hand the air over to any monopoly; there are none to hand it to, in the first place. Soviet TV, like the theater and the concert hall is truly a public servant, since they are not dominated by commodity relations. Soviet TV reflects Soviet society. A day spent before a TV and the dynamic life of this society passes in review. You have a front seat at the birth of the great Nurek and Ust-Ilim hydroelectric stations and you meet the men and women who built them. You feast on a rich cultural fare. The ballets and operas produced by the famous Bolshoi Theater and presented in full are a regular TV feature. So are concerts by Emil Gilels, Svyataslav Richter and other international artists—as well as plays staged by theaters in Moscow, Leningrad and Kiev.

Thus, with all our talk of "free" air waves and the ballyhoo about the "controlled" Soviet media, one may well ask: Which is truly more democratic? The Soviet, which gives the Soviet citizen a front seat at all the nation's great cultural, social and sports events, or our "free enterprise" media which base their programs on profits?

Moscow TV has four channels (there are also four radio programs). Channel I is an all-Soviet program and is relayed to all local stations; Channel 2 is directed primarily to the central region of the USSR; Channel 3 is entirely devoted to educational and scientific programs. It is an extremely important and regular educational program that includes physics, mathematics, language, and literature. Teachers assign lessons to their students on the basis of its programs. Channel 4 is exclusively devoted to theater, symphony, poetry, films, and variety music.

About the closest thing to a regular cultural program in our country is the Public Broadcasting Service, which broadcasts good theater and cultural programs. But PBS broadcasts only a minor fraction of such programs, compared to Soviet TV. Moreover, it leads a very precarious financial existence. It is compelled to make constant financial appeals to its very limited audience. And, like every institution in our monopoly-dominated country, it is subject to the big business financial (and political) pressures—direct, as well as indirect.

One other aspect of Soviet TV distinguishes it from ours. It is truly multinational. I watched Soviet TV programs in the 14 other Republics. Their TV stations compare quite favorably with their Moscow counterpart in all modern techniques and equipment (there are 127 TV centers in the USSR). They broadcast in their own national languages and feature national films, dramatic, and musical productions. Viewers in the 15 Soviet Republics also watch the programs broadcast from Moscow on Channel I.

What TV stations are devoted to broadcasting programs for the 10,500,000 Spanish-speaking people in the United States? There are Spanish-language radio programs but these hardly compare either in quantity or quality to the national programs in the 15 Soviet Republics. It is only in recent years, as a result of the great liberation struggles of the 1960s, that one has begun to see Black people and programs on the TV screen. Most of these programs do not do justice to the rich culture produced by Black Americans. Nor are 210 million Americans in any way as familiar with the great cultural and historical contributions of Black Americans, as 250 million Soviet citizens are with the cultures and histories of the 100 peoples who make up the socialist family of nations. As for the 800,000 Native American Indians, their culture is either distorted and vilified or ignored.

The theater, ballet, opera, writers and poets of Kazakhstan, Kirghizia, Turkmenia, Azerbaidjan, Uzbekistan and Tajikistan are almost as well known in the cities and villages of the Russian Federation as they are in their own Republics. During the entire year of 1973, when the 50th anniversary of the formation of the USSR was celebrated, Soviet TV literally brought the culture of 100 peoples into the living rooms of the Soviet people. The gala programs at the Kremlin Palace of Congresses celebration, unmatched in multinational richness, were broadcast in full.

Soviet TV plays a vital role in stimulating the development of amateur dance, song, and dramatic groups. A large part of the TV cultural program is given over to them. Most of the groups are factory and farm cultural groups like the ones in the VEF radio plant in Riga and the collective farm festival in Ogre, Latvia. The cinema is not a threat to TV, as it is in our country. Both are flourishing. Thus, you see the best new and old films, without commercial breaks.

Perhaps the most distinguishing feature of Soviet TV is its working-class character. Some of my colleagues from our "free enterprise" press, may have found this boring, but for me it was a pleasure to see workers as the stars of Soviet TV. The coal miner who fulfills his planned quota, the dairymaid whose cows produce the most and best quality of milk, the machine-tool worker who discovers new methods to increase productivity—these are the most highly honored Soviet citizens on TV, as they are on the front pages of the newspapers and magazines.

I saw some excellent documentaries that had the quality of drama in their warm human portrayal of the labor and lives of workers. This was particularly the case with an unforgettable documentary on the coal miners. It was difficult to think of it as a "documentary." What unfolded before your eyes was the life history of the Soviet coal miners. Skillfully woven together were scenes tracing the incredibly difficult and heroic upward climb of the coal diggers. We saw the black pit hellholes and barracks of czarist days that made this not only the most dangerous but also the most miserable of all labor. We were there as Stakhanov dug his way to history and made his name the symbol of socialist labor. We relived the terrible day of Nazi invasion and occupation. There were the deep Donbas mines that became the tombs of thousands of martyred miners. And here were their wives, sisters, and sweethearts marching with their picks and shovels to take the place of their men who were at the front.

We rejoiced in their triumph and their reconstruction of the new and more beautiful cities (like Donetsk). And we realized these men laboring in the bowels of Mother Earth were regarded and treated as the heroes of the Soviet Union. This deep, human treatment incidentally, could well be applied to Soviet handling of news, which often suffers from a too dry presentation of the facts.

Soviet Theaters

Soviet theater plays an important role in the cultural life of the USSR. Here I confine myself to some general remarks.

As a mirror reflecting contemporary life, it focuses on the problems, especially the old that obstruct the advance toward Communist society. And as a mirror, it also reflects the Soviet heroes and heroines of our time. No theater in the world has a richer store of traditions to draw upon. The spirit of Chekhov, Ostrovsky, Tolstoy, Gorky, and the great innovators, Stanislavsky, Nemirovitch-Danchenko, Meirhold, Okhlopkov, all of whom exerted a profound influence in the United States and in world theater, hovers over the Soviet stage. Contemporary Soviet theater, contrary to cold-war myth, which portrays it as conservative, uniform and dogmatic, is vital, varied and versatile.

Americans familiar with the problems of our theater were amazed to find that most Moscow theaters were not only packed, but were constantly surrounded by eager ticket-seekers. Moreover, professional theaters, which in our country are largely confined to a few metropolitan centers and university areas, exist in practically every Soviet city and town. This is the meaning of Soviet statistics on theater: almost 600 drama and music theaters performing in 42 languages.

The Soviet cultural stream flows into the most inconspicuous mountain hamlets, isolated desert settlements as well as into the lusty towns and cities springing up in the far North and the Siberian taiga. The theater is built along with the homes for the builders of new Soviet cities. And, as repertory theater, it brings incomparably rich and varied dramatic fare to its audience. Each of Moscow's 25 dramatic theaters has a repertoire of from 8 to 30 plays. Moscow patrons are annually offered a choice of about 500 plays from world and Russian classics to contemporary plays by Soviet and foreign dramatists.

Humanism and Cinema

Moscow's International Film Festivals, held every two years under the slogan "For Humanism in Cinema, For Peace and Friendship among Nations," attract an increasing number of countries. Perhaps no cinema festival in the world draws so many young and promising film studios from African, Asian, and Latin American countries.

The Soviet film industry lives by the festival's slogan "Humanism." It is promoted by an industry encompassing 19 feature and 34 documentary and popular science studios. And it is multinational. Fifteen feature studios are in the non-Russian Soviet Republics, which produce about half the films annually made in the Soviet Union. Among the Republic studios that have established international reputations are: Kiev Film Studio, named for the Ukrainian cinema genius, Alexander Dovzhenko (its entry, *White Bird with the Black Mark, won a gold medal at the 7th Moscow Film Festival)* Georgian Film Studio (its *Soldier's Father* won second prize at Rome International Film Festival); Lithuanian Film Studio, one of the Soviet Union's youngest, which made the extremely effective film *No One Wants to Die;* and Kirghizian Film Studio, the youngest of Soviet studios, which made a number of good films based on the works of Chingiz Aitmatov, one of the outstanding contemporary Soviet writers.

Ossie Davis, the celebrated U.S. actor, playwright, film director and producer—a militant fighter for Black liberation—summed up the role played by the Soviet film, in an interview in July, 1971, at the 7th Moscow Film Festival. Davis told me: "I was extremely impressed because Soviet film makers have a completely different approach to cinema. Take the *Liberation* series (a five-part Soviet chronicle of World War II). *Liberation* is an attempt to express a national epic. Who else could conceive of doing that? Moreover, it seems to me the Soviet film is imbued with a conscious effort to apply art to everyday problems of the Soviet people. And this is particularly demonstrated in that beautiful film *By the Lake* (directed by Sergei Gerasimov). The film deals with the question of ecology, of nature versus machinery, beauty versus utility, and the right of a community to determine its own destiny. All these questions are handled with tenderness, beauty, and all the resources of dramatic and film art. One doesn't see these kinds of films in other places."

Liberation is as important to Americans as it is to the Soviet people. It portrays the terrible days when the Nazi blitzkrieg was unleashed against the Soviet Union. To millions of Americans the names of hitherto unknown Soviet towns and villages became not only familiar but precious. The Hitler blitzkrieg had rolled over the capitalist countries of Europe. Could the Soviet Union stop what then appeared to be the invincible Wehrmacht? For most U.S. military experts, it was only a question of how much time before Hitler defeated the Soviet Union. The Soviet Union's performance in the fight against fascism and the military cooperation of the USSR and the United States in the anti-Hitler coalition, seriously weakened the poisonous influence of anti-Sovietism and anticommunism and raised respect for, and interest in the Soviet Union to unprecedented heights.

This comradeship-in-arms in the fight against fascism is the powerful story and lesson presented in *Liberation*. For almost three decades this history has been largely buried in our country. The last of the Soviet Union's 20 million war-dead had hardly been laid to rest when the whitewash began. Nothing reveals the deadening effect this has had in our country more then the "objectivity" with which the U.S. press has greeted Solzhenitsyn's praise for General Vlasov, who fought with Hitler's fiendish army against the United States as well as the Soviet people. The film shows the Vlasovites in action. *Liberation* revives the memory of the great alliance which defeated fascism, the memory of the joyful meeting of Soviet and U.S. troops on the Elbe. It is, therefore, a powerful force for extending normal relations between our two countries and for promoting detente and peaceful coexistence.

The Soviet camera has also focused its penetrating lens on the surging national liberation movement. A good example of this is *Black Sun*, based on the story of Patrice Lumumba's martyrdom. But Americans, especially Black Americans, will also recognize in *Black Sun* the story of the martyrdom of Dr. Martin Luther King, Jr., and Malcom X, the murder of Black Panther activists and the persecution of Angela Davis. It is a Soviet-African film about new Africa. The Soviet author of the script and director of the film Aleksei Speshnev, enlisted the assistance of three African countries. Most of the leading roles are played by African actors, with supporting roles played by students of Patrice Lumumba (Friendship) University in Moscow and by U.S. Blacks and their Soviet offspring living in the Soviet Union.

Another Soviet film *That Sweet Word, Liberty*, portraying the heroism and resourcefulness of Latin America's fighters for liberation from U.S. imperialism and its gorilla juntas, won a gold prize at the 8th Moscow Film Festival. It was directed by Vitautus Zalakevisious of Soviet Lithuania, one of the most imaginative directors of the stage as well as screen. His unique combination of realism and symbolism is revealed in that excellent film *No One Wants to Die*.

Soviet cinema was prompt in creating a sharply indicting documentary film on Chile. It was produced and directed by Roman Karmen, one of the geniuses of the Soviet documentary film (who saw fascism first-hand in Spain), in conjunction with a group of Chilean students at Moscow's cinema studio institute.

The Soviet screen also deals with the complex human problems that are involved in molding Communist man and woman. A good example of this is *Let's Live Till Monday* (Gorky Central Studio for Children and Teenage Films), the Soviet feature film entry in the 6th Moscow Film Festival.

The story, direction (it was directed by Stanislav Rostotsky), and acting are as honest as the film's chief character Ilya, a teacher in a Soviet secondary school, played by Vyacheslov Tikhonov. The camera conveyed this quality with such simplicity and tenderness that the audience burst into enthusiastic applause at the conclusion of the film. Its theme is the search and struggle for understanding and integrity in a Soviet classroom. It is a struggle that takes place within as well as between generations, within the ranks of teachers and students, as well as between them, and goes beyond school walls. No society, even the most advanced in the world, is immune from these struggles. Because of the film's utter honesty, we get an understanding picture of how that universal struggle takes shape in a socialist society in one of its most basic spheres, the school. The film, while describing the rigidity and insensitivity and even the backward concepts still existing among some Soviet teachers, shows the way this particular conflict takes place in the USSR. Anyone familiar with the crisis in our own schools will recognize the basic difference. *Up the Down Staircase,* the U.S. film entry in the 5th International Festival in Moscow in 1967, gave the Soviet audience a glimpse of this kind of crisis. The problem posed by the Soviet film is how to harmonize the functions of those who teach and those who learn, how to give full rein to the undisciplined but creative qualities of youth, while training them in the necessary disciplines demanded by study and life itself. The problem is how to impart to a generation which itself did not experience the Revolution, and the immortal lessons of that experience.

What gives this picture its optimistic spirit is that the society surrounding the school is a friend, not a foe, to the individual in the struggle for honesty and understanding. Moreover, socialist society not only leads the struggle but provides the material basis to make it victorious. Those who are rigid and timid represent not a system but the people in the system who lag behind the needs of a new and dynamically developing life.

Soviet cinema portrays Soviet men and women in the making, thus creating a powerful image that inspires the Soviet people. It does this by recreating the lives of the heroes and heroines of the Revolution, of the Civil War, intervention, and the Great Patriotic War, of the building of socialism, and now of the construction of Communist society. But there are weaknesses.

At the 24th Congress of the CPSU, the report of Leonid Brezhnev stated: "It cannot be said that all is well in the realm of artistic creative work, particularly as regards quality. We are still getting quite a few works that are shallow in content and inexpressive in form. We all have the right to expect workers in art to be more demanding of themselves and their colleagues."

Some of the Soviet films I saw could well have been made in Hollywood—in fact, they were poor imitations. But after the 24th Congress, there was a noticeable improvement in the quality of theme, content and form. There has been a decided improvement in dealing with the lives and problems of workers of the factory and field. Weaknesses are far overshadowed by the uplifting humanism of the Soviet film, its role as the educator of the Soviet people in the spirit of collectivity.

Sergei Eisenstein, the genius who revolutionized world cinema, best summed up the relationship between the individual and socialist society. When Eisenstein was asked to evaluate the impact of the October Revolution on him, he replied, " 'I' turned into 'we' and in this 'we' there was a place for 'me'". This can be said by millions of Soviet creative workers in all spheres of culture. Millions of "me's" both as professional and amateur artists, have found a place in a culture that stresses "we."

Culture—Not a Commodity

In the Soviet Union culture is regarded as *a social necessity which the government, the enterprises, the trade unions, collective and state farms, and all mass organizations, are duty-bound to provide and make accessible to the people.* It is not treated as a *commodity* but as a normal public service.

During the historic 1972 Moscow Summit Meeting, May 23rd, the late Ekaterina Furtseva, then Minister of Culture of the USSR, held a press conference to acquaint more than 200 U.S. newsmen with the status of Soviet culture. Assembled with Furtseva was a muster of who's who in the field of Soviet culture. She traced the unprecedented cultural revolution that transformed a land of mass illiteracy into a country that, according to UNESCO, *holds first place in the world in respect to theater, cinema, concert, museum, and library attendance.* The figures speak for themselves: more than 238 million persons annually attend theater and concert performances; more than 100 million frequent museums; 4,000 million, the cinema; *and about three-fourths of the population*—180 million—are library cardholders. As most newsmen gathered at the press conference knew well, our statistics hardly match these. To cite just one comparison: according to a 1967 Ford Foundation study, only 3.5 percent of the people in the United States have ever attended a live professional show.

The Soviet Union, Furtseva pointed out, had more than 134,000 clubhouses and palaces of culture; 1,144 museums, 360,000 libraries with more than three billion books and magazines; 547 drama and music theaters performing in 42 languages in 25 theaters in Uzbekistan, 8 in Moldavia, 24 in Kazakhstan, 10 in Tajikistan, 6 in Kirghizia and 6 in Turkmenia—all republics which, before the Revolution, had no national theatrical art or theaters proper (and some even had no written alphabets). In the Soviet Union, 23 million people—almost one-tenth of the population—go in for amateur activities (with facilities at their disposal such as those I have described in Riga and Lvov). The Soviet Union has 29 conservatories and art institutes, 11 institutes training highly qualified painters, 12 theater institutes, 16 choreographic schools, and 11 institutes of culture. And Furtseva pointed out it is all "free and students receive stipends." She outlined the setup which has made Soviet musicians and artists world-famous. It extends from primary to higher school and embraces 7,000 music and art schools and 445 secondary schools as well as 63 higher specialized educational establishments of culture and the arts.

These were the statistics of a cultural revolution that has never lost its momentum, that has been steadily gathering steam. The Soviet Union places high standards for admission to its institutes, universities and conservatories. And they are, indeed, demanding. But the demands are talent, ability, and hard work; and *never based on utility or obligation to pay*. What is more, adequate and constantly expanding channels are provided not only for the very talented but for the millions who want to express their talents, whether on a professional or amateur level. Free evening music schools are available to all, irrespective of age. If Furtseva's statistics had any meaning, it was that they expressed the real meaning of those much-abused words—cultural revolution.

The Soviet Audience

Culture in the USSR goes with everything and this includes political meetings. The agenda is usually one part politics and two parts culture. The mass character of Soviet cultural life has produced world-renowned artists on an unprecedented scale. It has also brought into being the world's most culturally advanced audience.

The people who pack Soviet concert halls and theaters are enthusiasts—critics—on a mass scale. This audience impresses visiting artists from all countries. They well know the *difference* between the composition of audiences in the Soviet Union and in the countries of "free enterprise." The 238 million who annually attend theater and concert performances in the Soviet Union constitute not only the world's largest but its most socially representative audience. In the United States, because of the commodity character of culture, it is largely an audience of middle class "concert and theater goers," students, and a sprinkling of workers.

My most impressive and most intimate acquaintance with the members of the Bolshoi Theater Orchestra was when I heard them perform at the Moscow locomotive repair plant (Sortirovichnaya) on April 12, 1969, on the occasion of the 50th anniversary of the Communist *subbotnik*. But I found this to be a normal and natural relationship everywhere I went. In Uzbekistan, during the cotton harvest, we couldn't meet any artists or attend any concerts—all were busy entertaining the mass army of collective farmers and volunteer cotton pickers. The miners of Donbas maintain regular contact with poets, actors, singers, and dancers. Moscow's popular Sovremenik Theater spent several days with the auto workers of Togliatti, getting intimately acquainted with their work and their life, before it started rehearsing "Tomorrow's Weather," a play about auto workers. The ballet, music, drama, and art studios of the clubhouses are the mass auxiliary force that augments the vast cultural network Furtseva described. They constitute an immense and inexhaustible reservoir of talent for the famous Soviet ballet, for opera, and dramatic theaters.

It is in the varied cultural activities of these clubhouses that a good deal of Soviet night-life takes place. Many of my colleagues from our bourgeois press found Moscow night-life dull. What they regarded as "night-life" largely consisted of night clubs, bars that are open into the early hours. Moscow and Soviet cities can't compete with us in that respect. Soviet cities could use more night spots. Basically, however, it is not a question of the "night-life" of a city, but its cultural character. Here the Soviet and U.S. cities do differ as night from day. There is another aspect to the cultural night-life of our cities. Fear has considerably affected the utilization of the available cultural facilities. Theater critic, Walter Kerr, in an article entitled "Can Broadway Move?" in the *New York Times Magazine*, June 3, 1973 points to the catastrophic effect which the climate of fear that envelops New York has had on attendance at Broadway theaters. The Times Square theater district, the heart of New York, Kerr notes with alarm "has grown dangerous. All those hookers, all those porno houses and massage parlors, all those junkies needing cash." Kerr recognizes that it is not just the Broadway area which has become "dangerous" when he adds: "Those who would defend midtown suggest that people aren't so much afraid of being robbed on 46th St. as they are afraid of going home to 76th or 94th St. afterwards. They don't want to go out at night in New York City *at all*." And Kerr points out that a similar situation exists in respect to Chicago and "other central cities." That he doesn't take his solution very seriously is indicated in his recognition that Broadway needs a "magic wand and $400 million" to move to a "vital center."

Nothing more forcefully points up the decay of New York City and the crisis of our cities than what has happened to Broadway and Times Square, the "vital square." It is a decay in the midst of "vital centers," plush apartment houses that are guarded like medieval castles with armed doormen and closed circuit television replacing moat bridges, breastplates, and halberds. It is a decay in the very midst of swanky restaurants and nightclubs and luxurious stores. Our climate of fear and the cultural poverty of our cities are closely related, just as the flourishing cultural life and the absence of fear parallel each other in Soviet cities. The very idea of moving to a safe "vital center," let alone the idea of spending "$400 million" in search of a haven of security is incomprehensible.

14 / CITIES WITHOUT FEAR

When we came to live in Moscow I was impressed that we could walk Moscow's streets day or night without fear. During our first months we rediscovered the simple pleasure of a brisk walk before retiring or of returning home late from an evening out without casting apprehensive backward glances or hastening our pace at the sound of footsteps behind us. I recall my first instinctive tenseness when late one night a Moscow youth approached me on the street for a cigarette. My first inclination was to ignore the request and rush past him. The young man regarded my hesitation with puzzlement and I felt a silent rebuke. When I lit up his cigarette, the *spacibo, dedushka* (thank you, grandfather) brought with it not only relief but embarrassment (it also reminded me of my age, incidentally).

As we walked along Leningradsky Prospekt one day with Alla Borisovna, we came upon a baby carriage outside a bakery—the infant in it swaddled tightly in Russian fashion, sleeping soundly. What made us stop and alarmed my wife Gail was that it was completely unattended. Alla hardly seemed to be concerned. She interpreted our lingering around the carriage as the normal love for a baby and after an affectionate peek or two continued on her way. But we still did not move. Puzzled, Alla returned and asked us if something were wrong. "Where is the mother?" Gail asked. "Probably in the bakery," Alla replied matter-of-factly. "But who is taking care of the baby?" Gail pressed her. Alla looked at us with bewilderment. "But why does someone have to take care of the baby?" she asked. As she spoke, women passing by paused momentarily to peek into the carriage and continued on their way. We have since learned to understand and fully appreciate Alla's attitude. It would never enter the minds of most Soviet mothers, to think that anyone could dream of harming their babies.

We also rediscovered the pleasure of sitting on a park bench to enjoy the quiet beauty of a summer night. At first we gazed apprehensively at the approaching dusk; instinctively we rose and prepared to leave. But none of those who were occupying neighboring benches made the slightest move. In the wooded lanes we could discern the fleeting shadows of casual strollers. We looked at each other and laughed. Since then we have enjoyed Moscow's numerous and lively parks in all seasons as well as at all hours. In the crisp, fresh Russian winter days and evenings, they are full of skiers, skaters, and sleigh-riders.

Major Vladimir Shuvalov told me that Izmailov Park, the largest city park in Europe and formerly the hunting preserves of the czars, has the smallest police detachment in his district. He never had to deal with mugging in his district. His militia, of course, had on occasion dealt with fights between hotheaded or intoxicated Soviet citizens. But muggers? Never.

Before coming to Moscow, we had an experience that makes up the frightening statistics the entire world is familiar with today. But this time it was not a statistic, it was our son.

Our son, Joe, aged 18 at the time, and our two nephews were walking in the Times Square district. The time was 9 o'clock in the evening. Without provocation, they were attacked by a gang of teenage hoodlums. My son was knocked unconscious; my nephews hailed a passing car and asked for help to rush my son to a nearby hospital. The two officers, who hardly appeared concerned, replied brusquely that this was a daily occurrence and they could scarcely involve themselves in such matters. It was only hours later, after our son was brought home in a dazed condition, that we could rush him to a hospital.

We have not been the only Americans upon whom Moscow's normal streets produced this effect. Cyrus Eaton, the well-known U.S. industrialist, told the *Moscow News*, English-language Soviet newspaper, that what particularly impressed him was that "one can go out on the streets of Moscow any hour of the day with perfect safety." This has been the sentiment of many visiting Americans we met who welcome Moscow's peaceful streets as if they had just come from a battlefield. "Battlefield" about describes the atmosphere of our city streets. The *New York Times* characterized it as *"coexistence with fear."*

Coexistence with fear has become even more grim. The Gallup Poll (*International Herald Tribune*, January 15, 1973), which made a survey of the nation's cities reported: *"One out of three* living in densely populated center-city areas of the nation has been mugged or robbed or suffered property loss *during the last 12 months."* It noted "21 percent of the adults had been victims of *one or more* of the crimes surveyed." The Gallup Poll also notes, "while the figures are lower for less urbanized areas, they are still frightening." The *U.S. News and World Report*, May 25, 1970, noted that during the period 1960-68, crime outstripped population growth by "11 to 1."

The very opposite is the picture in the Soviet Union. Nikolai Shcholokov, Minister of Internal Affairs of the USSR, noted: "The increase in the country's population (nearly 100 million since 1913) did not produce a corresponding increase in the number of crimes. Quite the contrary, the level has dropped considerably." Shcholokov, in an article in *Pravda*, November 17, 1973, noted that there was a 4.6 percent decrease in more dangerous crimes in the Soviet Union from 1972. He pointed out that there are thousands of populated places and enterprises where "for a long time there have been no serious violations of the public order."

The Crime Behind "Crime in the Streets"

In the United States, the most racist and reactionary forces are attempting to distort the crime problem into a race issue. They are portraying crime as *"black crime."* They well know it is the hugely disproportionate share of poverty and governmental neglect that are responsible for the disproportionate share of crime affecting the Black ghettos. The *New York Times Encyclopedic Almanac*, 1970 notes, "Poverty remains a dominant characteristic (sic) of nonwhite people—41 percent are poor in contrast to only 12 percent of the white." A presidential commission, headed by Dr. Milton S. Eisenhower, brother of the former President Eisenhower, which was formed to investigate violence in the United States after the assassination of Senator Robert Kennedy, flatly stated in its report November, 1969: "The correlation is not one of race with crime . . . the correlation is poverty with crime." And it pointed out, "more than 5 million families, one-sixth of the nation's urban population were inhabitants of overcrowded, dirty, disease-ridden slums" (the overwhelming majority being Black, Puerto Rican and Chicano). Racists and reactionaries not only portray crime as "Black crime" but as "Black crime against whites." It is on this false premise that an increasingly menacing vigilante spirit is being whipped up among fear-ridden whites.

Yet, the very contrary is the real situation. It is Blacks who are by far the greatest victims of the most vicious crimes and this includes crimes committed by other Blacks. This is stressed by the *International Herald Tribune*, August 5, 1973, which noted: "A Black resident of New York City is *eight times more likely* to be murdered than a white resident of the city, a computer analysis of police records indicates. A second finding of the study is that in slightly *more than four out of five* New York homicides, the killer and victim are of the same race." Blacks are the chief victims of the most brutal crimes, for the same reason that they are the chief sufferers from all of capitalist society's social ills. The same issue of the *International Herald Tribune* quotes Dr. Alvin F. Poussaint, a Black psychiatrist, as pointing out that "the economic and social frustration of a sharply segregated society and the pressures of poverty might lead to violent acts against *the first available target*." Black Americans are the "first available targets" of crime, as they are the first available targets of unemployment, disease, police brutality, drug addiction, discrimination, poor housing, second-class schools and all the "blessings" of our racist U.S. society.

The aims of the racists and reactionaries are: to exploit fears and prejudices by playing on the desperate frustrations of millions of American urban dwellers who can no longer *coexist with fear*; to divert the exploding mass dissatisfaction with a social system and a government that has led the American people to have this desperate state of affairs, into racist reactionary channels, into a struggle of white against Black.

That is why it is so important to understand the reasons for the stark *contrast* between our cities of fear and Soviet cities without fear. Soviet cities are cities without fear because they are cities without landlords, without crises, without doctor bills; cities where polluters can't pollute; cities of culture; cities where 100 peoples daily live in brotherhood; cities without financial crises and back-breaking tax loads on the people. They are cities in a nonpredatory society, a society without exploitation, without slums, without ghettos, without Murder Inc. and crime syndicates, without drug pushers, without rackets and payoffs, without incessant glorification of violence, without public promotion of pornography.

And Without Police Repression

The Soviet militia would be the last to claim that the basis of the far more peaceful condition of Soviet cities rests primarily on their work. On the contrary, the character of the Soviet militia, which is a true people's police, is based on the kind of society that gave birth to it and brought it up. Let me illustrate what I mean by citing one experience. During my tour of Moscow's militia facilities and activities, I spent a day in one of its precincts in the Frunze district. The district is in the center of Moscow. It embraces a population of 210,000 and includes 420 enterprises, numerous restaurants, stores, and hotels. During my day in the precinct, I kept up a running discussion with Colonel Aleksei Nozdryakov, the deputy head of the district. Occasionally the phone rang and a citizen's complaint was noted and acted upon. Phone calls also came in regularly from militiamen making their reports from their beats. Once or twice a citizen came in to complain against a noisy neighbor or a drunken one. I remarked to Nozdryakov that this was probably an unusually quiet day. He asked whether our police stations were not also quiet during the day. I replied dryly: "Not this quiet." "Well," Nozdryakov responded, "how can we be busy? Everyone's at work now." He didn't know it but he was hitting the nail on the head. Neither in Moscow nor in any of the many Soviet cities I visited have I come across the sight of unemployed youth standing on street corners or aimlessly walking the streets, their eyes smoldering with resentment against the upper-class affluence flaunted before them. Article 118 of the Constitution of the Union of Soviet Socialist Republics states: "Citizens of the USSR have the *right to work*, that is, the *right to guaranteed employment* and payment for their work in accordance with its quantity and quality."

There are, of course, some who manage to avoid that right, to shirk work. It is not easy to do this in a society based on the concept that everyone (unless physically unable) must work. It is from among these shirkers of labor who try to live a parasitic life in a workers' society that a good deal of the still existing social misbehavior and crime comes. There wasn't a single street killing in the Frunze district in 1969 and only one murder which took place at home and was the result of a violent quarrel between two youths who had been drinking heavily.

I asked Nozdryakov how many hold-ups of banks, stores, restaurants, and other places of business occurred in his area last year. He replied:

"I've worked in the Frunze District 15 years, I can't remember a single case of a hold-up of a bank, store, factory, restaurant or enterprise!" I asked him whether there were cases of stick-ups or murders of taxi drivers such as are quite common in our great cities. He never had any such cases in his district. In the more than five years we lived in Moscow, I never once witnessed or heard of any such crimes. Only an insignificant part of the crimes in his district, Nozdryakov told me, were committed by those 18 years of age or less. Nor had Nozdryakov come across any group muggings. On rare occasions, there are stick-ups in isolated areas on the outskirts of the city. The weapons are usually a penknife or a household knife. The possession of guns and dangerous weapons is unlawful. The law is strictly enforced, not only by the militia but by the citizens.

By contrast, here is the crime picture in an area in New York that is similar in size and population to Moscow's Frunze district, as portrayed by the *U.S. News and World Report,* May 25, 1970: "In just one month of this year, in one New York City police precinct, which covers an area measuring one mile by one mile, more than 1,000 major crimes were reported—homicides, rapes, assault, robberies, burglaries, larcenies and auto thefts." Contrast this with New York City's 1972 crime statistics as presented by the then Police Commissioner Patrick V. Murphy. According-ing to the *International Herald Tribune*, March 8, 1973, Murphy said, "that the city had 3,271 rapes last year, an increase of 35.4 percent; 37,130 aggravated assaults, an increase of 9.6 percent." New York, in 1972, also had 1,691 murders, an increase of 9.6 percent.

In the Soviet Union, organized and professional crime have been eliminated, but not without a struggle. Soviet films honestly depict the serious crime problem they had to contend with. It would be utopian to expect all crime, bred by centuries of unjust and inhuman conditions of past exploiting social systems to be eliminated under socialism. Pick-pocketing occurs. We witnessed and experienced petty thefts. Shoplift-ing, though not on a large scale, also occurs. And assaults and even killings in the heat of passion and largely under the influence of alcohol, still take place. On occasion, citizens are also terrorized by psychotic killers.

From the point of view of Soviet society, these still constitute and are regarded as serious social problems. Soviet society does not judge itself by comparing its life to that of a decaying social system such as ours. It has standards based on its far higher moral and social criteria. The question is not how or when the Soviet Union will reach its goal of complete eradication of crime, but *how have Soviet cities become cities without fear*?

Soviet Experience Explodes Some Pet Theories

Soviet experience demonstrates that crime is not primarily a police problem calling for an ever expanding and tougher police force. The dead end such a solution brings was pointed out by the *New York Times*, June 3, 1969, when it noted: "It was estimated, for example, that it would cost *$25 billion a year*—a third of the total budget of the Defense Department—to have one patrolman around the clock on each of the city's four-sided blocks." But the *Times* stresses even this would not solve New York's problem. "And even if this were possible, policemen say it would not stop crime since *more than half of it is committed in areas that they do not patrol—homes, restaurants, hallways and elevators*."

One of the pet theories circulating in the United States attributes growing crime to rapid industrialization, migration from rural areas to urban centers and the rapid expansion of cities. This is exploded by Soviet experience. No country in history ever achieved such a rapid industrialization as the Soviet Union, which, in the brief period of half a century, was transformed from one of the most backward, overwhelmingly agricultural countries to one second only to the United States in industrialization. No cities in the world have grown as rapidly as those of the Soviet Union in the past half-century.

Today the Soviet Union has more large cities than any other country. The Soviet Union, of course, faced more serious crime problems in certain periods. Shcholokov, the Minister of Internal Affairs, states: "Of course, it wasn't plain sailing all the time. Take the mid 1940s—there was a certain growth of crime in the country then—the aftermath of the war with all its destruction, family tragedies and material hardships. Or take the relative upswing in child delinquency caused by the so-called population explosion in the postwar years." It was an "explosion" that took place under conditions of unprecedented destruction and social disruption. But Soviet experience shatters the theory linking crime to rapid industrialization, migration and urbanization.

Dr. Igor Karpets, a professor, Doctor of Law and a member of the Collegium of the Soviet Ministry of Interior, and V. Kudryavtsev, Doctor of Law, noted in an article in *Pravda,* February 9, 1972: "In reality, socialism provides such social conditions for human life under which technological and scientific progress play a positive part in the education of discipline, in strengthening law and order and citizens' morality and consequently ultimately promotes the reduction of the number of antisocial phenomena. Thus, the past decades of vigorous development in the USSR were marked by a spiritual growth of the Soviet people, by their growing consciousness, by the strengthening of society's morality. No wonder the number of immoral acts in that period decreased in the country and the number of persons sentenced for crime fell by more than 50 percent. Over the past 50 years, Moscow has become one of the largest cities in the world. Its population more than doubled. Yet the number of those convicted for crimes has dwindled. For the same population, the number of robberies in the city has decreased to a third of the former level and that of swindling by almost 95 percent."

Our "Heritage" of Fear and Repression

Frankly, it took me a while before the full realization that Soviet police were really servants and protectors of the people sunk in, even though I knew they were products of a new and most humane social system. And I knew many readers would find it hard to believe. It is quite understandable. The words that characterize our police, particularly for Black, Puerto Rican, Chicano, Asian and Native American Indian minorities, are *fear and resentment*. During the Great Depression of the 1930s, when as New York City organizer of the Unemployed Councils and WPA workers, I participated in daily eviction and relief bureau struggles, I learned another word that went with police: *brutality*. They were the overseers of the evictions of unemployed families and mercilessly clubbed those who protested this inhumanity and tried to return the pitiful belongings of the unemployed to their homes. No one, of course, knows our police better than those who are confined to the Black, Puerto Rican and Chicano ghettos, and barrios, for most of whom the depression of the 1930s never really ended. U.S. city police are also rife with corruption.

In 1972, Dr. Jerome H. Jaffe, head of the Federal Special Action Offices for Drug Abuse Prevention, estimated the nation's heroin addicts, users and ex-addicts to be between 500,000 and 600,000. It has long been an open secret that supplying this huge army of addicts was made possible only by police cooperation and protection from the very *top*. Such corruption contributes to the rise in the crime rate. The tens of thousands of addicts are driven to commit the most desperate crimes to maintain their habit, which costs a minimum of $25 to $40 a day. (The price mounts with inflation.) It is they who constitute a huge part of the muggers and housebreakers (one out of three arrested for lawbreaking is a drug addict). But even more menacing is the racist and ultrareactionary character of many of our police departments. This is shown in the off- and on-duty wanton killings of Black youth. Such killings have triggered many of the outbursts in the ghettos in recent years. The ultrareactionary John Birch Society has found our police departments fertile ground for recruitment. One of the most menacing developments in the United States in recent years is the active entrance of police on the political scene. Utilizing their strategic positions, they have become a powerful and dangerous force for reaction. Thus, with such experiences with "free-enterprise" police, many readers unacquainted with socialist society and deluged by half a century of propaganda on the "repressive" role of socialist police and the Soviet "police state," may approach this question with some reservations and skepticism. My observations are based not only on daily living experiences but a three-week intensive study of the Moscow militia in 1970.

Soviet Militia—a People's Police

In Moscow—as well as everywhere in the Soviet Union—"people's power" and "community control"—are living realities. You can see it daily in the mutual respect between citizen and militia. You see it in the salute with which the militiaman greets you whether you are seeking information or being summoned for an infraction of a law. Rudeness toward, let alone abuse of, citizens, is considered intolerable, and the militiaman who violates that cardinal rule has, indeed, a short future. There are, of course rude militiamen but they are rare. And what goes for rudeness in the Soviet Union would barely cause a ripple among our long-abused citizens. I was hardly in Moscow a week when I had a run-in with a militiaman. I was as yet unfamiliar with Moscow's underpasses, which make passage across its busy thoroughfares secure, so I made a typical New Yorker's dash across Leningradsky Prospekt. I was hailed by a militiaman's sharp whistle. The militiaman saluted me as I approached him, then proceeded to scold me for risking my life. I felt properly abashed—especially after that unexpected salute—and lamely explained that I was a foreigner and unaccustomed to Moscow's traffic rules. This only heightened his concern. "And suppose something happened to you, what then would we do?" he asked me more in plaint than anger. I must confess since then I get a particular kick out of watching the reaction of visiting Americans—familiar with the brusque ways of our "finest"—to their first contact with Moscow militia.

I recall the impression such an experience made on Monsignor Charles Rice, when he visited Moscow in the summer of 1972. The Monsignor, a kind, gentle soul, requested me to aid him in locating the Roman Catholic Church in Moscow, where he planned to attend mass. I knew the general direction but not its specific location. So, when we reached Dzerzhinsky Square, I hailed the militiaman who was some distance away, in the center of the square directing the busy traffic. I must say the Monsignor seemed to regard my efforts as somewhat presumptuous and perhaps futile. What New York or Pittsburgh policeman (the Monsignor is from the Smoky City) would respond in a similar situation? The militiaman had acknowledged my appeal, waited a moment until he got traffic under way, then walked over and saluted us. He listened to my request and proceeded to explain the church's location. The Monsignor was astonished.

I got to know some militiamen personally during my tour of the Moscow militia. Lt. Col. Evgeny Kretchet, who served as my guide, typifies them. Kretchet just didn't fit in with the kind of police I was accustomed to. For one thing—no one, but no one—was in the slightest degree afraid of him. Nor did this kind-looking man seek—in the many little ways our own police are so familiar with—to inspire such feelings. On the contrary, no one would be more upset than Kretchet if he "succeeded."

I've seen many run-ins between Muscovites and their militia. I did not come across one case which reflected police brutality or the overbearing authority so common in the United States. I saw nothing of our instinctive fear upon coming in contact with the "arm of the law." I've seen militiamen patiently taking the kind of verbal abuse from intoxicated Soviet citizens that would have resulted in quite a roughing up by our "finest." The use of force by the militia is strictly limited. They carry no clubs. Those who direct traffic employ a lightweight baton, which is never used as a weapon. Some years ago, clubs were issued to militiamen but practice showed they were unnecessary. Under no circumstances are militiaman permitted to beat a prisoner, even if he is resisting arrest. Militiamen do carry small pistols but they are largely for purposes of warning in cases of danger. A militiamen may use his gun only when he is confronted with armed attack and the lives of other citizens are also endangered, and only after he has exhausted all other means of subduing a criminal. Even under these circumstances, he must first fire a warning shot in the air. Even after this fails to eliminate the danger, the militiaman must not shoot to kill. He can shoot only to wound in the leg or arm. *And under no circumstance—even if facing personal danger from an armed adversary, may a militiaman use his gun against anyone under 16, or a woman.*

Moscow's top militia officers told me that there has not been a single case of a police slaying either a youth or a woman and no slaying of any citizen since 1961. Any violation of the strict orders on the limitation of the use of force is severely punished and the citizen is given the benefit of the doubt if any questions arise.

The Soviet and Moscow militia had their casualties. They were casualties that reflected the struggle in the transition from the old czarist past to the new socialist society. Most of the casualties were inflicted during 1918-21, when the young militia was fighting savage battles against bandit gangs, the remnants of the criminal elements left by czarism and capitalism. Another sizable number fell in the fight against armed kulak bands during the early 1930s. But of course by far the bulk of the casualties among militiamen were inflicted in the Great Patriotic War against fascism. The Moscow militia (and the Soviet militia as a whole) demonstrated its character as a people's fighting force. It played a special role in organizing heroic partisan bands. More than half of its members fought in the front lines. The Moscow militia was awarded the high Order of the Red Banner, November 2, 1944, for bravery. And when they went to the front, their wives, sisters and sweethearts—about 10,000 of them, took their places.

I asked Moscow militia leaders: With all these restraints on your militiaman, how does he bring in his man? "Our citizens help him, if necessary," was the answer. Ordinarily resistance to arrest is rare (unless it involves a dangerous criminal). The culprit not only knows he has to contend with his fellow citizens, but is aware of the scorn that will greet him.

Soviet citizens find it hard to understand the passivity, indifference, and fear of Americans who witness criminal attacks on their neighbors.

I have, of course, come across Soviet people who are also indifferent to the problems and troubles of their fellow citizens. But they are so rare, they stand out sharply. The dominant characteristic of the Soviet people, as I have observed, is their *involvement and concern for each other*. It comes from the collectivity that is the characteristic feature of Soviet society. It is nourished by their relationship with a police that is *under* rather than *over* the people. That is why it is natural for them to assist and cooperate with their militia in the apprehension of those who break the law. Our people, especially those living in the Black, Puerto Rican and Chicano ghettos, are reluctant to cooperate with our police because they know them as killers and clubbers of strikers, militant Black liberation fighters and fighers for peace. They know the widespread corruption that links crime syndicates with our police departments.

The People's Character of the Militia

To understand the people's character of the Soviet militia, one must know something of its origin. This was graphically depicted to me in the Museum of the Moscow Militia in the central headquarters. My guide was Col. Dmitri Kiselov, who lived through and helped make much of that history.

I stopped before a picture of a ragged group of determined workers clutching rifles. It was a picture of a new kind of police, the world's first worker's militia, which was formed in 1917. One of the first acts of the October Revolution (which drew lessons from the Paris Commune of 1871) was the destruction of the old, oppressive, corrupt czarist and capitalist apparatus and particularly one of its pillars, the brutal police force.

Another picture—it was a facsimile of Lenin's first address to this new kind of a police force where Lenin called on them to "set examples in honesty, politeness, socialist legality," from top to bottom. "Only then will the citizen respect the militia," and submit to its directives, he said. These have been the guidelines of the militia. Revolutionary history marched in review before me. Here were the organized militia detachments going off to fight the numerous counterrevolutionary criminal bands, including those which committed their crimes under the banner of anarchist and ultra-Leftist slogans of those days. Such bandit groups, capitalizing on the chaos and disruption wrought by the bloody civil war and imperialist intervention, constituted a serious menace to the new socialist Republic. The militia played an important heroic role in wiping out this threat to socialist law and order. Many prominent Soviet citizens served in the militia, among them Aleksander Alekhine, the famous chess master, and the novelist Ilya Ilf (of the team, Ilf and Petrov).

The people's character of the militia is revealed in how they are recruited; how they are educated and trained; in their class ties with workers in plants, as well as with the community; and in their systematic accounting to the people.

A large part of the militia is recruited right out of the factories; another big section comes from demobilized army men. The recruiting in the plants demonstrates the concern with the *quality* of future militiamen. Applicants are discussed with their shopmates. The new militiamen often return to their factories and discuss their work with former shop workers. Prospective militiamen must be advanced workers who are respected by their fellow workers for the quality of their work as well as their conduct. They must have good records of labor discipline and, of course, of social behavior.

Not only must they be recommended by the shop, but the recommendations must be signed by the Communist Party, Komsomol and trade union secretaries and the plant administrator. The signers bear a heavy responsibility. If a militiaman is found to be unqualified or commits a serious violation, those who recommended him are held to account.

I visited the Lenin reading, study and meeting room of the 108th precinct in the Frunze district (each district has one). Militiamen come here during leisure hours to read classics and theoretical journals and to discuss latest developments on the world and national scene. Seminars and study groups are conducted on all levels, from the elementary to the most advanced. The job of the militiaman is one of education and not just enforcement. The key word, here too, is *prevention*. Thus, militiamen, on all levels, are called on to do a great deal of educational work with individuals as well as with large groups. They hold regular discussions with workers in plants, trade unions, schools, community clubs and organizations.

The fight against crime and social misbehavior is hardly regarded as the job of the militiaman alone. All the massive means of education, culture, and communication at society's command are *constantly* thrown into this struggle. Incidentally, it should be noted that Soviet children are *denied* films and television programs which make heroes out of gangsters and glorify violence or promote pornography.

The Soviet people would hardly respect their militia if it failed to keep in step with them. Thus, study never stops and, like workers in Soviet plants, the percentage of militiamen who take night or correspondence courses or go to institutes is very high. All heads of departments are graduates of higher institutions. Ninety-seven percent of the department heads of Soviet militia have higher or specialized secondary education.

Not all education is formal. An important role as a gadfly is played by the wall newspaper. The monthly wall newspaper in the Lenin room of the 108th precinct had its share of commendations. I also noticed satirical cartoons. Under them were articles that expanded on the theme. They were directed against lagging militiamen and they hardly pulled any punches. The laggards were identified by name as well as likeness. Such criticism has been part of every Soviet enterprise and organization since the October Revolution.

Soviet "Community Control"

District inspectors of Moscow militia's microareas (they usually include a population of 5,000 to 7,000) are obligated to account for their work before public meetings every three months. A very critical or hostile attitude leads to an investigation and, if necessary, to removal.

I attended an "accounting" meeting of the representatives to the city Soviet from my district. Soviet citizens, as the meeting revealed, and as I have since frequently observed, are hardly reticent in citing their grievances. Not only at account meetings. One has but to read *Pravda* and other Soviet newspapers to get some idea of how outspoken Soviet citizens are about shortcomings. Complaints against militiamen or officers can be, and are, made to local and city Soviets. Similar "account" meetings are regularly held at factories and a notice is posted well in advance on the plant wall newspaper informing workers when the representatives of the militia will be present.

In the United States bribery is a highly organized "business" embracing every aspect of evasion and violation of the law with the biggest bite, the "pay-off," starting among the top police echelons. The pay-off is viewed by the huge crime syndicates as part of normal expenses. The pay-off makes possible (and protects) the big business character of crime in our cities. The estimated take, indeed, rivals and exceeds the combined income of some of our largest corporations.

In the light of this, it is almost ridiculous to speak of bribery in the Soviet militia in the same breath. For all the reasons already stated, there is very little bribery in the Soviet Union. Among other things, there are no crime syndicates to be protected. Bribery is treated very severely. The militiaman who commits such a crime is considered to be worse than a hooligan. The militiaman and the bribe giver are both severely punished by jail sentences, sometimes as high as eight years each. And not only the guilty militiaman but those who recommended him are held to account.

No Drug Addiction Problem

Every U.S. family knows the vast extent of drug addiction and not just through alarming statistics. Today there are few U.S. families that can feel they are "immune" to the threat. There are some cases of drug addiction in the USSR, particularly in cases where such practices once had a hold. But it is on such a minor scale that it can hardly be described as a "drug problem." More of a threat is the "importation" of the problem. Soviet militia, well aware of the extent of drug addiction in capitalist countries, are alert against such "imports." This kind of "free exchange" between the two world systems will not be permitted.

The Problems of Hooliganism

I don't want to minimize the extent and character of hooliganism in the Soviet Union. It constitutes a blot on socialist society and is completely incompatible with moving toward Communist society. But the Soviet version of hooliganism is like a Sunday-school frolic compared to our typical Saturday night brawls. As the *New York Times*, June 2, 1969, noted: "Most of the hospitals *excel* in emergency treatment of stab and gunshot wounds *their stock-in-trade* after the bars close Fridays and Saturdays." Soviet hospitals enjoy no such stock-in-trade and consequently they do *not* measure up to ours in "emergency treatment of stab and gunshot wounds."

By far most acts of hooliganism fall into the category of "light cases" of public misbehavior. Many acts of hooliganism fall into the category of potential rather than actual acts of violence which in our country would hardly be given a second thought. Incidentally, in contrast to our fear of getting "involved" in such situations, large numbers of Soviet citizens usually "interfere" in brewing street brawls, and often effectively nip them in the bud.

But there are serious cases of group hooliganism. This was especially the case following the terrible disruption of family life as a result of the Great Patriotic War. Hooliganism is viewed as a serious offense, Lt. Col. Aleksei Nezdryakov of the Frunze district told me, because it concerns not just the individual but the "public peace." Most cases, he said, are handled by either the militiamen or *druzhina* by "education and persuasion" rather than fine or imprisonment. "We search his soul" is the way Nezdryakov put it.

Stronger measures are employed when the acts enter the realm of criminal offenses. If the offense is light, the offender may be fined; if a little more serious, he can get 15 days imprisonment or 15 days at hard labor, but the crime is not yet listed on his record. If the act involves a serious assault, he is tried, and if found guilty, he may receive as high as a several year sentence in a corrective work camp. But it is the public attitude toward hooliganism that is one of the most effective restraints. Few words in the rich Russian language bear the scorn associated with the word "*gooligan*" (there is no "h" in Russian). I often witnessed boisterous youth silenced by elderly women with the mere utterance of that terrible word.

Here let me say a word on the general Soviet approach to crime. It emphasizes *rehabilitation* rather than *punishment*. In our country, too, there is talk of "rehabilitation," but the brutal racist and class character of our prisons exposed in the numerous prison outbursts (like Attica) make a mockery of these pious pronouncements by government officials. In the Soviet Union, not only are those serving time given every opportunity to study and acquire a trade, but Soviet law demands such people be provided with a job and housing within a fortnight after their release. It is the responsibility of the militia to see that this law is adhered to.

The Soviet government adopted a decree in 1970 on "conditional convictions," under which some categories of criminals sentenced up to three years deprivation of liberty do not go to corrective labor camps but for reeducational labor on construction sites determined by the courts. Thus, they work on vital Soviet projects together with other Soviet workers. This participation in collective construction has been found to be extremely effective in producing social rehabilitation. Nikolai Shcholokov, Soviet Minister of Internal Affairs, noted that "repeated crimes have been reduced to practically nil among such offenders."

The contrasting social ostracism suffered by those convicted for crimes in our country, especially Blacks and other oppressed minorities, is well known. The "record" usually hounds the ex-convict for life. It bars him from all but the most menial jobs under the most humiliating conditions. The awareness of and the contact with these social bars help keep our prisons filled with constant "repeaters." And the inhumanities suffered by those who are not even convicted as yet are enough to guarantee their lifelong hostility to society. The *International Herald Tribune*, January 6, 1971, noted that a "federal census of city and county jails shows that 52 percent of their inmates have not been convicted of a crime and that many inmates, whether convicted or not, endure less than human conditions." It points out that "there are jails where prisoners have been held for five years or longer." Of these jails, "85 percent have no recreational nor educational facilities of any kind. About half lack medical facilities. About one-fourth have no facilities for visitors."

The Problem of Public Drunkeness

Public drunkeness is recognized as a serious problem. Rooted in the habits fostered by centuries of czarism and capitalism that once made public drunkeness, particularly among the downtrodden peasants and workers, a way of life, it has been immeasurably reduced in the course of 58 years of socialism. Russian literature depicts the mass character of horrible drunken brawls and wife beatings, especially on weekends and holidays, that so tragically scarred Russian life. This ugly and shameful situation still exists in our country as the vicious barroom brawls, wife and child beating, the battle casualties of hospital emergency wards, the tragic statistics of New Year's Eve celebrations, testify. The *"kabachok"* (saloon) disappeared in the Soviet Union with the czarist past. In the Soviet Union there are no private enterprises profiting from drunken misery. Nowhere in the Soviet Union are bars, saloons, and cocktail lounges as numerous as food stores. If anything, in my opinion, Soviet cities could use a few more beer halls. In the Soviet Union, the production and sale of liquor, like all other products, is state-owned and directed. And in no country in the world is there such an effort to decrease the sales and the profits of such a "lucrative" business. Not only is there no all-pervasive, psychologically sophisticated advertising aimed at encouraging drinking, but the Soviet government and all the vast instruments of propaganda are directed at discouraging excessive drinking. Moreover, steps are constantly being taken to restrict the sale of vodka and other hard liquors. In 1972, the Soviet government and the Central Committee of the Communist Party of the Soviet Union adopted new and more severe measures to restrict the sale of liquor and to deal with drunkenness. They include: greater restrictions on the channels and hours for sale of hard liquors; more severe punishments for salespeople who violate these limitations; stricter enforcement of penalties for repeated drunkenness; more intensive educational campaign against heavy drinking; increased medical treatment of habitual drunks.

But drunkenness in the Soviet Union is widespread enough to be considered a serious problem. It is a grave health, safety, social, and economic liability. Thus, there is considerable concern and discussion in the press, at congresses and conferences.

Some letter writers (in response to articles in *Komsomolskaya Pravda*) advocated a form of prohibition. But the more realistic view recognized the practice cannot be resolved by administrative decree alone. It is being dealt with by a combination of persuasion, propaganda, public disapproval, punishment, and medical treatment. And it is in the fight to curtail and eliminate public drunkenness that the *druzhina* are particularly active. The militia or *druzhina* report those guilty of public drunkenness, who fail to respond to persuasion, to their places of work. They are called in and "talked" to by their shopmates and the Party, trade union and Young Communist League representatives. If this brings no results, their misbehavior is discussed in the plant's monthly newspaper. Further acts of hooliganism or drunkenness lead to the replacement of the worker's ordinary work pass by a *"pazhorny propusk"* (shameful pass). The new pass is distinguished by its size; it is too big to carry in one's pocket. Thus, it is on display before his shopmates every time the offender enters and leaves the plant. The normal pass can only be restored on approval of his shopmates. It is often far more effective than a jail.

TV is also used to give expression to public disapproval. I witnessed a televised trial of a habitual drunk before his shopmates in a large plant. What impressed me was the combination of persuasion and firmness that was employed by all in dealing with the culprit. There are other effective forms of punishment, short of judicial measures. A habitual drunk has to bear the full cost of his 24-day, yearly vacation (ordinarily the trade union assumes 70 percent of the cost). He is denied the bonus and the extra month's pay that the others get as a result of accomplishing the plant's plans. He is placed lower on the list for new apartments. Finally those who persist, despite all efforts to correct them, are ordered to submit to medical treatment. They work in the hospital and most of their pay is not given to them but directly to their families. Increased stress is being placed on the role of psychiatric clinics in the fight against alcoholism. Nowhere in the world are drunks as humanely treated as in the Soviet Union. Unlike in the United States, they are not denied jobs, thrown on the scrap heap until they become derelicts and end up lying on the streets of our Boweries and Skid Rows, homeless, familyless, unknown and unclaimed when they die.

I've watched the special militia patrols (especially in winter when exposure is hazardous) searching for helpless drunks, activated by concern for their health and safety. They are picked up and brought to a special clean-up station. They are given a thorough washing and change of clothes; their bruises and fractures (the results of falls), if any, are treated. They "sleep it off" in a clean bed and are then discharged. For all this, they are made to pay only 15 rubles. Then, systematic attention, beginning with letters to their places of work and house committees, follows.

One is only too familiar with the "treatment" drunks (especially if they are Black) get from U.S. police. In many cases they are simply ignored, left to the perils of exposure as well as the prey of muggers who wait for such easy victims. When they are picked up, they are thrown into jail, treated as criminals and roughed up if they become in any way "abusive."

Drunkenness and socialism—what a contradiction in terms they express! But socialism, as one who lives it in daily life gets to understand, inherits people with contradictions. It has come to grips with the products of its heritage. One of the most pernicious of these and most difficult to eradicate is excessive drinking. For many, it is an escape from personal unhappiness (socialism and even communism make no claim to eliminating personal unhappiness and tragedy—these are part of the human condition). There is yet the considerable influence of age-old customs which "justify and give license" to heavy drinking. There is also the problem of how best to use increased leisure time, though nowhere in the world has culture been made more accessible to the people and it has been a powerful factor for vastly curtailing drunkenness in a country where it was once a mass curse.

Crime Prevention

The militia's crime prevention work starts with early potential violators. As a result, in the overwhelming majority of cases, the potential is rarely reached. There is a "Children's Room" in every microarea, usually located on the ground floor of a large apartment building. I met with Olga Stepanova, a mother and a graduate of a pedagogical institute, who directs the Moscow militia's work among children. Mrs. Stepanova told me that the main approach was aimed at early detection of behavior problems. Thus, she works very closely with schools, parents, house committees of apartment buildings and Pioneer groups. School absenteeism and frequent serious acts of misbehavior are carefully observed and acted upon promptly. The rest of the problem usually lies with some problems in the family—a drunken parent or broken families. Everything is done to try to improve the home environment for the child. But if all efforts fail, the child is sent to a boarding school (an ordinary school and in no sense a corrective institution).

The children are given special attention. Their particular abilities are studied and school work is directed toward enhancing their special talents. I asked Mrs. Stepanova if she confronted any drug cases among children. The surprised expression on her face compelled me to explain that this was a serious problem in our country. She never had come across such a case. I asked if she met with cases of theft. "Very rarely," she replied. Crime among children hardly exists in the Soviet Union. But as even the most unsympathetic U.S. visitors to the Soviet Union have observed, children in the Soviet Union are, indeed, the privileged "class." It is all-pervasive—nowhere have I seen such universal attention, concern and affection bestowed on children. Nowhere have I observed this kind of family involvement in sports and recreation. An abused child not only calls forth the wrath of the militia and the courts, but of every neighbor and the Pioneers in the child's school.

There were quite serious problems of child crime in the early years of the Revolution, as a result of the disruption of the families caused by the Civil War. The human and understanding Soviet approach toward the problem was unforgettably depicted in the famous film *The Road to Life*. The principles of child education, which have since exerted a wide international influence, were to a large extent formulated by the beloved and highly regarded Makarenko. One of the most moving experiences is to observe the annual get-togethers of the "alumni" of the special schools that were established for the *"bezprizorni"* (vagrant homeless children) of the 1920s. Among these "alumni" are some of the Soviet Union's most prominent scientists, writers, artists, generals, and plant and collective farm heads. Of course, some serious problems again arose as a result of the disruption of World War II, but they were rapidly overcome by the all-out attention Soviet society showered on its "privileged class."

The Militia's More Advanced Role

The militia's role changed radically in the course of more than a half-century of socialist living. Shcholokov, Soviet Minister of Interior, on the

militia's 52nd anniversary, November 11, 1969, summed it up as follows: "During the years of Soviet power, radical socioeconomic trans-
formations have taken place in the country. The social structure of society
has changed and a cultural revolution has been accomplished. The
educational standards have immeasurably improved." Thus, he stressed
that the "tasks facing the militia have also changed, as distinct from the
early days of the October Revolution. It is fulfilling its tasks under the
conditions of exclusive domination of Communist ideology, of Communist morals. One can say that never in the past has the militia worked
under such favorable conditions." But these new conditions place in the
foreground the "problem of *preventing* crime." "Thus," he added, "the
Soviet militia must increasingly become an intellectual force."

Just imagine any U.S. attorney general (let alone the late J. Edgar
Hoover) discussing the solution to our crime problem and the role of the
U.S. policemen in that spirit! Or the President of the United States, for
that matter! The vastly different approach to crime is based on this solid
reality: the very source of lawbreaking is different. Shcholokov summed
it up in *Pravda*, March 17, 1973, as follows: "Under socialism crime is
not a form of social protest against living conditions but, above all, the
result of moral personal degeneration, intellectual backwardness, and
low culture. Investigations reveal that violators of law are much more
frequent where educational work with people is neglected, where there is
a low labor discipline, where little attention is devoted to organizing the
life of people, where the problem of wisely utilizing free time is poorly
dealt with, where there still exist serious deficiencies in the work of
administrative bodies."

In the Soviet Union community control over the police is indeed
practiced. It is particularly demonstrated in the mass character and the
role played by the *druzhina*. Those in our country who prate about the
superiority of democracy in the United States may well take a good look
at the *druzhina*.

No one hailed the formation of the *druzhina* on March, 1959, more
than the militia who not only understood its role and significance but fully
cooperated with it. Together they formed a formidable people's team.
The decision of the Central Committee of the Communist Party of the
Soviet Union and the Council of Ministers of the USSR setting up the
druzhina was based on the conclusion that "in the atmosphere of growth
of the consciousness and political activity of the working people, and the

further development of Soviet democracy, the struggle against crime and antisocial behavior must be carried out, not only by administrative organs but by broad involvement of the working people.''

The *druzhina* is a volunteer organization. Its members, who participate in patrols one night a week (from 6 P.M. to 12 A.M.) once or twice a month are not paid for their services. I spent a night with the *druzhina* of the First of May district on the outskirts of Moscow. I observed them at work, discussed with them their role and organization and participated in one of their patrols. The headquarters of the First of May *druzhina* (as is usually the case) is on the ground floor of a typical Moscow apartment building. As I walked in, *druzhina* members, red armbands on their coat sleeves, were getting ready to go out on patrol. They had just come from their shops and offices. More than 50 percent of the First of May *druzhniks* are shopworkers—many of them come from the same shop and are organized on a plant basis. A good many are engineers, technicians, and professional workers.

The *druzhina* have no power of arrest and carry no weapons. They do not resort to force. Their power lies chiefly in the people's authority and the respect they command among Soviet citizens. Most cases are handled by persuasion. Those who are more aggressive, and especially repeaters, are either brought to *druzhina* headquarters or to the militia. The record of each violator of the law is kept in a notebook, with a special one for repeaters. Persistent acts of drunkenness and abusive behavior lead to medical treatment in a hospital.

The May First *druzhina*, which was organized in October, 1963, has demonstrated the effectiveness of these people's patrols. It broke up a number of hooligan gangs, including one that had a particularly bad reputation. It reduced by more than half the number of hooligan acts in one year.

The *druzhina* is an independent organization separate and apart from the militia with whom it works closely. *Druzhinas* not only patrol streets, they are at all public places, parks, and sport stadiums. Large restaurants and hotels have their own *druzhinas*. Moscow is a city without fear because, in addition to everything else, its citizens have nothing to fear from its police (militia). Only a people without such fear can regard crime and the maintenance of public order as a people's responsibility.

The *druzhina* is as different from the vigilante type of *citizen's* patrols in the United States, that have largely been organized by racist police-backed groups, as socialism is from capitalism. The *druzhina* and Soviet militia can effectively perform their functions because the basic cause of crime—capitalist exploitation—has been eliminated. The very existence and the mass nature of the *druzhina demonstrate the vast contrast in the approach to the problem of "law and order" in the USSR and the United States.*

Many years ago the founders of scientific socialism, Karl Marx and Friedrich Engels, wisely noted: *"There is something rotten in the very core of a social system in which crime grows even faster than the size of the population."* (Karl Marx and Friedrich Engels, *Works*, Russian Edition, Vol. 13, p. 515.)

Our cities, where coexistence with fear is a way of life, are becoming unlivable. No people can long accept coexistence with fear. Racists and reactionary forces are consciously attempting to exploit the unbearable frustration of millions of American urban dwellers and direct it into racist channels. Soviet experience demonstrates that there is no short cut, least of all at the end of a policeman's club, to achieving real safety in the streets. *Safe streets can exist only in cities without crisis. And cities without crisis are the fruit of a social system which cares for the needs of the people.*

15 / CITIES WITHOUT FINANCIAL CRISIS

To Soviet people and officials in Moscow, Leningrad, Kiev, Lvov, Kishinev, and Riga, with whom I discussed the situation, our cities present an incredible paradox. The wealthiest country in the world, gripped by constant city budget crises? Great metropolitan centers like New York, Chicago, Detroit, San Francisco, economizing by curtailing basic school services, charging up to sixty cent fares for deteriorating transportation? And all this while taxes on the people continue to mount?

Here is a comparison between Kiev's 1971 budget and New York City's budget for 1968 to 1969. Kiev spent 71 percent of its budget on housing, schools and health, whereas New York spent only 35 percent of its budget on these basic needs. For housing, Kiev spent 27 percent on this most essential need. New York appropriated four-tenths of one percent for "housing and urban development." Kiev expended 22 percent of its budget on health—New York, 11.2 percent. (These figures hardly give the full picture, since the entire Soviet economy considerably augments the contributions made by the cities.)

On one item, New York spent three times the amount spent by Kiev for "the administration of justice" (mainly police and prisons)—9.3 percent of its budget. Only an estimated 3 percent of Kiev's budget went for that purpose. Translated into concrete terms, Kiev's budget meant: 237 nurseries and crèches for 60,700 children, 280 secondary schools in the day and 60 for the evening, 98 libraries, 67 hospitals with 18,350 beds, 28 factory polyclinics, 273 medical stations and 6 huge beautiful parks.

Something valuable is lost when one begins to take socialism for granted. This goes even for Soviet citizens who have good reason to do so, since for most of them, this is the only life they have ever known. And for progressive people in the West, such "sophistication" actually dulls one's ability to grasp what it all means in terms of everyday living. After all, it is this everyday socialist reality that a half-century of anti-Soviet propaganda has sought to conceal. A vital part of that daily reality is revealed in the difference in taxes.

Besides a federal income tax and innumerable excise taxes, New Yorkers, for example, are saddled with a city income tax of 7.35 percent (up from 4.20 percent when the tax was imposed in 1966) state income taxes that go from 2 to 14 percent and a city-state sales tax of 8 percent. All told, taxes bite off about one-third of one's income.

There are no sales taxes in the Soviet Union. There are a few excise taxes such as for plane and train tickets (which one hardly notices because the fare is so much cheaper than ours). There is an income tax with a top of 13 percent—and that's it as far as taxes go. Incidentally, living without sales, theater and amusement taxes, tolls and countless excise taxes, without federal, state and city income taxes makes life not only less expensive but less complicated for the Soviet resident.

Soviet cities are not in hock to bankers. Neither Kiev nor any Soviet city pays a penny in interest to private bankers, for the simple reason that the Soviet Union is not burdened with such institutions as Rockefeller's Chase Manhattan.

Of the 1968–69 New York City budget, 11.1 percent went to the bankers in payment for interest on loans. This amount, which largely went to a handful of big money bags, was equal to the total sum New York spent on health services for 8 million people. At annual budget hearings in City Hall, the paring knife is callously applied to minimum demands for schools, parks, and hospitals. It is never applied to the banker's sacred pound of flesh—the mounting payment for interest.

Our cities are drained from two directions. On the one hand, the handful of very rich skim off the cream in the form of huge profits. On the other hand, social inequities have created a constantly growing army of permanent poor. For these millions crammed into ghetto slums, the Great Depression of the 1930s has never really ended. Here is a description by the *Los Angeles Times*, July 15, 1973, of the South Bronx slums in New York, whose population is 65 percent Puerto Rican and 35 percent Black:

"The concrete blocks placed over the doors and windows to replace shattered wood and glass have themselves been smashed and squatters furtively slip deeper into ruined interiors which smell of urine and feces. People live here scarcely better than men did in caves at the dawn of civilization or perhaps as they may in its twilight. People dying a little each day on heroin, exist in ruins like the doomed troglodyte survivors of some science fiction holocaust."

Is it any wonder that in this seething hell created by our sick society "violence is waiting to happen at every corner. An argument which would mean harsh words elsewhere means the letting of blood here." And the *Los Angeles Times* reporter notes: "Angry spokesmen for slum dwellers charge the society *warehouses* the poor in its *wastelands*, letting them prey upon one another, providing them just enough care to keep the ghetto functioning." Nowhere in the Soviet Union can one find such wastelands. Nowhere in the Soviet Union can one find the other end of our polarized society—the palatial homes for the very rich. For the two, which go together, are distinctive capitalist products.

Nothing is as expensive (to working people) as social decay. The price is exacted not only in a vast and growing police force, which acts like an army of occupation, in the ghetto area but in the myriad of profitable vices—narcotics, prostitution, theft, and gambling, whose "direct costs to government in trying to control these are incalculable" as the *New York Times,* June 1, 1969 noted.

The cost, however, is not only in crime—it is, above all, in poverty. In 1969, one person in eight in New York City depended on welfare relief. It took 26.6 percent of the budget (up from 10.8 percent in 1963). By September, 1972, it was about one in seven—1,184,599 out of a population of little less than 8 million (15 percent of the city's population (*International Herald Tribune,* November 24, 25, 1975). Much of this welfare aid goes to the slumlords, who charge welfare clients exorbitant rents for rat- and roach-ridden, decaying housing. Many needy are either unaware that they are entitled to relief or so harassed and intimidated by welfare authorities that they surrender these rights. About a half-million more people are eligible for welfare than are on the rolls at present.

Few things in our monopoly-dominated society are as revolting as the calculated campaigns to portray the poor on welfare as plunderers of our national treasury. Well-fed representatives of powerful real estate and banking interests dare to inveigh against the welfare poor as the cause for the city's financial difficulties. They demagogically incite workers, small business people and small home owners, driven to desperation by the unbearable tax load, against the most destitute victims of our society. And since Black people form a substantial share of those on welfare, the fuel of racism is poured over the flames of resentment. In 1971, one-fourth of the Black population could only exist by resorting to public welfare. But the justified resentment of the mass of the suffering city dwellers was directed away from those who really were milking the city to the chief victims.

The slanderous charge widely spread by the capitalist press—that the welfare poor are loafers and shirkers—is made with the full knowledge of the falsity of these claims. In analyzing the composition of New York City welfare rolls, the *New York Times*, June 1, 1969, pointed out: "In New York a Department of Social Services report says that 59 percent are children too young to work, 19.1 percent are mothers kept from work because they must look after these children; 5.6 percent are too old to work; 8.6 percent are disabled; 2.7 percent have jobs but earn too little to support themselves and 4.5 percent are unable to work because of alcoholism, narcotics addiction, emotional instability or other problems." Added up this means that 99.8 percent of those on welfare rolls in New York City are either unable to work or are placed in that position by our capitalist society (particularly the 19.1 percent who are mothers with small children). Only two-tenths of one percent are eligible to work under present conditions, yet this in no way inhibits the big-business inspired campaign against the "loafers on welfare."

Pay is so low for many, especially for Black, Chicano and Puerto Rican, Asian and Native American Indian unskilled workers that, as the *New York Times* points out, "welfare becomes competitive with work." The father has to make the choice either to get along on an impossibly low wage or to surrender his dependents to a welfare system that can give them more money than he can. Thus, the cruel welfare regulations are responsible for breaking up many poor families and many a father is forced to move "away from his family and thus make them eligible for full welfare assistance."

The Soviet solution to the social problem was the very opposite of the one proposed by the big monied interests in our country. Welfare rolls were eliminated by doing away with unemployment and national discrimination and the social system and classes which bred them. Thus, from the financial as well as the social point of view, Soviet cities are relieved of two major financial drains that are present in our cities—interest payments to bankers and the necessity to maintain a huge and constantly growing army of destitute and unemployed.

Why No Budget Crises

Soviet cities face financial problems but these are linked to those faced by Soviet society as a whole. The financial health of Soviet cities depends directly on the health of the economy, on industry and agriculture. The hardships in the years of the war and of postwar reconstruction were reflected in financial stress. This was manifested in the severe housing crisis, shortages of schools, inadequate transportation, serious lack of store facilities, inadequate and often poor road and street construction. No Soviet city executives are complacent about their problems, financial or otherwise.

The basic reason why Soviet cities are not plagued by annual budget crises can be traced to the fundamental difference between the two social systems. The main revenue for Soviet cities, making up 90 percent of their budgetary income, comes from the accumulations of enterprises in industry, transport, trade, and service. In the United States, nine-tenths of budget revenue comes from *taxes*, which fall most heavily on the people. Every Five Year Plan fulfilled, means vastly increased financial resources for the cities. City Soviets thus have an added incentive to assist in the fulfillment of Five Year Plans.

The story of the Soviet Union's flourishing cities is told in the steady advances of its nine Five Year Plans. There is a close and complementary relationship between Soviet cities and the Republic and All-Soviet branches of government, which is reflected in their budgets. More than three-quarters of the Soviet budget goes for the general welfare and culture and for further developing the people's national economy. Soviet cities rarely incur budgetary deficits. Soviet cities, like Soviet society as a whole, are based on a planned socialist economy.

On the other hand, the estimated U.S. federal deficit for fiscal year 1971 alone was $18,562,000,000. The huge deficits are made up by borrowing from private banks and by issuing interest-bearing bonds (which are tax exempt and largely bought up by big monied interests). The interest paid by the federal government on these debts was $19,455,000,000 for 1971 (almost $5,000,000,000 more than spent on health). U.S. cities spend from 11 to 13 percent of their budgets on interest on loans from banks and tax-exempt bonds. Interest rates frequently go up. In January, 1975, a syndicate headed by Chase Manhattan and First National banks forced New York City to pay 9.49 percent interest, the second highest in history, at the cost of $58.1 million, on $620 million worth of short-term loans. This "dictated economies" on public services, as well as tax increases. Soviet cities are immune from such pressures.

Soviet city and all governmental budgets are also immune from another financial and social ill natural in our "free-enterprise" society—*inflation*, "the new terror of U.S. cities." The financial stability of the ruble is based upon the ever increasing wealth produced by the Soviet economy. Its products, sold at stable prices, constitute the most reliable guarantee of the ruble.

The fate of our cities, too, is linked with that of our economy and industry. This especially hits home to us when our one-industry towns suddenly lose that one industry and become ghost towns, because the industrialists no longer consider the area sufficiently profitable. Booming industry does not automatically spell financial affluence for our cities.

Nothing demonstrates this more than the fact that it was during one of the greatest and longest periods of economic well-being, the 1960s, that our urban centers suffered their most intense financial crisis, and the crisis of our cities deepened. This was so because the crisis was enormously aggravated by the expenditure of tremendous national resources on destroying the villages and towns of the Vietnamese people. And today, with the most severe depression since the 1930s our cities face not just crisis but disaster.

A Decade of Peace—A Decade of War

As Moscow correspondent, I observed what a decade of peace means for Soviet cities. This was impressed on me when I visited Tbilisi, the capital of Soviet Georgia in 1971. Ten years before, I was a guest of that socialist Republic.

Georgia's often tragic history produced a people who can be warm friends or fierce enemies. This is symbolized by Mother Georgia, who stands guard over Tbilisi holding a sword in one hand and a wine cup in the other.

I shared the wine cup with my Georgian hosts in 1961 for the first time. They told me: "Come again ten years from now and if we have peace, you will see what we will accomplish." And in 1971, together with a large group of correspondents from many countries, I saw what ten years of peace had brought to Georgia. There was Tbilisi's Metro, a palace of art like its Moscow model, but with a distinctive Georgian charm. There were miles of new apartment buildings, with the accompanying schools, nurseries, polyclinics, cinemas, and stores. New factories, a huge hospital and medical complex, a 20-story Intourist hotel, scientific institutes were all under construction.

As I surveyed these constructive fruits of peace, I thought of the terrible harvest the decade of dirty war had brought to the Vietnamese people and our own. The contrast was all the more vivid to me because only a year before, in 1970, I had traveled 360 miles in a Soviet jeep from Hanoi to Ngue Thuy, a small fishing village in Quang Binh province only five miles from the 17th parallel. That 360 miles was a trail of U.S. shame, a cemetery of cities, villages, schools and hospitals. And it was a ghastly picture of the tragedy that billions of dollars had brought to the people of Vietnam.

North Vietnam's beautiful earth was mutilated with mathematical precision by fiendish U.S. "scientific" minds. Here, in the ugly gashes torn into North Vietnam's bleeding rice fields, also lay buried the schools, homes, and hospitals that were never built for our crisis-ridden cities and our Black, Chicano, Asian and Puerto Rican ghettos. Here in Vietnam's tortured soil, sprouted the seeds of the Johnson-Nixon-Ford inflation. Here our yearly city budget crises were created; each crater spelled death and taxes. Death for thousands of Vietnamese; taxes and death for the American people. Mayor John Lindsay estimated that the people of New York annually paid $3 billion to finance this shameful destruction.

The flourishing Soviet cities are one of the impressive results of more than a quarter century of peace. This does not mean that they are unaffected by the arms race. Even though far less of the Soviet budget goes for arms than that of the U.S. budget, the funds set aside for the protection of the Soviet Union constitute a drain on the country's economy. And there is no question that Soviet cities could provide their inhabitants with many more services if that arms burden were reduced or eliminated. At the 24th Congress of the CPSU, two programs were put forth: one, the historic Program for Peace implemented by the greatest peace offensive in history; and the other, the 9th Five Year Plan, which provided for far-reaching improvements in the material and cultural well-being of the people. Both were based on an estimate of the world relationship of forces, an estimate which concluded that the forces of socialism and peace now had the upper hand.

When Brezhnev projected the slogan *Make Moscow a Model Communist Capital*, the resplendent Kremlin Hall of Congresses rocked with applause. Every Soviet citizen realized that the slogan signalized a Soviet offensive on urban problems.

The signing of the U.S.-USSR agreement on the prevention of nuclear war and the limitations on strategic armaments were hailed by Soviet citizens not only because they constituted historic steps towards guaranteeing world peace but also because they foretold new possibilities to intensify the struggle to limit and stop the arms race, making available additional resources for improving life for the Soviet people and all mankind.

No Federal-State-City Conflicts

Soviet cities are also free from the crippling effects of the insane system of federal-state-city relations that exhaust and hogtie our cities. Leningrad is not at war with Moscow for its fair share of financing. No delegations (let alone demonstrations) of irate Soviet citizens need descend on the Soviet capital to plead for relief from municipal budget crises.

Few things in our crisis-ridden social and political system are as outmoded as our system of federal-state-city relations, especially in respect to finances. They are even outmoded as a system of relations in terms of capitalist forms of political structure, as comparison with many of the leading capitalist countries will confirm. Federal-city financial relations in the United States add up to an almost one-way procession of tribute from the municipalities with only a trickle returning to them in appropriations to meet their mounting needs. About 73 percent of the federal income comes from the cities. The General Revenue Sharing Act was passed in 1972, supposedly to adjust this imbalance but what it gave the cities with one hand, the federal government took back with the other through impoundments, freezes, and program cutbacks.

The one-way tribute is particularly reflected in the tiny share of school costs for 1972-75 borne by the tax-devouring federal government. It was only 7.8 percent, down from 8.8 percent in 1967-68, its highest point. Likewise, while an estimated 60 percent of the state's revenue comes from New York City, only 40 percent or less comes back to the city. One of the main reasons for this inequitable division of revenue is the political domination exercised by the up-state rural areas. It is the manipulation of city-rural differences by the huge financial interests which control both. Carefully drawn legislation favors the more conservative rural areas for representation in the state legislatures.

The archaic structure of federal-state-city relations constitutes an ideal roadblock against public pressure. It is one huge obstacle course that exhausts and enmeshes the harassed citizenry in a diabolically devised tangle. The cards are stacked against the frustrated city dwellers. The main sources of revenue are reserved by law for the federal and state governments, in that order. The most limited and most onerous taxes are left to the cities. This, among other things, explains why cities are particularly at the mercy of the bankers. While their financial sources are circumscribed, the cities bear the main burden for providing the bulk of everyday services.

At the same time, the tax burden has been shifting increasingly onto the shoulders of the mass of working and small business people as the more affluent people flee the cities for the suburbs. There is a growing contradiction between restricted revenue and mounting needs.

Moreover, the structure enables the most reactionary forces to utilize regionalism in discriminating against the needs of the working people. In none of the major capitalist countries does regionalism, combined with racism, so fragmentize the functions of government, particularly in housing, education, welfare and health. It permits Mississippi to spend on education about one-third the amount expended by New York State.

The relations between Soviet cities and their regional administrative centers, their Republic capitals and Moscow, are not "blessed" with our federal-state-city antagonisms. This is as true of finances as it is on all questions. All share mutual problems. At times there may be differences among them on how to resolve these problems, but these are based on difference of opinion, not on a clash of interests. The revenue derived by some cities may be greater than that of others (since much of it is linked to the productivity of the plants in their environs, which may vary from city to city) but this is not large enough to make meaningful differences. Moreover, the basic social and cultural needs of the Soviet people are on the whole equally provided for in all 15 Republics.

Soviet cities do not confront their rural "up-state" areas as political rivals or opponents. Soviet workers and collective farmers are nonantagonistic classes for the simple reason neither exploits the other. For the same reason, they are in constant cooperation. This is reflected in every

Five Year Plan. The cities provide agriculture with the technical equipment that is industrializing Soviet farms, the training of their cadre, the cultural enrichment of rural life that is fast bridging the age-old gap between town and country. Soviet cities at harvest time are transformed into staging areas for the huge urban volunteer armies of students, workers and professionals who help bring in the harvest.

This cooperative relationship is carried over to the political field. It is reflected in the composition of Soviet political bodies on all levels. Here is the general composition of both chambers of the Supreme Soviet (1970), which is similar in city Soviets: 31.7 percent were workers, 18.6 percent collective farmers, almost 20 percent (18.5) were under 30 and almost one-third (30.5 percent) were women. There are more women deputies in the USSR Supreme Soviet than in the parliaments of all capitalist countries taken together. The deputies also represent sixty-two nationalities.

As for our Congress, a Ralph Nader study (*Who Runs Congress?* Bantam Books, 1972, p. 48), points out: "The fact that members of Congress come almost exclusively from professions that almost exclusively serve business clientele or from business itself, gives the corporate community a several-step headstart over other citizens in making Congress work for them." It notes there is almost never a congressman under 30, only nine Blacks (in 1969), and that the "disproportionate representation is even more skewed for women and blue-collar workers." The relatively few farmers in the government of the United States usually represent the rich rural interests, who, in turn, are closely allied with, and subordinated to, the huge food processing corporations and conglomerates. Even the taxes the huge corporations do "pay" are *not paid by them* but by the mass of working people. This is detailed by Ferdinand Lundberg, in the chapter "The Great Tax Swindle," in his book *The Rich and the Super-rich*. (Bantam Books, p. 398.)

Noting that in the 1961 federal budget, revenue from corporation income taxes was listed as 21 cents on the dollar, Lundberg points out: "Corporations, however, are no more taxed than were the aristocratic pre-revolutionary French estates . . . all taxes supposedly paid by corporations are passed on *in price of goods or services to the ultimate buyer, the well-known man in the street.* This is not only true of federal and state taxes (where levied) but it is also true of *local real estate and property taxes paid in the name of the corporations. The corporations in nearly all cases merely act as collection agents for the government.*" Lundberg exposes how the multimillionaires get away without paying any taxes, while the burden correspondingly is shifted onto the backs of the working people.

An analysis by economists of Brookings Institution disclosed that the wealthy received $14 billion a year through capital gains loopholes and nearly two-thirds of the $14 billion goes to the richest 3 percent of families. As Lundberg points out, 86 percent of all federal revenue "comes from the lower brackets." Soviet society, in eliminating the greatest swindle of all, the expropriation of surplus value, is likewise immune to our tax swindles. Tax swindles, after all, are only another way for big business interests to protect or augment their profits.

The Public Consumption Fund—"To Promote the General Welfare"

What is the specific source of the ever increasing social services the Soviet cities and Soviet society provide the people? Let me describe the role played by the public consumption fund in Soviet life. It is this fund that makes a Soviet reality of what is only piously proclaimed in the preamble to the United States Constitution. Article 120 of the Soviet Constitution stipulates that Soviet citizens are entitled to the following *rights*, which must be implemented by their government: free education up to and including the university; complete and free medical and health care; material assistance in old age and in case of sickness and the inability to work (for as long as necessary in the latter); free or partly paid accommodation at sanitoria or rest homes; vocational training, maternal leave and assistance.

These are not statements by individuals or even by the government. These are written into the Soviet Constitution as inalienable rights; these rights have not only been steadily implemented but expanded in all aspects of daily Soviet life. They are made possible by the public or general welfare fund, as I prefer to call it. The general welfare fund is the ever expanding golden egg laid by Soviet economy and particularly its industry. It is a big part of the surplus value that in our country goes to the Rockefellers. It is the services provided by the general welfare fund that so vastly augment the average Soviet wage.

Soviet people draw on it even before birth, since it is out of this fund that working mothers receive paid maternity leave of 112 days, medical aid for themselves and their newborn children (there are 24,000 maternity and child care centers). From the fund comes the maternity payments and confinement care, grants for the baby's clothing and special food needs, and the time necessary for the mother to breast-feed the infant on the job.

Contrast this with the scandalous neglect suffered especially by Black, Chicano, Puerto Rican and Native American Indian mothers and their newborn babies and infants. The 1972 census report revealed mortality rate among Black infants was twice that among white infants. It is even greater among Native American Indians. Moreover, these rights (to care), which are freely granted and steadily extended in the Soviet Union, are only partially achieved in the United States, at the price of bitter struggle. An unceasing war has to be sustained to keep them from being either completely eliminated or nibbled away by Washington, state and city governments. In addition these rights are *regionalized and frag-mented*. Working mothers have to deal with 50 sovereign powers (state governments) and wage war on 50 fronts. There are no "Southern differentials" in either social services or wages in the Soviet Union. There are no "Mississippis" which deprive Soviet citizens of education, health or culture. The benefits provided by the general welfare fund are uniformly applied in all 15 Republics.

This fund made possible the nurseries attended by about 10 million children in 1972, 80 percent of whose cost is borne by the state; the stipends for Soviet college students; a worker's training in a skill or profession; annual rest and recreation by more than 25 million working people and their families. It frees the Soviet worker from the fear of financial disaster that haunts U.S. workers stricken by serious illness. Soviet workers receive the highest sick pay in the world relative to wages (in some cases equal to a person's full pay) for as long as necessary. The general welfare fund makes possible the world's cheapest rents and most intensive housing construction program. Tenants pay rent that is only a fraction of what it costs the state to maintain and service apartments. The fund also makes possible the lowest retirement age in the world.

Nowhere are the aged more respected and more involved in every sphere of life than in the Soviet Union. Soviet citizens receive pensions amounting to 70 percent of their pay. In money terms this would be smaller than ours, but nothing is more deceptive than such a comparison. To begin with, in the Soviet Union these pensions are not whittled away by inflation, devoured by high rents or spent largely on medicines and doctor bills. Moreover, the pension system differs from ours in at least two respects: it covers *all* Soviet citizens, and the *entire cost* is borne by the state.

One of the greatest tragedies of our "free-enterprise" system is the plight of the aged. Here is how the situation is described by Ralph Nader's study group in their book *Old Age, the Last Segregation* (Bantam Publishers, 1971, p. 135): "Some 7 million older people, more than one-third of the over-65 population, are impoverished and must depend on someone else—their families or the government—for assistance. The average social security payment to a couple retiring in 1950 met half the budget cost estimated by the U.S. Bureau of Labor Statistics as necessary for self-support; *today it meets less than one-third*. In *urban areas*, the percentage of living costs covered by social security is *even lower*. About two million get public assistance under Old Age Assistance. This aid is not only inadequate, but differs from state to state so that the elderly in South Carolina get about one-half of what the aged receive in New York." Many have been driven to eat dog food and the lives of many aged have been shortened in hell-hole nursing homes.

The general welfare fund makes it possible for Soviet society to be the first in history to bridge the gap between pious proclamations and reality in respect to those who are handicapped. Nowhere in the world do those suffering from any kind of handicap, physical or mental, incurred through birth, disease or accident, receive more human care than in the Soviet Union. I describe this at great length in another chapter on mental health. But this is equally demonstrated in Soviet treatment of the blind and deaf. All blind receive pensions, and those who work have a six-hour day and a month's paid annual vacation. They pay no income tax or fare for any municipal or district transportation; they get priority in housing and sanitoria accommodations; they receive free universal education. They get special training at enterprises operated by the Society of the Blind. All who want to work are guaranteed employment. They work not at special "work for the blind" but on products including transformers, electric motors, telephone exchanges, and on oil filters for trailers and automomobiles. There are nearly a thousand libraries and hundreds of clubs and houses of culture for the blind in the Russian Federation alone. Many work as teachers and scientists, including 25 who have Doctor of Science and 110 Master of Science degrees. There are special nurseries as well as boarding schools and specialized secondary schools where the deaf are taught trades. They are fully engaged in all industries permitted by their handicap and, aside from their wages, they receive pensions. No Soviet "employers" have to be implored to hire physically handicapped people as in the United States, where the handicapped are not only made to feel they have to be eternally grateful but also usually pay for the "benevolence" bestowed on them, by working at lower wages.

Children born out of wedlock and their mothers enjoy fully the same rights as all other children and mothers do. Neither they nor their mothers are stigmatized by Soviet society. They are fully provided with the vast services normally extended to all. No unwed Soviet mother is compelled to abandon her child to a foundling institution or surrender it for adoption by legally married mothers, as in our country.

The kind of scurrilous campaigns directed in the United States against unwed mothers and their children—children who are compelled by our society's heartlessness and discrimination to go on welfare relief, are unthinkable in the Soviet Union. Nowhere in the world are children born in or out of wedlock treated with more universal love backed by material assistance than in the Soviet Union. And those who are unfortunate enough to have parents who cannot properly care for them are given added care. Abused children, abandoned children, in the rare cases where this occurs, are fully provided for.

The unceasing war that goes on in the United States among Washington, the 50 states, and hundreds of cities as to who shall provide for the handicapped and the unfortunate is unthinkable in the Soviet Union. No Soviet citizen is driven to scour the country in search of a city where a little more human care is provided. And no Soviet city is beset by the "problem" of erecting a barricade of inhumanity in the form of severe welfare laws to divert this search for human care from their borders.

To sum up, the general welfare fund immunizes Soviet cities from the constant crises that have become a "normal" part of existence in the United States. It makes it possible for Soviet cities to meet the critical problems posed to all urban centers by the complex pressures of modern life. But more than that the general welfare fund *heralds the Communist future toward which the entire Soviet society is exerting all its efforts and for which nine Five-Year Plans have laid a solid foundation. It is the great leveler, even now, under socialism of the still existing differences in incomes. These funds are used to satisfy the needs of Soviet citizens without regard to the quantity or quality of work they perform (the guiding principle of socialism). They are provided to all, on the basis of need, the guiding principal of Communist society, "to each according to his needs."*

U.S. correspondents ignore this all-important role played by the general fund in determining the living standards of the Soviet people. They focus attention on the admittedly higher wages received by U.S. workers. Thus, the impression is created of a low Soviet standard of living as contrasted to a high one in the United States. Typical of this approach is the article in the *International Herald Tribune*, on February 11, 1974, by Murray Seeger, *Los Angeles Times* Moscow correspondent. To begin with, Seeger's article was captioned "Soviet Workers Showing Signs of Restlessness," and "Wages Among the Lowest in Industrial Nations." The sole basis for the "restlessness" was Seeger's report of the results in one plant of a questionnaire (which, incidentally, appeared in *Izvestia*) that showed Soviet workers wanted higher wages and particularly a greater supply of consumer goods.

But here is the pay-off. Seeger states that "a western labor leader studying the annual report of the centrally planned Soviet economy, would see a ripe target for negotiation." Why? Because, says Seeger, "profits of state enterprises rose by 12 percent in 1973 and labor productivity by 6 percent, according to the official figures; still, the average wage paid Soviet workers rose only 3.7 percent." Seeger makes no mention of the fact that the 3.7 percent increase was a real one, since Soviet prices have been and are stable. In the same year that Soviet wages rose 3.7 percent (1973), U.S. real wages declined 3 percent.

To read Seeger, one would think that Soviet enterprises were owned by the USSR equivalent of our General Motors, IBM or ITT, since he is so concerned about the 12 percent increase in profits in 1973. Seeger's and the *Los Angeles Times*' "concern" is not shared by Soviet workers who know that these profits are the source of the general welfare fund, that there are no monopolies to skim off the cream. That's why, unlike the situation in our country, workers engage in competition with each other to increase profits, to raise labor productivity. Thus, Seeger's arithmetic is not only tendentious; it is downright deceptive. The 3.7 percent wage increase comes out of the 12 percent profit (and much more comes out of it, as we have indicated). This kind of arithmetic has been benefiting Soviet workers for 58 years and nine Five Year Plans. An honest and objective comparison between the USSR and the USA standards of living can only be made on the basis of comparing what the Soviet worker gets from the general welfare fund and its manifold social services, *in addition* to his wages, with what the U.S. worker gets in the form of wages and social benefits. Such a comparison is avoided by our Moscow correspondents — for obvious reasons.

In terms of direct wages and many consumer goods (especially the automobile) the United States is still ahead. One of the reasons is that labor productivity (in our country — read "speedup") is still a good deal higher than in the USSR, though with every Five Year Plan, the gap is steadily being narrowed. Increased labor productivity is the last, the most difficult and most decisive hurdle that still has to be jumped in the race with the capitalist system. And it is on productivity, based on the latest scientific and technological development, that the construction of the material base for communism depends. It is on productivity that the implementation of the principle "from each according to his ability, to each according to his needs," depends. The only "restlessness" one can really notice in the USSR is the desire to move faster toward this goal.

The Soviet City's Secret Weapons

The Soviet city has an invaluable ally in the organized activity of its citizenry. In our society, ridden with racist pressures and class conflicts, the city is an exploding battleground. How can the residents of Harlem, Watts or central Detroit even think in terms of aiding the city when their daily lives are made up of fierce struggles with the city's blue-coated army of occupation, with the rats that feed on the garbage in the streets, with the dope pushers who are allowed to destroy the lives of their children, with the schools most of which provide custodial care instead of teaching? All the tremendous energy, initiative, and talent which our capitalist society compels our frustrated citizens to expend in a protective battle for sheer existence, is turned to productive labor and service for the common good in the Soviet Union. *This is the great strength of Soviet society and Soviet cities. It is their secret weapon that makes them immeasurably superior to our own, despite our vast wealth and unrivaled industrial machine.* And in the advance to communism, the involvement of the people in the administration as well as planning of society is rapidly extending.

Nothing reveals this future more than the *present role of the trade unions in Soviet society.* Among their many functions, the trade unions in the Soviet Union administer and manage the entire vast social insurance and welfare programs. The budget of the social insurance program alone is 20 billion rubles. Soviet trade unions have at their disposal 94,000 clubs, palaces of culture, libraries and cinema halls; 440 sanitoria and holiday hotels; 535 rest homes; 650 tourist bases, camping sites, ships; 6,200 factory weekend holiday centers; 11,000 Pioneer camps, accommodating two million children; 2,470 stadiums; 8,170 gymnasiums; 5,640 skiing places; 475 swimming pools, and 370,000 athletic grounds. More than 25 million are members of trade union sports clubs. In addition, the trade unions direct three million inspectors in the observance of labor safety.

Soviet cities are without budget crises because they draw on all the vast resources of their country; because they are not in hock to a Chase Manhattan Bank; because they are not drained at one end by the profits siphoned off by big business and from the other by the poverty and misery it brings in its wake; because they are not battlegrounds involving racist, regional and class interests; and because they can draw on the incalculable initiative of the Soviet people.

16 / CITIES WITHOUT CRISIS

t was painful to return to find New York not only deeper in crisis but on the brink of disaster. San Francisco's Mayor Joseph Alioto warned at the 43rd gathering of the U.S. Conference of Mayors, "The seeds of New York are in every American city."

New York is my town. I grew up on the teeming and exciting streets of East New York and Brownsville in Brooklyn. To this day, every street holds a memory. East New York and Brownsville in those days were working-class areas, "poor neighborhoods." They were populated by Jewish immigrant workers who had fled from the pogroms of czarist Russia. Many of these workers brought with them the inspiring traditions of the revolutionary movement in Russia, which burst into full flame with the victorious October Revolution.

We lived in dank, dark tenements made more dismal by the fluttering bluish glare of gasjet lights. In the winter we lived around the only bit of warmth—the coal stove in the kitchen. Steam heat and electric lights have long since come to my old tenement home but that has hardly brightened up or warmed the lives of its present inhabitants—Black and Puerto Rican families.

During the 1930s, as organizer of the Unemployed Council, I got to know more intimately and to love more dearly my Brownsville neighbors. Those were days of hunger and bitter struggle. But even in the midst of the Great Depression life was not as depressing in my old neighborhood as it is today. Nothing has more forcefully revealed to me the decay that has gripped my town than the sight that greeted me when I returned to the scene of my childhood and youth. It is a sight that is common to Black, Puerto Rican and Chicano ghettos and barrios in all our great cities. It is an accepted part of the street scene of our cities, bewailed in countless studies that lie, gathering dust on bureaucrats' shelves in Washington, New York, Chicago, Philadelphia and elsewhere.

The sight that greeted me reminded me of the devastated areas I had seen in Okinawa and Japan as an infantryman during World War II; devastated hulks of tenement houses, their windows gaping holes, a revolting odor of decay and urine escaping from the dark, abandoned buildings. These were deserted buildings now inhabited by derelicts and dope addicts. But this was not an abandoned, dead city; it was decay and degeneration that children were surrounded by as they played and went to school. It was decay that poisoned the very existence of the tens of thousands of people who lived in the midst of it like refugees of war.

Mayor Lindsay visited Brownsville after it had exploded in angry, desperate revolt in 1965, to "calm" its furious inhabitants. The mayor, surveying the scene, described Brownsville in one word "bombsville." Yet little has changed in Brownsville since the mayor's visit.

When we returned to the United States in December, 1975, we visited another old neighborhood of ours, the East Bronx, where the same scene met our eyes.

No one in the Soviet Union could walk the streets of his or her childhood with a similar feeling of pain. No one in the Soviet Union can come upon scenes of decay and degeneration in his or her old neighborhood after an absence of 30 to 40 years. On the contrary, the outstanding characteristic of Soviet cities is dynamic, progressive change, not only in physical appearance but in the quality of living. The changes are so swift and all-embracing that it is hard to recognize one's neighborhood in five years, let alone four decades. And it is a recognition of pleasure in the Soviet Union, not pain—and this in a country that has had far more than its share of pain, that had to rebuild from the ground up hundreds of cities and towns, thousands of villages.

Naturally I looked with different eyes at Soviet life than the Soviet citizen. Perhaps this is why the contrast between Soviet city life and ours struck me so forcefully.

A Word on and to My Soviet Friends

I was a little taken aback when I first found that the pleasures of life without landlords and Rockefellers hardly occasioned the same enthusiasm among the Soviet people that I exuded. My Soviet friends accepted all their ways of living quite matter-of-factly. After all, it was the only life they knew. But I found that many had considerable illusions about "affluent America." Why couldn't every Soviet person see the obvious superiority of their own way of life to our dog-eat-dog existence, notwithstanding the serious shortcomings and unresolved problems in Soviet society?

I was not quite fair to my Soviet friends. I had a decided advantage over them. I not only had lived in two worlds, I continued to live them every day of my more than five years in the Soviet Union. Mine was a life of daily comparison and contrast. My Soviet friends did not live with the image of the Brownsville of my childhood and 40 years later; it was hard for them to grasp the essence of capitalist existence. Once I jokingly told a group of Moscow youth, who regarded our abundance of automobiles as a symbol of mass affluence, that they had the misfortune of never having lived under capitalism. Of course, they laughed and hardly appeared to regret their "misfortune." But there is a small element of truth in what I said. More than 80 percent of the present Soviet population never lived under capitalism. That means that they never lived with exploitation. It is not to say they did not suffer. Few people in the world suffered as they did from the ravages of war. And that suffering was inflicted on them from the outside by fascism. This, the Soviet people will never forget. But it is hard for them to grasp suffering that comes from within the social system itself, especially in a country as rich and as industrious as ours, which has not felt the ravages of war on its soil for more than a century.

This became clearer to me with every day of life in the Soviet Union. Reading the *International Herald Tribune* in Moscow was like reading reports from Mars. Incidentally, William Buckley, the ultrarightist columnist, blamed the *International Herald Tribune* for the dismal picture of U.S. life (March 4, 1974). Buckley's reasoning is in the spirit of the absolute rulers of old who used to put to death the bearers of ill tidings.

Soviet journalists, writers and educators, indeed, face a challenge to make this strange, brutal and inhuman world fully real to the Soviet people. This is not an easy task. From my own reading of the Soviet press and experience with its TV, radio, cinema and stage, my feeling is that while in many respects an effective job is being done, there is still much to be desired in this respect. For example, the decay of our cities, one of the most damning indictments of our social system, has not yet been fully and forcefully portrayed to the Soviet people.

Socialism is vastly superior to capitalism not only because it increasingly provides better material conditions for the *mass* of the people, but because it gives them the most purposeful, most moral, most *human way of life*. Never has it been more important than now to emphasize the *moral superiority of socialism*.

If making the capitalist world real to Soviet youth involves understandable objective difficulties for the Soviet press media, this is hardly the problem we face. From the reports of our big business press correspondents, one would imagine that the big news in the Soviet Union was not that its cities were cities without crises, not that in the Soviet Union, prices (with the exception of vodka and cognac) remain stable while inflation mounts in the capitalist world. The "big news" was the opposition to this way of life on the part of a miniscule and dwindling group of what our press termed "dissidents," a squeak which is drowned in the gigantic roar of Communist construction. By amplifying this grunt the U.S. press hopes to create the impression of mass discontent in the USSR.

I realize I am stating the problem from the standpoint of one portraying Soviet life favorably, superior to life in the United States. A half-century of unremitting anti-Soviet, anti-Communist propaganda has created an atmosphere in which there is one *unforgivable sin*—to portray Soviet life and communism favorably. No single subject so occupies our newspapers and TV as communism. Moreover, attention is centered on the most advanced land of socialism. And for all the talk of "dialogue," it has for more than half a century been an overwhelmingly one-sided discussion.

The massive outpourings of successive generations of Sovietologists have one central objective. To "prove" that workers cannot govern society. Here is the way it was put by *Novoe Vremya* (the New Times), a reactionary newspaper in czarist Russia on the eve of the Great October Socialist Revolution: "Let us assume for a moment that the Bolsheviks will win. Who will govern us then? Maybe the cooks, those beefsteak and cutlet proficients? Or firemen? Stableboys? Stokers? Or maybe the nursery maids will hurry to State Council sessions after they have washed the diapers? Which is it going to be? What are these statesmen? Perhaps the fitters will take charge of the theaters, plumbers of diplomatic service and joiners of the post and telegraph? Is this the way it is going to be? The Bolsheviks will get an authoritative answer to this mad question from history.''

Nine Five Year Plans have demonstrated how the cooks, stokers and nursery maids, plumbers, and joiners can govern. But the anti-Sovietologists, though hardly so crude today, still play endless variations on the same theme. And it is largely on this *theme* that the "discussion" on the Soviet Union and communism has been based. The rules governing the discussion and "debates" seem to be that everyone can discuss communism—Sovietologists, outright anti-Communists, liberals and radicals of various hues, renegades from communism, defectors and "dissidents" (they are held up as the experts from the "inside")—everyone but Communists. Americans are gagging at this daily one-dish diet.

Socialism has long ceased to be a mere goal to be *theoretically* explained. Socialism is and has been a reality for more than a half-century. It is the solution that has led "somewhere." Life and intense experience in building and defending socialism have provided the answers far better than "theorists" who disdainfully brush aside the actual example of the most human society in mankind's history.

Time is running out for the wily manipulators of this shell game though they have become more dexterous through half a century of practice. The need for a way out to "somewhere" is too great and that "somewhere" too bright and too real today to be concealed. Millions of Americans will see what Tom Druax, an Ohio coal miner who visited the Soviet Union in 1973, saw. Draux noted: "Over there, coal miners are the best treated and most respected of all the workers in the whole country. Miners have everybody's respect." In an interview printed in the *United Mine Workers Journal*, November 1-15, 1973, Druax added "I don't care where the idea comes from. If it is going to save the lives of our men, then we ought to try it."

Of course! What is unpatriotic about seeking a more human, peaceful life for all the working people in our decaying cities? Why shouldn't we have *cities without crisis* also?

After our return home we were particularly struck by the moral and physical decay that has spread throughout our land in these last six years—like mushrooms after the rain. The Times Square area at 42nd Street in New York is a showcase of this degeneration. (Every large city in our land has its own.) Six years ago, Times Square was already a jungle; a hangout for pimps, prostitutes and muggers. Now it is more than a mere hangout: it is the center of the pornography and filth industry. Forty-second Street is big business. Manhattan has its financial and garment industries and Times Square is just another "business" district—selling sex and sadism.

The moral decay is hardly confined to a "district" or to pimps, prostitutes and muggers. Today it is so all-pervasive that you inhale it with the polluted air you breathe. Moral pollution is given license in the name of "freedom of expression." There is no such "freedom of expression" in the Soviet Union. There is no license to spread the pollution of immorality; there are no Forty-second Streets in the USSR.

Much has been made of the need for an exchange of information between the United States and the USSR. An honest and meaningful exchange would be very good for we have much to offer the Soviet Union. No one realizes this more than the Soviet government and people. Soviet leaders are eager to learn from us—how to improve their services, how to streamline management, how to run their expanding tourist facilities more efficiently, how to produce consumer commodities more economically, how to modernize their system of retail stores, etc. But, isn't it time to recognize how much we stand to gain from an honest exchange—that detente is a two way street?

Among questions guiding such an exchange I would suggest: Why are Soviet cities, cities without crisis? Why are they free from our annual budget crises and Big Mac receiverships? Why are there no ghettos, no "hot summers," no Atticas or Wounded Knees? Why are rents almost nominal and housing being built for millions annually? Why are Soviet cities, cities without fear? Why is it possible to operate palatial subways at a stable and cheap fare since 1935?

I submit that these points of information, hardly dealt with by Moscow correspondents of the U.S. commercial press, are of utmost concern to most Americans.